American Historical Press
Sun Valley, California

MASSACHUSETTS

From Colony To Commonwealth
An Illustrated History

Judith Freeman Clark
& Robert J. Allison
Picture Research by Ruth Owen Jones

To my grandparents
Frederick L. Worby and
Mary Andrea (Riedel) Worby

As early as 1638, their families took
part in Massacusetts' growth from colony to commonwealth.
—Judith Freeman Clark

© 2002 American Historical Press
All Rights Reserved
Published 2002
Printed in the United States of America

Library of Congress Catalogue Card Number: 2002112122
ISBN: 1-892724-30-8

Bibliography: p. 331
Includes Index

A scene in Wellesley on a wonderful cloudy day. Photo by Jim Gipe, Pivotmedia, Florence, Massachusetts.

CONTENTS

AUTHOR'S FOREWORD

Provincetown, Cape Cod's outermost town, is seen about 1902. There are board sidewalks and new telephones, but no automobiles in sight. In 1904 work began in earnest on the Cape Cod Canal, which would make the Cape an island. Photo by Clifton Johnson. Courtesy, The Clifton Johnson Collection, The Jones Library, Inc., Amherst

Few assignments could have been more challenging than this one. To chronicle events and issues specific to Massachusetts history was a welcome, if somewhat daunting, task. A resident of the state for most of my life with a family history that reaches back to colonial times, I felt it a privilege to describe the individuals, places, and experiences that make Massachusetts one of the more unique states in the Union.

Drawing on various sources, from newspapers and government documents to other historians' written and verbal interpretations, I soon learned that writing Massachusetts' biography was a mammoth job. Where to begin and where to conclude? What facts were most critical, which ones were most entertaining, which the most obscure? Many sources had favorites; my problem was to select the most representative. Sometimes I faced eliminating particular tales or descriptions of famous individuals, a necessary but dissatisfying exercise. On the other hand, preparing this book meant sampling different accounts of Massachusetts as well as learning how the state has been viewed by others at various points in time.

Massachusetts claims a proud heritage. It is the "land of the Pilgrim's pride . . ." as the song goes. But it is also made up of more than dead, dry facts. Many things that make the Bay State an interesting, exciting place to live in the late twentieth century have existed in some form for several centuries: fine cultural and educational institutions, a demanding political arena, natural resources that offer everything from hydropower to fishing industry to dairy farming. The early settlers recognized the potential in Massachusetts, and surely entertained many hopes for that potential, even as the ink dried on the Mayflower Compact.

No matter how compelling the subject, a single volume cannot possibly detail every fact about so dynamic a state peopled by so complex a group of citizens. But this book is meant to be an overview, a taste, a sampling. All that, and perhaps something more. It is meant to provoke further exploration, to encourage curiosity the same way that early settlers' interests were kindled by tales about the New World.

Enjoy these chapters, the accompanying photographs and illustrations. This book, a journey into America's past, will tell you about the heritage all Americans share. This book will tell you many things about Massachusetts, and may tell you something about yourself.

Judith Freeman Clark

THE PLYMOUTH AND MASSACHUSETTS BAY COLONIES (1620-1700)

★　　★　　★　　★　　★　　★　　★　　★　　★

The Mayflower II, *a replica of the ship used for the Pilgrims' 66-day voyage of 1620, is docked at the Plymouth waterfront. This 106½-foot vessel actually crossed the Atlantic in 1957, soon after it was built. Photo by Justine Hill*

Some three and a half centuries ago, one of many immigrant groups reached our shores. This group—a small band of English men and women—came in search of religious freedom and a new life which they could fashion according to their particular needs. To most people today, Plymouth Rock represents the foundation of that new life. That rough gray stone half-buried in the sandy Plymouth shore has become a symbol for all Americans—a visible reminder of our nation's humble, earnest beginnings.

The symbolic significance of Plymouth Rock notwithstanding, the first landfall of that hardy group was not on the coast by Plymouth but at Provincetown on the tip of Cape Cod. Subsequent generations have marked this first landing spot by raising, amid tide-swept dunes assailed by harsh winds, a stone tower that stands in mute testimony to the Pilgrims' sojourn. Swept north from their Virginia destination by

stormy weather, the Pilgrims weighed anchor in Provincetown Harbor in November 1620. After five weeks spent exploring the coast, their ship finally anchored in Plymouth, and the Pilgrims established a settlement there.

The Pilgrims came to the New World seeking respite from religious persecution. However, their journey had begun not in 1620 but in 1607, when they left England for the Netherlands where they hoped to be able to worship God in peace. It soon became clear, however, that the toleration and comfort they sought was not to be found either in Amsterdam, where they first settled, or Leiden, where they moved next. Although the Pilgrims could worship together in the Netherlands, life there was difficult, jobs were not plentiful, and as a group they feared for the future of their religion. Furthermore, their children were acquiring foreign ways and manners. Economic hardship and fears that their

On the day before they decided to settle at Plymouth, some of the Pilgrims explored Clark's Island and held a Sunday service there. This illustration from an 1869 book depicts John Carver (1575-1621), who had already been elected governor aboard ship, reading the Scriptures. From Mudge, Views from Plymouth Rock, *1869*

children would forget their homeland and their religious teachings made the Pilgrims decide to leave the Netherlands. However, their departure took time to arrange. The freedom the Pilgrims sought was impossible to obtain in England, but since King James I sought to rid his land of dissenters, the Pilgrims had been able to obtain a charter for land on the James River in Virginia. This charter was granted to the Pilgrims through the London Company, a joint-stock company controlled by London merchants. After more than a decade of deliberation, planning, and much disappointment, the Pilgrims finally left Leiden in 1620 and proceeded to Southampton where they set sail for America aboard the *Mayflower.*

Led both by a need for freedoms not easily found in Europe and by a desire to be self-governing, the Pilgrims envisioned their future in a community in which harmony and cooperation abounded and which was, above all, led by God's gracious will. They were not anxious to invest their government with all-encompassing powers. Instead, they sought a separation of the secular and the sacred. The Pilgrims had too often experienced the oppression resulting from the combined power of church and state in their native England. They felt the church should be independent of state control, and this desire for religious autonomy resulted in a church separate from secular government but with spiritual power over its members. The Pilgrims were known as *Separatists,* a religious group broken away from the Church of England, although it did retain some of the basic teachings of England's

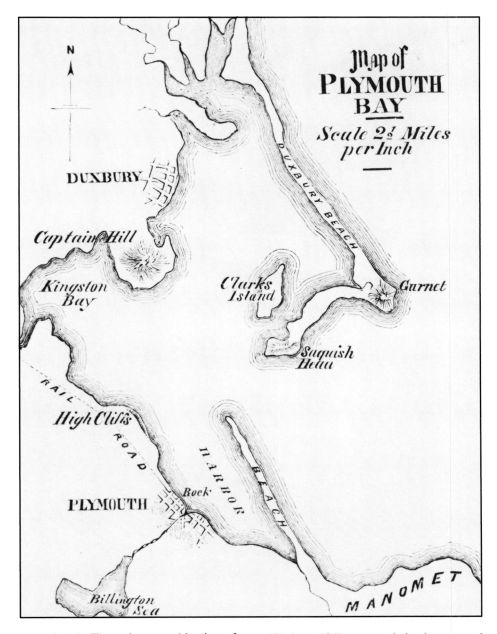

This 1869 map of the Plymouth area (including a recently added railroad line) explains why the Pilgrims chose to finally disembark from the Mayflower *in December 1620. The geographically protected settlement site, combined with a mild winter, meant that some of the Pilgrims could survive despite being ill prepared for a New England winter. Bartholomew Gosnold was probably the first European to explore what is now the Massachusetts coast at Martha's Vineyard, Nantucket, and the Dartmouth area in 1603. From Mudge,* Views from Plymouth Rock, *1869*

state church. The unique combination of enterprise and piety that characterized their search for freedom spurred them to hard work and a determination to live according to God's laws. These ideas put their indelible stamp on the future both of Massachusetts and of the United States.

The relief the Pilgrims felt upon ending their long journey to the New World is not difficult to imagine. According to William Bradford's *A History of Plimoth Plantation,* after weeks of a confining voyage fraught with every imaginable discomfort and doubt, the Pilgrims "fell upon their knees and blessed the God of Heaven, who had brought them over the vast and furious ocean and delivered them from all the evils and mysteries thereof, again to set their feet on the firm and stable earth, their proper element."

FREEDOM DEFINED

On December 21, 1620, when the Pilgrims anchored at Plymouth, their search for a suitable site on which to build permanent shelter was over. They numbered 101 souls, including an infant, Peregrine White, born on board the

Many of the earliest shelters at Plymouth Colony were mud-daubed cottages with English-style thatched roofs similar to this reproduction at Plimoth Plantation. Photo by Justine Hill

Mayflower while it was anchored in Cape Cod Bay. He was the first child of English parentage born in New England. The Pilgrims stayed on board the ship while waiting for a break in the weather. Some of this time was spent discussing the form of government they were going to have. Since they had landed far north of Virginia and out of London Company jurisdiction, their charter was of no legal value. The Pilgrims therefore drew up a new charter known as the Mayflower Compact, which was signed by 41 freemen aboard the ship. The compact pledged allegiance to the English king but established a form of government by the will of the majority. Among the stipulations contained in the compact, one noted that, "We whose names are underwritten do by these Presents, solemnly and mutually in the presence of God and one another covenant and combine ourselves together into a civil Body Politick . . . and by Virtue hereof do enact . . . such just and equal laws . . . as shall be thought most meet and convenient for the general Good of the Colony." The agreement was similar to the church covenant that also guided them. It provided for full and equal participation of all signers in issues and concerns of the colony, including the annual election of a governor. The compact remained the basis of government in Plymouth for 10 years, and all later governments in the colony developed out of the compact.

Their government taken care of, the Pilgrims waited nearly a month before going ashore. Cramped and short of food, some became ill and all were without proper sanitation facilities or warm clothing. When spring finally arrived, they ventured onto land. By now, their faith and patience had been sorely tested—almost half of them had died. Yet despite disease, starvation, or exposure, none of them chose to return with the *Mayflower* to England. Among the surviving men were John Alden, William Bradford, William Brewster, Thomas Prence, Myles Standish, and

Variegated Indian corn was photographed in the fall at a roadside stand in Deerfield. Native to the Americas, corn was brought to Europe by Christopher Columbus, where it became popular as a vegetable dish and as a grain for bread. Corn bread, Indian pudding, succotash, corn meal mush, and other humble dishes were staples of Europeans in colonial Massachusetts. Photo by Paul A. Sherry

Edward Winslow, all of whom left an outstanding legacy of service to the new colony. William Bradford was governor of Plymouth Colony, serving several separate terms of office from 1621 to 1656, succeeding John Carver, who had been elected while the Pilgrims were still aboard the *Mayflower*. Carver had signed the famous compact but he died in the spring of 1621, so it was Bradford who served the colony with dedication for many decades. Dealing both with people and a harsh, primitive environment demanded foresight, patience, and skill, all qualities that Bradford possessed. It was his abilities that undoubtedly made the critical difference between Pilgrim

success and failure. Too, Bradford's *A History of Plimoth Plantation* has long been admired as a fascinating social history and valuable contribution to written accounts of English colonial life in America.

The sickness and privation that marked the Pilgrims' first winter in Massachusetts was mitigated somewhat by friendly support from Wampanoag Indians. Without their help, Plymouth Colony may not have survived to become a permanent settlement. The Wampanoag chief, Massasoit, who first approached the Pilgrims, remained steadfastly faithful to them for more than 40 years. Massasoit initiated the first agreement—the Seven Point Peace treaty—that aided both sides in settling

disputes for decades. The degree of peace and tranquility the two populations enjoyed was relatively constant until about 1660 when a growing white population encroached more and more on Indian lands.

The story of the first Thanksgiving has been told and retold and its origins now lie hidden in myth and folklore. But we do know that during October 1621, after a small harvest of corn, the Pilgrims celebrated their first Thanksgiving Day. Some 90 Indians joined the Pilgrims, who felt grateful to be alive and offered thanks to God at a meal that included four wild turkeys.

FREEDOM ESTABLISHED

Pilgrim men and women all made

NATIVE AMERICANS IN MASSACHUSETTS

Few people today give much thought to the human inhabitants of Massachusetts in the centuries preceding European colonization of North America. Thoughts of aboriginal Americans generally evoke images of either Pilgrim encounters with "noble savages" or somewhat later clashes between western settlers and the Indian tribes of the Great Plains. Seldom does the casual reader find an accurate, in-depth view of the North American continent and its inhabitants prior to its settlement by European colonists.

This lack reflects the dearth of extant written history from the pre-Columbian era. Although some artifacts and tools from that period have survived, the native Americans did not leave overabundant records of their existence before the arrival of the French, Spanish, and British. What does remain has been pieced together by anthropologists, archaeologists, and historians who have attempted to determine exactly who these early peoples were. But such piecemeal deductions can only partially satisfy our curiosity about pre-colonial culture in America.

Historical accounts of early Massachusetts colonization seem to relegate native Americans to a historical position of only auxiliary importance. The natives of Massachusetts who met and traded peacefully with the English—or made war on small bands of settlers who tried to carve a lifestyle out of an often forbidding land—have usually been overlooked in regional histories. Native Americans enter history only when they gave land to white settlers, or when they converted to Christianity at the urging of English clergymen.

However, native American culture flourished in the Northeast for thousands of years before European settlers took control of the land. Some 12,000 years ago, in the region we know today as Massachusetts, people were hunting, gathering, and eking out a simple life amid the woodlands and heavier forests

and along the coasts and marshes. These Indians had reached the Northeast from the south and the west. Until 10,500 B.C., the area had been covered for many millenia by a thick glacial ice cap. This ice cap retreated slowly, leaving in its frozen wake a growing profusion of flora and fauna which eventually encouraged human habitation. The Paleoindian culture of the region is known today principally through its stone implements, used in hunting and attendant tasks. Largely due to scrapers, points, and other items made of flint, chalcedony, and jasper, archaeologists have identified an Indian site in the northeastern region of Massachusetts by the New Hampshire border. Excavations at this site, called Bull Brook, indicate its inhabitants lived there for more than one season of hunting, fishing, and gathering. They hunted a variety of animals, including white-tailed deer, black bear, and elk, along with many smaller mammals and birds. They also fished in freshwater ponds, gathered shellfish, and collected roots and berries from plants growing wild in the region.

Later Indians practiced agriculture, growing corn and beans primarily. They eventually taught the white settlers to cultivate these crops. Still, the Indians

Camouflaged paleo-Indians are depicted hunting barren ground for caribou that lived as far south as Massachusetts about 10,000 years ago as the last glacier receded. Drawing by Marie Litterer. Courtesy, Pratt Museum, Amherst College

relied somewhat on hunting, particularly during the long New England winters. Shellfish added an important component to their economy, serving as tools, ornaments, and food. Most of these native Americans were Eastern Algonquins whose extended family groups lived in portable structures made from animal skins and wooden poles.

Calculating the number of Indians living in Massachusetts during the pre-colonial period can only be done by estimation. Some archaeologists have identified apparent fluctuations in demography around the first millenium A.D., although there are no reliable clues as to why the population declined nor to why it subsequently increased. Some suggest that disease may have been a factor in demographic change, but this is pure speculation. Other experts cite

environmental change as a likely explanation for population shifts. However it happened, before the European colonists arrived Massachusetts' native population had decreased somewhat from its former peak. By some accounts (meant only as a general guide rather than a definite index of tribal population) there were about 45 people per square kilometer in early seventeenth-century Massachusetts and the surrounding region.

As time passed, Indians formed more or less specific tribal groups. By A.D. 1600, they were identifiable as what we now term the Eastern Algonquin tribes in Massachusetts. By 1630, the major tribes had subdivided into fairly specific territories. These tribes were: the Pocumtucks, the Nipmucks, the Massachusetts, and the Pokanokets (or Wampanoags). While these tribes all belonged to the larger Eastern Algonquin nation, each had developed customs and language deviations setting them apart from others. Their territories, although identifiable, apparently shifted and blended, and by the late seventeenth century were less and less distinguishable.

War, both intertribal and with white settlers, combined with assimilation to the European culture and disease to change the native American way of life in Massachusetts. Change had formerly been internal or brought on by the environ-

This drawing of life in a Massachusetts Woodland Indian camp shows the people at everyday tasks in summer. Much of what we suppose to be their way of life is based on Europeans' early contact and reports to their sponsors or friends back home, but also from archaeological findings. Drawing by Marie Litterer. Courtesy, Pratt Museum, Amherst College

ment. Once Europeans settled in Massachusetts, external change was imposed on Indians through voluntary or enforced alteration of cultural patterns. The noble savage of myth and folktale in Massachusetts' early history was transformed almost beyond recognition by the late 1600s—and the "city upon a hill" envisioned by Governor Bradford was one in which there were no native American neighborhoods. The tribal lifestyles disappeared quickly through virtual genocide and assimilation of native American culture. By the time the U.S. Constitution was signed in 1789, aboriginal lifestyle in Massachusetts had become as much a part of the past as the era of the Founding Fathers seems to us today.

contributions of inestimable worth to the building of that first colony at Plymouth. By June 1621, title for land in Plymouth had been assigned in 100-acre parcels to each person. Fifteen hundred acres was set aside also as common land for the use of all settlers there.

As more ships arrived from England during the decade of settlement following 1620, the region's population grew. New colonists swelled the ranks of those who had arrived earlier, prompting the establishment of new communities. Most people hoped for a parcel of land on which to build a house, keep some animals, and raise enough food for their family's needs. Settlements grew, founded by *Mayflower* Pilgrims and their direct descendants, as well as by subsequent travelers arriving on ships similar to the *Mayflower*. Duxbury, a few miles to the north of Plymouth, was settled in 1631 and granted its own charter five years later. It was the second town in Plymouth Colony and relied primarily on farming in its early years. Later, Duxbury would see fishing, trading, and shipbuilding become part of the town's growth and development. The Congregational Church in Duxbury was organized by William Brewster, a signer of the Mayflower Compact. A church elder, he was an important leader in the colony, and the town of Brewster on Cape Cod, settled in 1656, was named in his memory.

Another well-known Pilgrim settler was Myles Standish. The first military leader of the colony, he successfully maintained cordial relations with neighboring Indians. In 1649, Standish purchased a large tract of land from Chief Ousamequin, which subsequently became part of what today is Bridgewater, Brockton, and surrounding towns. Standish was also instrumental in the founding of Duxbury along with William Brewster and John Alden.

The story of Myles Standish's courtship of Priscilla Mullens, with John Alden as go-between, was published in 1858 by Henry Wadsworth Longfellow in the poem, "The Courtship of Miles Standish." The story has no historical basis, but it remains a charming legend. In it, Alden plays the part of the romantic messenger for the couple, and the most often quoted line is Priscilla's parrying comment, "Why don't you speak for yourself, John?" Standish's intentions backfired, for, in reality, Priscilla Mullens married John Alden and the couple led a happy, fruitful married life. They are interred in Duxbury's Old Burying Ground, where Captain Myles Standish is also buried. The Jonathan Alden House in that same town, built by the couple's son, was their last home.

The number of towns in Plymouth Colony grew in response to the settlers' desires for larger farms and more spacious surroundings. Scituate was incorporated in 1636, followed by Barnstable in 1638 and Taunton in 1639. Marshfield was founded in 1640 and Eastham in 1644. The latter was a hoped-for relocation site for the original Plymouth Colony, but the proposed resettlement was discarded by the majority of settlers, who felt Plymouth should remain the central town of the colony. Rehoboth was founded in 1645, Bridgewater in 1656, Swansea in 1668, and Middleborough in 1669, to name a few other Pilgrim communities of those early years. The Indian chief Massasoit relinquished tribal jurisdiction over what is now West Bridgewater in 1645, according to legend, in exchange for a handful of "knives, hatchets, skins, hoes, coates [sic], and cotton."

Yet another settlement—one quickly earning a reputation for loose morality and questionable activities—was Mount Wollaston. It was founded in 1625 by Thomas Morton and was known also as Merry Mount. The town became a gathering place for traders and Indians who trafficked in firearms, furs, and spirits. William Bradford, then governor of Plymouth Colony, sent Myles Standish to arrest Morton on a variety of charges, among them encouraging celebration of

pagan festivals. Although he was banished to England in 1628, Morton returned to Plymouth Colony, only to be sent away once again in 1630. Mount Wollaston is located in the north part of Quincy, an industrial city south of Boston.

THE PURITANS SEEK FREEDOM

The Pilgrims, though generally thought of as the first, were not the only settlers of Massachusetts during the seventeenth century. In 1628, the nucleus of a Puritan colony was established at Naumkeag, in what is now Salem. Under the leadership of John Endecott, it displaced Salem's few English inhabitants (led by Roger

Top: *This is an 1869 artist's idea of what the Pilgrims' first meetinghouse probably looked like. It is known from a drawing that by 1683 they had built a larger, two-story structure of a much more sophisticated design with a belfry, clapboard cladding, and shingle roof, and a five-over-four window configuration similar to houses of the period. From Mudge,* Views from Plymouth Rock, *1869*

Above: *The John Alden House, built in 1653 in Duxbury (the second Pilgrim town, after Plymouth), is a timber-braced frame house that illustrates the early use of shingles for siding. From a circa 1910 postcard*

COLONIAL HOUSING AND APPAREL

Political and economic considerations aside, a people describes itself in general terms by means of various everyday practices and effects common to their social structure and culture. Among these are housing and apparel, inventions, and innovations. The early European colonists of Massachusetts accrued a record of such practices and effects throughout their first century that tell us a great deal about their individual and collective aspirations.

The tangible realities of life prior to the War for Independence are enumerated in all manner of private and legal documents—account books, diaries, wills, and marriage contracts. Some, such as William Bradford and John Winthrop, told of community happenings and described personal joys and sorrows. Others, such as firebrand patriot James Otis and his equally patriotic and articulate sister Mercy Otis Warren, left speeches, essays, letters, and pamphlets to illustrate points of honor and law. These records are invaluable, for they tell us about Massachusetts in its early years. But there are forms of records other than written ones, and they, too, define colonial life in eloquent, if unspoken, ways.

Although no pictorial record exists to chronicle the Pilgrims' landing at Plymouth, we know that when they came ashore they were weary, cold, and anxious to establish a means of shelter—however temporary—as soon as possible. The Pilgrims realized that New England's climate necessitated tight, weatherproof structures, and with warmth in mind they erected simple wattle-and-daub cottages. Humble homes perhaps, but welcome after a three-month ocean voyage. They were buildings which were thus to be replaced quickly with something more permanent. By 1623, according to one visitor to Plymouth Colony, there were about "twenty houses, four or five of which are very fair and pleasant." He noted that the homes were built with "clapboards, with gardens also enclosed behind and at the sides with clapboards." In just a few years at least some of the Pilgrims were thus able to satisfy their wish for more permanent dwellings.

Still, the houses were neither large nor elegant. They usually had only one-and-a-half stories, a thatched roof, and one or two tiny windows. After 1635, shingle and board roofing generally replaced thatch because of the threat of fire. Windows were thought of as luxuries and until 1640 were usually made from oiled paper or fabric rather than glass.

Edward Winslow, one of the original proprietors of Plymouth Colony, wrote to England with advice to a group of would-be emigrants to "bring paper and linseed oil for your windows." This meant that the Pilgrim houses were dark inside, and with often no more than one room at ground level, they lacked privacy as well. A fireplace on one wall dominated the room and provided the only source of heat as well as the cooking area.

Above, accessible by ladder or steep stair built close to the chimney, was a room often described as a "chamber"—the Pilgrims' term for bedroom. Some houses built with a larger floor plan had two rooms downstairs and a divided chamber upstairs, with a central fireplace, but these larger homes generally date from a slightly later and more prosperous period.

Only after the Pilgrims had attended to the colony's most basic needs did houses gain additional rooms. A lean-to was the most common addition. It sometimes served as a kitchen, but was just as frequently used for storage or sleeping. Some homes as early as 1640 also had cellars, which were either built under a portion of the main house or as part of the lean-to.

By twentieth-century standards, interiors of Pilgrim homes were sparsely furnished. However, inventories of the colonial period indicate that a wide range of prosperity existed in Plymouth. One man, Web Adley, was listed in 1652 as

A kitchen in a Massachusetts home circa 1700 would have probably looked like this, albeit more cluttered with food, ashes, and things like towels or potholders. Open-hearth cooking was the method of cooking until well after the Revolution. There was often a small oven in the wall of the brick fireplace. Courtesy, Connecticut Valley Historical Museum

having a total personal wealth of £3.7s., and another man, William Pontus, was assessed at just under £13. Yet another colonist, William Thomas of nearby Marshfield in Plymouth Colony, had land and possessions valued at £375. From the very beginning, economic diversity characterized life in Massachusetts.

The inventories list items such as chairs, beds, tables, and wooden cooking and eating implements, as well as pewter and—less frequently—silver cups, spoons, and beakers. Pilgrims possessed a few table knives, but forks were nonexistent since they were not yet in common use even in England. Many of these artifacts have been preserved and can be seen in museums and historic restorations such as Plimouth Plantation.

Another measure of wealth in Plymouth Colony (and in Massachusetts Bay Colony as well) was linens—bedsheets, napkins, petticoats, and handkerchiefs. All were woven and sewn by hand. The wealthier colonists had coverlets or bedspreads, blankets, and rugs as well as bed curtains. Feather pillows and feather beds were found in homes of the very richest people, but poorer folk slept on mattresses stuffed with scraps of wool and rags or hay and husks.

Pilgrim clothes were handmade of natural fibers—wool, linen, and leather. Cotton was rare in the seventeenth century and available only to the very rich. Some clothes were valuable enough to be left to ensuing generations, especially if they were heavy and very durable or very finely ornamented. This accounts for the careful listings in wills that show certain garments given as legacies to heirs, and it provides posterity with a very intimate peek at colonial life. In 1650, a woman's fine petticoat might be valued at £1.10s. The same amount of money would purchase a man's suit of clothes or be equal to the cost of a herd of goats or a large portion of wheat.

It is inaccurate to think of Pilgrims as dressing exclusively in somber colors, although it is true that they did not indulge in bright colors or elaborate clothes or ornamentation. Jewelry was frowned upon; Pilgrim husbands and wives did not even wear wedding bands. The most common colors for daily wear in Plymouth Colony were hues of red or brown, but some blue, green, and yellow garments were also worn. The colors reflected the availability and range of homemade vegetable dyes rather than any desire to limit brightly hued clothing. Pilgrims did favor black for their best clothes, but this may have been because these were expected to last at least one generation and therefore needed to be conservative and serviceable.

Style of clothing varied little in Plymouth Colony. Most men wore a close-fitting jacket known as a doublet, knee-length breeches which were cut quite full, and a three-quarter length cloak. Sometimes a heavy sleeveless jacket known as a jerkin was worn in colder weather as a supplement to the doublet. Underneath was a linen shirt, stockings, and leather boots for everyday wear; shoes were used only for special occasions. Men also wore a hat or a cap, but this was by no means required.

Women's clothing generally consisted of a three-piece dress with skirt, bodice, and sleeves. The latter were tied or laced to the armholes of the bodice. In colonial inventories sleeves sometimes were listed as bequeathed to a person separately from other portions of an outfit. There was usually a petticoat under the skirt and often an underskirt under that. A chemise was worn under the bodice, and a loose smock was the basic undergarment. Leather shoes and woolen or linen stockings covered women's feet, although they often wore wooden clogs to protect their leather shoes from mud. A neck scarf and a cap completed the clothing for Pilgrim women. In fact, a woman's hair was bound tightly and covered completely

This dowry chest built in the 1770s is reminiscent of 1600s Pilgrim furniture. Made in the Northampton area for Sarah (Hooker) Strong (who married Caleb Strong, later governor of Massachusetts in 1777), the chest is one of the type called Hadley chests. From 1670 to 1730 this kind of hand-carved chest was especially popular up and down the Connecticut River. Courtesy, Northampton Historical Society

by a cap—it was considered immodest and wanton for women to be bareheaded, indoors or out.

The strict mores dictating style of apparel and the hardships of earlier colonial life gave way by the mid-1700s. Puritanism relaxed and Massachusetts became more cosmopolitan as its population grew, but these changes were slow to evolve.

Conant). In 1630, John Winthrop located the main Puritan settlement at Boston, which soon became the capital of the Massachusetts Bay Colony.

The Puritans, who settled the Massachusetts Bay Colony, differed from the Pilgrims (Separatists) in Plymouth Colony. Wanting only to *purify* the Church of England, the Puritans did not want to break away to form their own church. The Puritans' views, radical for their time, were not widely held and were as much concerned with governmental issues as with church issues. By 1630, 17 ships bearing more than 1,000 English Puritans had arrived on Massachusetts' shores and settled numerous towns, including Dorchester, Lynn, Roxbury, and Watertown.

Boston, founded on September 17, 1630, soon became the most prominent town in the Massachusetts Bay Colony. An important harbor community, its economic development flourished due to the constant influx of immigrants from England, many of whom stayed to contribute their talents to the growth of the city. Boston was designated the capital of the colony in 1632, and its settlement was guided principally by its third governor, John Winthrop, who in 1630 had led a migration of 900 Puritans from England. The Massachusetts Bay Colony was worthy of great admiration according to Winthrop, whose diary

entries anticipated that the Puritan settlement "shall be as a City upon a hill." Most Puritans worked tirelessly to promote their colony's success as envisioned by Winthrop and others like him. By 1642, there were nearly 10,000 people in the Massachusetts Bay Colony, some freemen and others who were servants or other non-property-owning individuals.

FREEDOM'S PARAMETERS

Initially, church membership was required of those sitting on the General Court. This being the case, decision-making rested firmly in the hands of the governor and a small body of clergy and church members. Later in the century, a 40-shilling freehold was substituted for the church membership requirement. This changed Winthrop's plan for a "holy commonwealth" and paved the way for a variety of other secular changes that soon transformed the entire colony.

During the first years of the colony, education was deemed of paramount importance. Boston Latin School, opened in 1635 as a school for boys, was the first free public school and the first secondary school in America. It was modeled, as were English private schools, along classical lines. Since the colony needed a college for training clergy, one was established in 1636 with a grant from the General Court. In 1638 it was named for

John Harvard, its first benefactor, who died that year, leaving an extensive library and half of his fortune to the school. The importance of education to the Puritans is evidenced by a 1647 Massachusetts General Court ruling that communities with more than 50 families must provide a teacher for their children. Towns with 100 families or more were required to establish a grammar school so that children might be educated. Books were also important to the colonists. Four years after Harvard College was founded in Cambridge, the first printing press was set up in the same town. Owned by Stephen Daye, it published the *Bay Psalm Book,* the first book in English printed in America.

Other General Court decisions affecting colonial life were less popular than setting up schools. By the 1650s, many people were unhappy with laws that extended voting privileges to church members only. These laws were related as well to church elders' worries that fewer adults were eligible for church membership. A decline in personal religious conversions—necessary for acceptance into membership—contributed to shrinking church membership. Everyone had to attend worship services each week, but this attendance did not automatically ensure church membership. Those seeking such membership had to publicly confess their sins. Each year, smaller numbers confessed and asked for acceptance into the communion of the church so as to receive community voting rights. The dwindling number of "visible saints," as this group of members was called, threatened church and community stability. By the middle of the century a solution to this legal and religious problem was deemed a critical necessity by the Puritans.

The *Half-Way Covenant,* adopted in 1662, permitted admission to church membership for those Puritans who had

This was Harvard as it appeared in 1721, 85 years after it was founded. On the left is Harvard Hall, built in 1672. Stoughton Hall, built in 1698, stands in the center, and Massachusetts Hall, built in 1720, is on the right. From New England Magazine, *October 1901*

By 1652 the Massachusetts Great and General Court authorized minting of the Pine Tree Shilling, the first coinage for use in the American colonies to be struck there. The motivation for this defiance of British authority was counterfeit coins that were plaguing the colony. In Boston's illegal mint the colonists minted their own coins: silver shillings, sixpence, and threepence. The obverse side had the pine tree surrounded by the word "Masathusets," while on verso was the year and the denomination. Courtesy, Berkshire Atheneum

not made a public profession of faith, but who led morally upright lives. As planned, the covenant strengthened the church and increased its membership— but only on a limited basis since a conversion experience, publicly confessed, remained an imperative qualification for full church membership.

This change in church doctrine was probably inevitable. Merchants in Boston and elsewhere were becoming increasingly prosperous and this prosperity extended to others as well. Manufactured goods flowed in from England, and the trappings of affluence were more available to the colonists. In 1651, the General Court passed laws regulating and limiting the wearing of fine clothes, which many Puritans considered an affront to God. This law indicates that the standard of living in Massachusetts Bay had improved somewhat since the 1630s.

FREEDOM AND COLONIAL INTOLERANCE

Children and grandchildren of the Puritans grew accustomed to material comforts greater than those enjoyed by the original colonists. Not surprisingly, attitudes about the fitness and legitimacy of amassing wealth shifted accordingly. This change placed a strain on Puritan spiritual life as the desire to "get ahead" overtook the need to be saved. Not all colonists were willing to confess their faith publicly, although most were anxious to remain part of the established church. By allowing for relaxed church membership rules, as with the *Half-Way Covenant,* Massachusetts Puritans acknowledged the colony's shifting social and economic fabric. At the same time, they hoped to maintain its moral stability and save the church from an untimely demise.

Although internal church structure accepted modification, Puritans (and Pilgrims as well) emphasized external adherence to church law. This was especially apparent in expressions of religious intolerance. Freedom of worship was not allowed in the colony, and Quakers were among those who suffered the most from this intolerance. In the summer of 1656 when the first Quakers arrived in Massachusetts they were imprisoned and then forcibly ejected from the colony. By October, the General Court legislated a fine against anyone hiding a Quaker, and by 1658 the court had prohibited Quaker meetings. Two years later, however, the persecution abated after Charles II, a friend of Quaker leader William Penn, was restored to the English throne.

It was not only Quakers who suffered. In 1636, Anne Hutchinson, wife of one of Boston's leading citizens, was charged with heresy and banished from Boston. A woman of learning and great religious conviction, Hutchinson challenged the Puritan clergy and asserted her view that moral conduct and piety should not be the primary qualifications for "visible sainthood." Her preachings, labeled "Antinomianism" by the Puritans, were termed heretical since church teaching dictated the need for outward signs of God's grace as well as for an inward, direct experience of grace.

Threatened by meetings she held weekly in her Boston home, the clergy charged Hutchinson with blasphemy. An outspoken female in a male hierarchy, Hutchinson had little hope that many would speak in her defense, and she was tried by the General Court. After being sentenced, she went with her family to live in what is now Rhode Island. Several years later she moved to New York where she and some of her family died during an Indian attack in 1643. A descendant, Thomas Hutchinson, later became governor of Massachusetts.

Another dissenter, Roger Williams, was likewise banished from Salem, where he was known for his unconventional dealings with the Indians. His original tenure there as a minister had actually begun in Plymouth but was terminated after he challenged existing church teachings. At Salem, Williams was in violent opposition to almost every

established law and practice, both church and civil. A religious man, he nevertheless favored complete and absolute separation of church and secular government, even to the extent of repealing taxes in support of the church.

Williams criticized Puritan authorities' dealings with the Indians and advocated that settlers return Indian lands to their original owners. In 1635, he was tried by the General Court and banished. Williams fled to Rhode Island where he helped found Providence. He secured a royal charter in 1644, which established the Providence Plantations as a separate colony.

In both these cases, dissent represented such a threat to civil and church authority that it was dealt with in the most expedient, thorough, and extreme way. In Massachusetts Bay, the clergy and the General Court acted together to preserve the sanctity and integrity of the community. But it would not be long before even more serious issues threatened community stability.

Through banishment, fines, and even hanging (in the case of witchcraft and some other serious misdeeds), Puritan rulers kept a firm hold on the Massachusetts Bay Colony. Likewise, the Pilgrims exercised strong control over the Plymouth Colony. But laws, sermons, fines, and trials could not permanently forestall change in the social, political, and cultural spheres, change which pressed on all of the colonists during the latter part of the seventeenth century.

INDIANS CHALLENGE COLONIAL FREEDOM

It was not only religious life that changed during the seventeenth century in the Massachusetts Bay and Plymouth colonies. The settlers' relations with Indians changed, too. Like Roger Williams and Myles Standish, some colonists tried to maintain cordial relations with the Indians and a few, such as "Praying John" Eliot, tried to convert Indians to Christianity. Eliot translated the Bible into the Algonquin Indian language in an attempt to carry God's word to native Americans. He helped establish a community—a "praying" town—at Natick in 1651, and by 1674 there were around 1,100 Christian Indians in Plymouth Colony. Eliot's ambitions for his Indian proteges included a conventional education, and at least one Indian, Caleb Cheeshahteamuck, graduated from Harvard College in 1665.

Despite Eliot's best efforts, relations between whites and Indians deteriorated. Most settlers considered all Indians potential enemies, while non-Christian

John Eliot (1604-1690) was born in England and sailed to Boston on the ship Lyon *in 1631. He was pastor of a church in Roxbury, where he first came in contact with the native Americans. Eliot undertook to learn their language in order to convert them to Christianity, which he felt was their only salvation. He, like other Puritans, believed that the ability to read, especially to read the Bible, was a necessity. He translated the Bible into the Indians' language, and so published the first Bible in North America, paid for by friends in England. His attempt to make the Indians like English colonists failed during King Philip's War in 1675-1676. From Spencer and Lossing,* A Complete History of the United States of America, *Vol. I, 1878*

Indians rejected converts as colonial pawns. There was, in fact, some basis for colonists' fears. Settlers in Plymouth and Massachusetts Bay had expanded their hold on land in the region, and as colonists encroached on areas formerly inhabited exclusively by Indians, the latter responded violently. After 1662, when Massasoit's son Metacom (known to whites as King Philip) became Wampanoag chief, relations between the two groups deteriorated steadily.

King Philip, unhappy with the white settlers' overbearing attitude, was convinced that Indians were doomed if they did not resist further expansion into their tribal lands. To complicate matters even more, Philip was unwilling to make treaties with colonial governors. He preferred to deal directly with the King of England as befitted his own status as tribal leader. Philip ultimately planned war against the colonists with whom he could not agree, a conflict which broke out suddenly. It occurred after three Indians were hanged by the settlers for their role in a Massachusetts Bay Colony murder in 1675.

Incensed by this act of white justice, the Indians, under King Philip's leadership, attacked Swansea in June 1675 and killed all of its inhabitants. Other towns fell to the onslaught—Brookfield was destroyed in August. In Maine, which was then a part of Massachusetts, Indians rose up against the whites, and in neighboring Rhode Island, settlers were attacked by Narragansett Indians sworn to support King Philip in his attempt to rid New England of colonists. Deerfield, in western Massachusetts, was destroyed in the fall of 1675; no whites returned to the town for almost a decade. In February 1676, King Philip's warriors destroyed Lancaster, killing all the males and taking women and children into captivity.

By the time King Philip was killed in a small battle in Rhode Island in August 1676, one out of every 16 white settlers in New England (most of them in Massachusetts) had died at the hands of Indians. Angry white survivors treated their conquered foes harshly and all of Myles Standish's diplomacy was rendered futile. As a result of King Philip's War whites forcibly emptied praying towns of their Indian residents. They were relocated, often to remote spots without sufficient hunting or fishing resources, and many of them died as a result. The Indian population in New England was irreversibly affected by King Philip's War and its aftermath: the Wampanoag tribe, for example, suffered almost total extinction.

THREATS TO ECONOMIC FREEDOM

It was not only hostility between Indians and whites that threatened colonial existence. Both Plymouth and Massachusetts Bay colonies faced increasing internal and external discord as the seventeenth century drew to a close. Despite efforts of civic and church leaders, change was inevitable. Sometimes it was effected peacefully, as with internal shifts to a wealthier lifestyle. This type of change was absorbed gradually, but externally, strife meant ultimate confrontation—both among colonists themselves and between the colonists and English authorities.

Clashes over trade spelled tremendous upheaval for the colonies. In 1676, England declared Massachusetts in noncompliance with the Navigation Acts. These regulations, passed in 1660, required colonists to trade exclusively with England. Eight years later, in 1684, Parliament revoked the Massachusetts Bay Colony Charter for violations of trade restrictions.

In 1686, following the ascension of James II to the English throne, the Massachusetts Bay and Plymouth colonies became part of the Dominion of New England along with New York and New Jersey. The dominion represented perhaps the biggest shift in political structure the colonists had yet known.

Chief among the differences apparent after dissolution of the Massachusetts Bay and Plymouth colony charters was that the Dominion of New England was a civil commonwealth. Simply stated, this meant an individual could vote without being a church member. Not surprisingly, this law had a far-reaching effect on church power in Massachusetts and contributed to a growing mood of religious tolerance in the colony.

Sir Edmund Andros became the first royal governor of the dominion in 1686. By then, colonists had learned to enjoy their relative autonomy, and Massachusetts residents did not welcome the

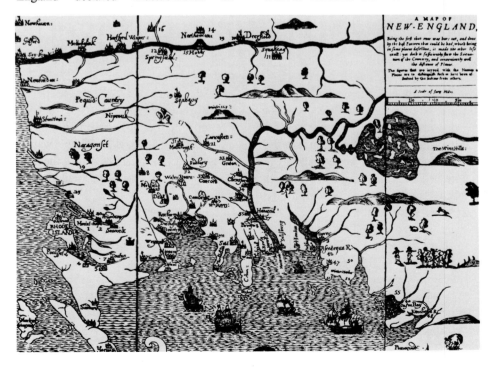

This early map by John Foster, first published in 1677 in the book Indian Wars in New England, *shows where the English had established themselves by the time of King Philip's War. Most of the towns were on the coast or along the Connecticut River. The map also tries to document which towns were attacked by Indians during the war. Ten to 15 percent of the English men, as well as numerous women and children, were killed. There were atrocities on both sides. For example, in Brookfield, colonists' heads were said to have been kicked around like soccer balls. And, after the war, Metacom's (King Philip's) head was displayed on a pike in Boston while his family was sold into slavery in the West Indies. From* Waters, Ipswich in the Massachusetts Bay Colony, *1905*

Left: *Built in 1681, the Hingham Meeting House is the only church from the 1600s remaining in New England, and it is still in use. It is known as the Old Ship Church because it was supposedly built upside-down in shipbuilding fashion by the seagoing settlers of coastal Hingham. The entryways were probably added later. Early meetinghouses were very simple in design; what is now considered the quintessential New England church, the white, end-gabled, Greek Revival edifice, was not built until the early 1800s. From Winsor,* Narrative and Critical History of America, *Vol. III, 1884*

Facing Page: *"The Landing of the Commissioners at Boston" illustrates the time when, after the end of Puritan Oliver Cromwell's rule and the crowning of Charles II, royal commissioners were sent to Massachusetts. The new king sent his commissioners in 1664 to correct whatever abuses they could find. The colonists were told to stop coining their own money and to say "God Save the King" after the reading of royal proclamations. From Stark,* The Loyalists of Massachusetts and the Other Side of the Revolution, *1910*

newly-appointed governor, who had a reputation as a military man. Quickly becoming unpopular, his efforts at ruling seemed both arbitrary and harsh. Angry citizens heard of the overthrow of James II in England and therefore deposed Andros in 1689 at Boston's Rowe's Wharf. Andros returned to England where the Glorious Revolution had restored William of Orange, and his wife Mary, to the throne, uniting England and Scotland as Great Britain.

Some colonists hoped the Glorious Revolution would reestablish an independent Massachusetts Bay Colony, but this did not occur. Two years after attempts to obtain a revived Massachusetts Bay charter failed, in 1691, the crown colony of Massachusetts was established, uniting the former colonies of Plymouth and Massachusetts Bay. The new royal governor of the colony was Sir William Phips, a Maine native, who arrived in Boston in 1692 just in time to play a role in one of Massachusetts' most infamous episodes.

THE UNEXPECTED FRUIT OF FREEDOM AND CHANGE

Puritan social order was disintegrating.

Plymouth's Pilgrims had been incorporated into Massachusetts, now a single political entity. Religious tolerance, while not flourishing, was permitted to the degree that Anglican church services were now held in Boston, that original bastion of Puritan dogma. But soon, the tragedy of the witchcraft trials at Salem in 1692 came to symbolize the intense disarray into which Puritan lifestyles had fallen.

In March 1692, a 73-year-old Salem woman—Rebecca Nurse—was accused of witchcraft. In July, along with four others, she was hanged as a witch. Just two months before Nurse was put on trial, a young girl named Betty Parris, daughter of local minister Samuel Parris, was afflicted with a strange, convulsive sickness: she writhed in pain and screamed that devils were tormenting her. Ultimately, her illness was blamed on witchcraft.

A curiously prevalent charge leveled against offenders in seventeenth-century Massachusetts, witchcraft was blamed in 1688 for the illness of several girls in Boston. Later, a woman was executed after being charged with witchcraft in connection with the girls' symptoms. In

This 1880s depiction of the witchcraft hysteria shows the men with Lincolnesque beards which Salem men of 1690 did not have. However, the picture does illustrate the belief that prayers and fasting would deliver the afflicted one from the power of the witch. From Lossing, Our Country: A Household History of the United States, *1888*

Salem Village a few years later, a West Indian slave named Tituba, who lived in the Reverend Samuel Parris' household, was implicated in the case involving Betty Parris, her cousin Ann Putnam, and several others. Tituba, under intense pressure from her interrogators, confessed to being a witch. She described in fantastic and imaginative terms the procedures she and the Devil supposedly used to hurt their victims. "The Devil came to me and bid me serve him," she said at one interrogation. Parris and his supporters were delighted to blame the young girls' strange and disturbing troubles on something as reprehensible as witchcraft. They proceeded to prosecute with a vengeance and Salem soon rocked with controversy as scores were accused and 20 were actually executed.

On the surface, witchcraft in seventeenth-century Massachusetts seems to have been frighteningly capricious—its victims and perpetrators were everywhere. But a closer look reveals that those labeled witches often held little power in the community. Tituba, a servant in the Parris home, was a black woman with no education. Others accused of being witches had reputations as jades, or disreputable women, and

were in frequent quarrels with neighbors. In Salem, feuds between relative newcomers to the community and older, established families seem to have been a contributing factor in the witchcraft hysteria there. Also, many witchcraft victims were young. Betty Parris was only nine years old and her co-accusers were within a few years of that age. Nearly everyone identified as a witch in the early stages of the craze was virtually powerless even before the scare became widespread, and this may provide a clue to their defenseless positions.

The hysteria of young witchcraft victims—many of whom hallucinated, had convulsions, and suffered odd speech and behavior—was terrifying to a society based on order and obedience. One observer told of the girls at Salem "getting into Holes, and creeping under Chairs and Stools, and . . . uttering foolish, ridiculous Speeches, which neither they themselves nor any others could make sense of."

The Reverend Parris and other ministers and magistrates who examined the victims were baffled. Chief Justice William Stoughton, lieutenant governor of Massachusetts, presided over the Salem witchcraft trials. He questioned victims closely, was convinced that their testimony rang true, and was determined to convict as many witches as necessary to put an end to society's torment.

As weeks passed, more and more accusations were made against people in and around Salem. Eventually, a few grew skeptical, even critical, of the shrieking, wailing victims who sat at the trials. But those who questioned the validity of witchcraft charges often found themselves accused. By September 1692, the hysteria resulted in the jailing of more than 100 people, both men and women, in Boston alone. The Massachusetts General Court restored a law making witchcraft punishable by death, thus paving the way for executions. Eight people were hanged in Salem on September 22, 1692, and throughout Essex County numerous strange episodes involving animal, as well as human, behavior seemed to confirm the alleged witchcraft.

No matter how respectable one was, it appeared nobody was safe from the victims' rantings. John Alden, son of John and Priscilla Alden, was asked to present testimony before a Salem court. Ultimately, he was arrested and jailed for 15 months on witchcraft charges, but he escaped to New York and stayed there until the terrors subsided. Alden was not alone in his peril. Ministers' wives were accused, as were friends of the royal governor, Sir William Phips. Even Phips' wife, the Lady Mary Phips, was accused of being a witch.

Cotton Mather, a well-known minister from Boston, was not convinced that hysterical testimony from young girls was sufficient to condemn a person to death. His father, Increase Mather of Cambridge, agreed, noting in an October 1692 sermon that "It were better that 10 suspected witches should escape, than that one innocent person should be condemned." Many agreed with the Mathers' opinions and in early 1693, Governor Phips ruled that nobody could be convicted of witchcraft solely on the basis of spectral evidence, that is, testimony of afflicted persons saying they had witnessed apparitions doing terrible things.

Of 52 cases tried in the courts during this latter period, only three resulted in convictions—and those only because the accused actually confessed to being witches. The governor reprieved those found guilty and saved them from hanging—much to the dismay and expressed displeasure of Lieutenant Governor Stoughton, who had spent so much time prosecuting witchcraft cases in Salem. In May 1693, John Alden was cleared of charges lodged against him and all others jailed on witchcraft charges in Massachusetts were set free. No more witches were hanged from the so-called Witches Hill gallows in Salem. Governor Phips' actions were based on his concern that the witchcraft episode, if allowed to

Cotton Mather (1663-1728) entered Harvard at age 11 and went on to become a teacher and a minister. In 1685 he wrote about cases of witchcraft that he had heard of, so he was hardly an impartial investigator of the Salem problems. Engraving from Drake, Nooks and Corners of the New England Coast, *1875, after a 1727 mezzotint by Peter Pelham*

continue, would have a detrimental effect on all of Massachusetts. He wrote to the Earl of Nottingham in February 1693 that he feared "the black cloud that threatened this Province with destruction."

In Salem Village, the Reverend Parris was the subject of an April 1695 meeting that resulted in a mutual agreement concerning his departure. By July 1696, he had left Salem Village and the ministry to become a teacher in a neighboring town. Afterward, Salem tried to erase the events that held the community in the grip of fear and horror for 12 months. Despite these efforts, however, Salem's name has been tied by historic record and public memory to witchcraft trials and to the deaths of those unfortunates ensnared in the web of fantastic accusations.

In the wake of these unsettling circumstances, most people in Salem and elsewhere set aside dissenting opinions concerning religious practices and social and economic change. The colonists were as eager as Governor Phips to erase the unwholesome blot of witchcraft from Massachusetts and they worked diligently to promote prosperity and progress in the eighteenth century. What colonists could not foresee, however, was a change in British colonial policy that heralded a new era for Massachusetts and all of North America.

TRADE, TAXATION, AND THE WAR FOR INDEPENDENCE (1700-1780)

★　★　★　★　★　★　★　★　★

Compared to conditions suffered by colonists arriving in Massachusetts in the 1600s, eighteenth-century colonial life encompassed a considerable increase in material comforts and a wider latitude of individual freedom. In addition, political autonomy had developed to an extent satisfactory to most colonists. Although Britain established a board of trade in 1696 to regulate and deal with aspects of colonial administration, Massachusetts residents retained many decision-making powers, including legislative control, the right to levy taxes, and the right to approve governor's council appointees. For although named to his post by the king, the colonial governor consulted only with advisors acceptable to the colonists.

Some historians have referred to Britain's inability to regulate or effectively control affairs during this period as a time of "salutary neglect." Various results of this apathy would appear before the end of the eighteenth century.

A GROWING SEPARATION

During the late 1600s and early 1700s, a lapse in well-established censorship policies fostered the growth of numerous publishing ventures in Massachusetts. However, they were closely monitored by conservative magistrates threatened by a press that challenged their authority. On April 24, 1704, the first regular newspaper appeared in Boston. The *Boston News-Letter,* published by John Campbell, postmaster, carried the phrase "published by authority," indicating nominal approval by the governor's council. In time, postmasters throughout Massachusetts came to expect that publishing duties and rights would accompany their other responsibilities. By 1723, little censorship was exercised by either royal authorities or church officials. Unlike the previous 90 years, clergy now found it difficult to dictate what could be published in Massachusetts. Control was limited to threats of libel suits by civil authorities. However, not until well after the War for Independence was the press in Massachusetts truly free in the sense that it is today.

Though prohibited in theory, smuggling was another activity carried out on a large scale. When British Parliament passed the Navigation Acts in 1660, there was little hope of their enforcement in the colonies due to the number of ships and ports requiring surveillance. Therefore, until the War for Independence, a great proportion of shipping originating from Massachusetts was illegal. Up and down the coast, merchant ships from Cape Ann to New Bedford maintained healthy trade relationships with countries other than Britain. Sugar, molasses, naval stores, furs, grain, and other items found their way into holds of ships plying Atlantic and Caribbean waters. The lucrative business resulting from these unlawful dealings launched the fortunes of more than one Massachusetts family.

To better describe the magnitude of this illegal shipping trade, one historian estimates that by 1748 there were 491 colonial ships sailing annually out of Boston Harbor and another 131 ships sailing out of Salem, the most important colonial port north of Boston.

Of course, some of this activity remained lawful. Fishing represented a major industry only a few years after the founding of the Plymouth and Massachusetts Bay colonies. The fleets that sailed from Nantucket, Martha's Vineyard, and other smaller ports were instrumental in establishing the financial stability of Massachusetts' fisheries. Abundant supplies of fish in Atlantic waters, which are warmed by the Gulf Stream, provided an economic windfall to the colonists. Massachusetts later recognized this boon symbolically: at the end of the 1700s, a Massachusetts House of Representatives resolution declared the new legislative body would "hang up the representation of a Codfish in the room where the House sits."

Not by caprice did the cod become a sign of the state's enterprise. According to

By 1765 Peter Folger II of Nantucket could afford to build this fine house on Centre Street. The receipt that dates it reads, "From Jethro Hussey, housewright, to Peter Folger II for 28 pounds, 10 shillings on account of building his house." The Folger family was on Nantucket in the 1600s and consisted primarily of merchants and inventors. Peter Folger II was a cousin of Benjamin Franklin. Photo by John H. Martin

THE BOSTON POST ROAD

Transforming a raw, untamed country into a thriving and dynamic society had taken more than a century. The first 100 years or so in which the colonists carved out a new existence in North America are noteworthy for the innovation, thrift, passion, and determination with which the settlers approached the challenges of their new life. By the time of the War for Independence, Massachusetts colonists had earned a reputation for hardheaded individualism, a taste for economic gain, a concern for religious freedom, and above all an overwhelming interest in making things better.

One way in which they attempted to improve their condition was by upgrading what we might now call their communications system. In the seventeenth and eighteenth centuries, that system was limited to travel on foot or horseback, or by carriage, coach, or boat. Although roads were generally primitive, the need for good ones was recognized early. In order to improve communications between the various colonies, a post road was opened in Massachusetts as early as 1673; it was used to transport mail between New England and New York.

On January 22, 1673, the first mail carrier left New York on his way to the capital of the Massachusetts Bay Colony. That initial dispatch arrived in Boston around February 1. Springfield, Brookfield, Worcester, and Cambridge were among the communities served by this postal carrier along a route known variously as the King's Highway, the Great Road, and later, the Boston Post Road.

Both Governor John Winthrop of Connecticut (son of the Massachusetts governor) and the royal governor of New York, Francis Lovelace, shared an enthusiasm for a regular post between their two colonies. They were encouraged in this endeavor by King Charles II, who supported a better communications system among all the colonies.

Initially, the 200-mile journey began on the first Monday of every month. After several years of interrupted service—due to Indian attacks on such postal station towns as Brookfield, and also due to the Dutch takeover of New York—the Boston Post Road finally saw regular mail service. By 1691, service was regularized and a royal patent was given to the individual in charge of colonial post offices. By 1751, two deputy postmasters—one of them Benjamin Franklin—were named by the crown.

Among the records of post road travel that exist today, the journal of Boston businesswoman Sarah Kemble Knight is vivid and insightful in its observations. In 1704, she traveled unchaperoned on horseback from her home near Dedham to New York, guided by a post rider. Knight acknowledged that her trip, both long and hazardous, was an "unheard of thing for an unaccompanied woman to do." The task of guide and traveler's aid was part of the mail carriers' job despite the requirement that post riders average 30 to 50 miles per day in summer months.

The post road journey being a lengthy one, it was not long before taverns and public houses were commonplace along the route. Establishments such as the Golden Ball Tavern in Weston and the Bunch of Grapes on Boston's King Street flourished in the years prior to the War for Independence. The Green Dragon, also in Boston, became legendary for its role as the place where the Sons of Liberty met before the Boston Tea Party.

In his diary, John Adams describes a Shrewsbury tavern, Major Farrar's, which he visited in 1774. He records that there he "sat down at a good fire in the barroom to dry out my great-coat and saddle-bags." While most taverns provided common rooms in which food and drink were served, few afforded their guests any real comfort—or privacy. Many public houses offered only the most rudimentary and sketchy sleeping arrangements, often with up to eight beds in a room and four people per bed. In her diary, Sarah Kemble Knight refers with no little disgust to having to share her already uncomfortable sleeping accommodations with several strange men.

As time passed, post road improvements accrued. Milestones were erected, in part as a way of determining postal rates. Early in its history, the charge to send a piece of mail along the post road was about three pence for a distance of up to 100 miles. During the War for Independence, these milestones were invaluable aids to intelligence efforts, since they allowed the patriots to report accurately on the movements of enemy troops.

The Boston Post Road saw the gradual demise of postal riders after the advent of stagecoach and wagon travel. Although this change occurred somewhat later than is generally imagined, by the late 1780s stage and wagon travel had been introduced and soon flourished. On October 20, 1783, along the post road from Boston to Hartford, a stagecoach was available to paying travelers for the first time. It made the journey in four days, stopping in Northboro, Brookfield, and Somers, Connecticut. This means of conveyance quickly grew popular, and in 1785 stagecoach owners Levi Pease and Reuben Sykes were granted the first contract to carry U.S. mail.

★   ★   ★   ★   ★   ★   ★   ★

Codfish caught in season could be dried into fish "flakes" on racks in the sun, as depicted here in Provincetown. The fish were usually caught, cleaned, and salted at sea, and rinsed and resalted ashore. The flakes were either covered or brought in at night or in rainy weather. From a circa 1907 postcard

In the 1890s Clifton Johnson photographed this scene which could have taken place at least a century earlier. Gloucester fish cleaners are preparing fish for salting away in barrels in the days before refrigeration. Such barrels were shipped from Gloucester to places all over the world. Courtesy, The Clifton Johnson Collection, The Jones Library, Inc., Amherst

Jonathan Edwards (1703-1758), a Northampton Congregational minister, led a controversial return to more strict Calvinist principles in the late 1730s. He felt sinners must recognize their own depraved natures and have an emotional awakening in order to obtain salvation. In a famous 1741 sermon he reminded his followers of God's power: "The God that holds you over the pit of hell, much as one holds a spider, or some loathsome insect over the fire, abhors you, and is dreadfully provoked." Edwards died from a smallpox inoculation shortly after accepting the presidency of Princeton. Engraved by S.S. Jocelyn and S.B. Munson from a circa 1750 oil painting. Courtesy, Forbes Library

Francis Higginson's observations of Massachusetts waters in 1630, "the Abundance of Sea-Fish are almost beyond believing and sure would I scarce have believed it except I had seen it with mine own eyes." Peter Faneuil, a prominent Boston merchant who gave Faneuil Hall to the city, built his fortune by shipping codfish to foreign markets. By the early 1770s, Chatham, on Cape Cod, boasted 27 cod-fishing ships. George Cabot, another prominent Bostonian, was a ship's captain by the age of 18 and was later the first American to send a ship to St. Petersburg, Russia, in 1784.

Although critical to coastal communities, the Massachusetts economy as a whole did not rely exclusively on fishing. By the mid-1770s a triangle of trade flourished in the Atlantic, both with the British West Indies *and* the French West Indies. Its growth encouraged the emergence of a new merchant class in Massachusetts and created growing tension between colonists and British authority once the Navigation Acts deemed this trade triangle largely illegal.

The triangle was based on specific commodities: whale oil (principally originating from ports at Dartmouth—later known as the town of New Bedford—and Nantucket); naval stores; furs (at least until the late 1760s); and rum. These were shipped to Africa (rum was the principal currency traded there) where they were exchanged for gold—and slaves. Slaves were shipped to the West Indies and exchanged for molasses, which was then transported to Massachusetts distilleries and used in rum production. Medford was but one community known for its manufacture of this lucrative molasses by-product.

While few records exist of many Massachusetts-based slave ships, we know that in 1700 several such vessels operated out of Plymouth and Boston. By and large, however, slave traders were British-based ships and profits from slavery accruing in Massachusetts were only indirectly linked to that tragic and peculiar institution on which the southern colonies became so dependent.

Another century would pass before Massachusetts became heavily embroiled in the public controversy surrounding slavery. But in the early 1700s, awareness of this and other ethical issues provoked concern over moral decline and roused the question of religious degeneration.

The religious revival that began in Northampton in 1734 is another example of how colonial thought and culture changed in spite of itself. Like the growth of the free press and the triangular trade, both this revival and the Great Awakening (which began in Boston in 1740) were phenomena that both shaped and were shaped by their participants. The first of many religious revival movements to spread through New England, the Great Awakening signaled a change in colonists' views of themselves and their communities.

An eloquent preacher, Jonathan Edwards (1703-1758), grandson of the respected Massachusetts clergyman Solomon Stoddard (1643-1729), kindled a religious revival along the Connecticut River Valley. The fervor spread like wildfire from Northampton, where both men had parishes, along the valley north to Northfield and south to Suffield. Entire communities were transformed, and the conversion experience represented to the colonists a common bond among hundreds in Massachusetts as well as many who lived outside the colony. Missionary zeal and millenial hopes went hand in hand. Revivalists became evangelists as well, and in 1751 Edwards himself went to preach in Stockbridge, an outpost in western Massachusetts. There, another minister, David Brainerd, had worked earlier to bring Christianity to the Indians.

The Great Awakening, which burned out by 1744, was a unique, specific religious phenomenon infusing new life into a Puritanism that was creaking with age. Although the Puritans had guided Massachusetts for more than a century, their influence was by now diluted. Revivals helped rejuvenate the colony's spiritual and intellectual climate, intensifying religious influence and resulting in funding for new schools and colleges as well as the revamping of established educational institutions. These schools would train a new generation of clergy, many of whom were to become involved in missionary work throughout the world.

More importantly than its specific religious impact, however, the Great Awakening encouraged people to look optimistically at life in America. Colonists had imagined themselves dwelling in a redeemed land, and the religious revivals resulting from the awakening promoted the idea that the "city upon a hill" was still viable. It was in part due to this renewed sense of religious authority that the political and moral issues of ensuing decades affected the colonists so deeply. To a large degree, the Great Awakening of the 1730s and 1740s strengthened the colonists' resolve so that continued encounters with British authority were treated as unjust and tyrannical acts against a godly people.

ESTABLISHING AN IDENTITY

A growing economy, a more dynamic political structure, and a more complex social environment all contributed enormously to changes in Massachusetts between the mid-seventeenth and mid-eighteenth centuries. But another factor affected the colonists even more directly: war between France and Britain.

This war was made up of several separate conflicts, beginning with King William's War (1689-1697), the North American extension of the War of the League of Augsburg in Europe. Frontier towns in New England were raided by

Benjamin Franklin (1706-1790) was born on Milk Street in Boston, the 10th son in his family. He went to school in Boston for a few years but was educated at home and by himself for the most part. At age 12 he was apprenticed to his half-brother, a Boston printer who began the New England Courant. *After a dispute with the half-brother, Franklin, at age 17 already an expert printer, left for Philadelphia. He of course became more than a printer: his future occupations included author, inventor, statesman, foreign diplomat, and scientist. Drawn by C.N. Cochin, engraved by A.H. Ritchie, 1777. From Duyckinck and Duyckinck,* Cyclopedia of American Literature, *1866*

Indians attacked the stockaded frontier village of Deerfield in 1704, killing some and taking the rest captive—only a few escaped. This scene depicts Rev. John Williams and his family trudging north to Canada with their captors. Mrs. Williams was slain not far along the trail, as she was weak from recent childbirth. Two of the Williams children were also killed. Some of the captives (including a Williams daughter) chose not to be ransomed and stayed on with the Indians. From Lossing, Our Country, A Household History, *Vol. I, 1888*

the French, who subsequently lost Port Royal, Nova Scotia, to the retaliating British. In 1697 the Treaty of Ryswick declared original settlers to be the rightful owners of these areas. King William's War was followed by Queen Anne's War (1701-1713), known in Europe as the War of the Spanish Succession. Queen Anne's War was followed by King George's War, or the War of the Austrian Succession (1740-1748), which was followed by the French and Indian War (1756-1763). The last and by far the most important of this series of conflicts, the French and Indian War left

a lasting impression on Massachusetts' development. This war fostered the Indians' hatred of the French in Canada and the British in New York and New England. Both the French and the British claimed to have some Indian allies, however, despite the Indians' general antagonism toward white colonists. Opposing forces from Great Britain and France continuously used Indians against colonial settlers to further English and Gallic political goals.

In 1704, during Queen Anne's War, a party of French, along with hostile Indians from Montreal, descended on the

Massachusetts town of Deerfield. It had been laid waste by an Indian massacre in 1675 and was once again attacked and 53 people were killed. Another 111 were taken captive by the French and the Indians and marched through bitter winter snows as far as Canada. Lancaster, which lay further east, suffered similarly. In 1708, Haverhill, near the New Hampshire border, was attacked, and about 40 people in that community lost their lives.

Although some towns suffered from Indian attacks more than others, some made alliances with Indians and thus were spared any violence. The Iroquois Confederation, known as the *Five Nations,* became closely allied with the British in America. These natives sold furs to colonists and fought alongside the British during the French and Indian War. Opposing tribes allied with the French included the Delaware Indians.

When the French and Indian War erupted, many British settlers' lives were constantly threatened by Indian raids. Combined with the previous decades' conflicts, this promoted the colonists' willingness to fight back. British control of North America was finally secured with the Treaty of Paris in 1763, after British forces defeated the French in the Battle of Quebec. Among the leaders on the British side was General Jeffrey Amherst. The town of Amherst in western Massachusetts was named after this able soldier, who helped take Crown Point and Fort Ticonderoga in 1759. Fighting under the command of Amherst and numerous other officers, including George Washing-

Boston lawyer James Otis (1725-1783) was the intellectual leader of Massachusetts' opposition to the English colonial tax measures after his 1761 court battle against the "writs of assistance," or general search warrants, which Crown officials used to search for smuggled goods. From Grafton, The American Revolution: A Picture Sourcebook, Dover, 1975

Faneuil Hall, a gift to Boston from merchant Peter Faneuil, was to be used for public meetings and as a marketplace. Because of a speech by James Otis in 1763 dedicating Faneuil Hall to the cause of freedom for which he later fought, the structure became known as "The Cradle of Liberty" and in it were *hung portraits and memorabilia from the Revolution. In 1742 when it was built, Faneuil Hall served a new international trading center just blossoming near the waterfront, a shipping port of growing importance. From Barber,* History and Antiquities of Every Town in Massachusetts, *1839*

Right: *In 1762 a rumor spread around Boston and New England that the crown had appointed an Anglican bishop to sit in Boston, still a Congregational stronghold. Then in 1767 the spectre raised itself again when an Episcopal preacher was said to have written a letter to England requesting a bishop. The colonists were furious at the idea, and this cartoon shows the strong feelings aroused. There had been an Anglican church—King's Chapel—in Boston since 1754, and royal appointees were usually Episcopalian, but the thought of a bishop really rankled the anti-hierarchy Congregationalists. From Stark,* The Loyalists of Massachusetts and the Other Side of the Revolution, *1910*

Facing page, top: *On August 14, 1765, the Loyal Nine (a Boston social club of printers, distillers, and other artisans) and North and South End mobs rose up against the Stamp Act and the future stamp agent, Andrew Oliver. The mob hung Oliver in effigy, tore down a new building they assumed would be the stamp office, and built a bonfire with the wood near Oliver's home, where they smashed his windows. In this view sympathetic to Loyalists, the angry crowd is shown throwing stones and threatening the officials who came to disperse them. Andrew Oliver promised not to become the stamp agent. From Stark,* The Loyalists of Massachusetts and the Other Side of the Revolution, *1910*

ton, more than 6,000 Massachusetts troops lost their lives during these war years.

A separate set of events during this period marked a significant shift in British colonial policy. As victory over France became certain, British authorities began enforcing stiffer colonial adherence to crown policy. In 1761, Parliament had passed the Writs of Assistance authorizing general searches of homes and warehouses. The law seemed acceptable so long as war raged, but following the Treaty of Paris in 1763, colonists expected arbitrary searches to cease. James Otis, a noted Boston lawyer, carried their arguments against such searches and their demands for termination of the Writs of Assistance to the courts. Otis called on Britain to acknowledge the colonists' rights, but Parliament, deaf to his pleas, ignored these as well as subsequent demands for a hands-off colonial policy. By doing so, Britain unwittingly set the stage for colonial rebellion.

In 1764, James Otis published a pam-

Left: *Royal Governor Francis Bernard (1712-1799) was well liked by the people of Massachusetts when he was first appointed in 1760. By 1769 when he fled Boston back to England, he was despised as a person and as a symbol of British rule. While in office he acquired large tracts of land: all of Mount Desert Island in the Maine district, parts of seven townships in Vermont, one-third of a large town in the new Berkshire County, and a large estate on Jamaica Pond in Roxbury. He lived in Boston at the Province House, worshiped in the royal curtained box at Anglican King's Chapel, and had apartments at the fort on Castle Island in the harbor. This portrait was painted circa 1775 by John Singleton Copley. From Stark,* The Loyalists of Massachusetts and the Other Side of the Revolution, *1910*

phlet titled *The Rights of the British Colonies Asserted and Proved,* in which he avowed that Parliament could not legally tax colonial property. It was one of the early arguments in the most significant dispute yet between Britain and its colonies. Taxation without representation was the issue that would ultimately provoke the end of British rule in Massachusetts, as well as in the 12 other colonies.

Subsequent legal limitations placed on colonists were detailed in 1765 with passage of the Stamp Act, which required a stamp on all newspapers, pamphlets, legal documents, and other papers issued in the colonies. And the tightening of the 1764 Sugar Act, first passed in 1733, lowered a sixpence-per-gallon duty on imported molasses to three pence-per-gallon but threatened serious enforcement. It also meant that the British were less interested in regulating trade and more intent on raising revenues in the simplest way possible. The enforcement of duties on sugar affected the price of rum as well and further angered the colonists.

GROWTH OF DISSENT

Massachusetts had grown in population size and density since the 1680s. In 1643, the counties of Suffolk, Middlesex, and Essex had been established. Hampden County had been established in 1662, followed by Barnstable, Bristol, and Plymouth counties in 1685, and Dukes and Nantucket counties in 1695. The latter was named after the Indian word *nantican,* meaning "far-away land." Worcester County was established by the General Court in 1731. In 1760, Massachusetts' estimated population was 202,600, and in 1761, Berkshire County was established with Pittsfield as its county seat. It became more and more apparent that if challenged by Britain, Massachusetts would have both the moral inclination and the human resources and governmental structure to stand up to that challenge.

In June 1765, shortly after Parliament passed the Stamp Act, the Massachusetts Assembly proposed that an intercolonial Stamp Act Congress should meet. Here, representatives from the colonies could discuss ways of legally protesting the new law. Britain expected to collect about £60,000 annually from these colonial stamp duties, but Parliament had failed to consider the colonists' willingness to pay the tax. Instead of generating colonial revenue, the Stamp Act provoked unanticipated resistance.

The Stamp Act Congress met in New York City in October 1765. It immediately adopted the Declaration of Rights and Grievances, which declared that freeborn Englishmen could not be taxed without their consent. It further stated that since colonists were not represented in Parliament, any tax imposed on them without their consent was unconstitutional. It was a repetition of the point James Otis had made the year before, in 1764, when protesting against the Writs of Assistance.

Meanwhile, rioting mobs in Boston were sympathetic to the Stamp Act Congress' aims. These mobs looted and burned both homes and offices of British stamp officials. Lieutenant Governor Thomas Hutchinson's Boston mansion was vandalized as a protest against his harsh, unyielding, and autocratic views. Stamp Master Andrew Oliver's house was attacked and his office destroyed. By November, when the Stamp Act was actually to take effect, British officials were left without any alternative but to ignore the act's regulations. Massachusetts colonists had made their point.

Methods other than rioting also were effective in expressing colonial dissatisfaction with British authority. By virtue of Massachusetts law, the colonial assembly approved individuals whose names were submitted as candidates for the royal governor's council. In 1766, the assembly refused to approve names submitted by Governor Francis Bernard, and although the royal governor became furious, his anger only strengthened the opposition. A group of men calling themselves the Sons of Liberty—James Otis, John Adams, Samuel Adams, Paul

Facing page: *The Province House, built in 1716 nearly opposite the head of Milk Street in Boston, was home to the royal governors. It was an imposing three-story brick mansion, set back and well-landscaped, with a stone walk and massive stone steps. On the lofty cupola turned a copper Indian weathervane—now at the Massachusetts Historical Society— made by Shem Drowne. Before the Revolution the royal governor fled the country; the Province House was soon seized by the colonists. After the Revolution it became the property of the state until 1811, when this sketch was made. In 1864 it burned, but traces of its brick walls were still in evidence in 1910 and may still be there. From Stark,* The Loyalists of Massachusetts and the Other Side of the Revolution, *1910*

This view of the Boston Massacre, March 5, 1770, portrays the British Redcoats being set upon by a rowdy bunch. The British almost look apologetic and chagrined at having to keep order in front of the Town House, now called the Old State House. Painting by Alonzo Chappel. From Spencer and Lossing, A Complete History of the United States, Vol. I, 1878

Revere, Benjamin Edes, and others—publicly asked for resistance against the governor. The Sons of Liberty held meetings, published statements in newspapers, and encouraged all the colonists not to cooperate with crown officials. Governor Bernard saw only too well what might happen and how impotent he was politically. In a 1765 letter to the Lords of Trade in London, Bernard had complained that he was "only a nominal governor," and that he was a "prisoner . . . wholly in the Power of the People."

Governor Bernard was able to sense what Parliament, at such a distance, was unable or unwilling to admit. Encouraged by the Sons of Liberty, Boston merchants signed nonimportation agreements—indeed, merchants throughout Massachusetts signed such contracts boycotting British goods. Both in Boston and in smaller cities and towns, people refused to buy anything shipped from England. Those who did not comply with this new edition of colonial resistance were publicly denounced and derided by other colonists. The nonimportation boycott caused a trade loss resulting in the repeal of the Stamp Act by Parliament in 1766. This repeal occurred after British merchants complained that their businesses were in jeopardy.

Passed in 1765, the Quartering Act generated even more alarm and resistance in Massachusetts than had previous restrictive British regulations. Suddenly, residents faced the probability of increased numbers of British troops in Boston—troops toward whom Massachusetts colonists felt more and more hostile. The end of the French and Indian conflict led colonists to expect a respite from the presence of British regulars, but the British authorities decided otherwise.

In this version of the Boston Massacre by Paul Revere after a painting by Henry Pelham, the British are portrayed as the aggressors; the "poor colonials" were not really fighting at all and look quite innocent. The little dog in front was to remind the viewer that dogs licked up the blood when the fight was over and five colonials were dead. From Winsor, The Memorial History of Boston, 1630-1880, *Vol. III, 1883*

On October 1, 1768, two regiments of British redcoats—about 600 men—landed in Boston and disembarked at Long Wharf. The presence of these regiments (the 14th and the 29th) was in royal response to Massachusetts' call for intercolonial protest against the Townshend Acts. These acts had been passed the year before, shortly after repeal of the Stamp Act. Now, Massachusetts colonists hoped to provoke a nonimportation agreement similar to that launched after passage of the Stamp Act. In October 1767, Samuel Adams and his cohorts designated items taxed by the Townshend Acts to be boycotted if the acts were not repealed. The tax included such items as glass, lead, paper, and tea—materials and products in great demand in the colonies. Adams knew he would have little difficulty promoting a boycott. He also sensed that Massachusetts might be able to encourage other colonies to act against Britain and was soon gratified when Massachusetts took steps to ensure such group action. The Massachusetts General Court sent a circular letter to other colonial legislatures urging protest against the Townshend Acts. When word of this letter reached Lord Hillsborough, the British royal secretary of the colonies, he responded by sending two military regiments to Boston.

Ultimately, peaceful boycott of the Townshend duties led to the repeal of most of them by the British Parliament in March 1770. All taxes except those on tea were lifted. But news of that repeal reached Massachusetts too late to prevent a major clash between British troops and Boston residents. The encounter had been brewing for two years, since the troops had landed in Boston Harbor. Hostility ran high against British authority and sentries posted throughout the city were a too-visible reminder of that hated authority.

On March 5, 1770, fighting broke out in Boston's King Street, near the Custom House. Muskets fired—despite a British officer's orders against shooting into the crowd. Soon five men lay dead or dying, victims of the so-called Boston Massacre. The lieutenant governor was petitioned by a committee of colonists who demanded that the British troops be withdrawn from the city. The committee's message was direct:

That it is the unanimous opinion of this meeting that the inhabitants and soldiery can no longer live together in safety; that nothing can rationally be expected to restore the peace of the town & prevent further blood & carnage, but the immediate removal of the Troops; and that we therefore most fervently pray his Honor that his power and influence may be exerted for their instant removal.

Ultimately, nine British soldiers were arrested and put on trial for murder. Seven were acquitted of the charges and two were found guilty of manslaughter. These two were punished and discharged from the army. The two regiments were finally removed to Castle William, a fort

located in Boston Harbor.

Fanned to white heat during the two years leading up to the rioting, tempers cooled as time passed and repeal of the Townshend duties was publicized. By now, Massachusetts had a population of about 235,000, and few were eager to continue extremist opposition to Britain. Even Samuel Adams—the feisty, fire-eating Son of Liberty—recognized by 1771 that violent sentiment could not be maintained indefinitely: ". . . when at a lucky Season the publick are awakened to a Sense of Danger [and] a manly resentment is enkindled, it is difficult, for so many separate Communities as there are in all the colonies, to agree on one consistent plan of Opposition."

By this time, the current royal governor of Massachusetts, Thomas Hutchinson, relaxed a bit. For although British troops remained, the colonists seemed relatively calm. In fact, some of the more radical patriots such as Samuel Adams expressed open dismay at what

they feared was deepening apathy. The solution, according to these patriots, was to form a Committee of Correspondence. This committee helped promote the idea that there remained many complaints to be lodged against Britain. Other colonies followed suit and formed their own organized protests. A short distance away, in Narragansett Bay, colonists in Rhode Island burned a British customs ship—the *Gaspee*—in 1772. Responsibility was claimed by the Committee of Correspondence there. The following year a far more colorful incident took place in Boston Harbor. The provocation was once more an act of Parliament designed to interfere with colonial trade.

Britain passed a Tea Act in 1773, granting the British East India Company monopoly on tea sales in the colonies. Suddenly, colonial merchants were no longer involved as middlemen in the lucrative tea trade. And since tea was a most popular eighteenth-century beverage, colonial merchants' losses were

Castle William on Castle Island in Boston Harbor was the strongest fort in New England and contained apartments for the royal governors. Governor Francis Bernard often avoided pre-Revolutionary War problems by having a 12-oared barge always ready to take him to Castle Island. When the unpopular governor and his son fled Boston in August 1769, they went to Castle William and then to England. The delighted Bostonians celebrated with fireworks. From Winsor, The Memorial History of Boston, 1630-1880, *Vol. III, 1883*

considerable. But more important, interference in their trade arrangements once again worried colonists. How long would it be before the British crown became involved in other aspects of colonial commerce?

As in the past, Boston's response was swift and effective. When the British ship *Dartmouth,* with a hold full of tea, arrived in Boston Harbor in December 1773, its captain waited to see if the tea would be unloaded. He needn't have wondered. It was taken—at night—by a band of "Indians" who dumped the entire shipment into the water. Of course, the group was not made up of real native Americans, but disguised Sons of Liberty. Their action prompted retaliation by Britain, and the resulting Coercive Acts placed severe restrictions on Massachusetts government and closed the port of Boston to all commerce. It would remain closed until the East India Company was paid for the tea.

By 1774, Britain's General Thomas Gage, commander in chief in North America, had been appointed governor of Massachusetts. Town meetings, ordinarily in session as frequently as necessary, were limited to annual gatherings. Provisions of the Coercive Acts were combined with terms of the Quebec Act and were labeled the "Intolerable Acts" by the colonists. Finally, Massachusetts and all other colonies had a mutual complaint. Colonial resistance to British tyranny was unified once and for all.

The Massachusetts royal charter had been annulled by the British in May 1774. By the time General Gage took over as governor, Massachusetts had set up an extra-legal Provincial Congress with John Hancock as head of the newly formed Committee of Safety. This group was empowered primarily with responsibility to train and to call out the militia if necessary.

War seemed inevitable. In February 1775, the second Provincial Congress of Massachusetts met, and later that month British troops arrived in Salem where

military provisions had been stored. The redcoats were unsuccessful in their mission to seize those munitions and the colonists congratulated themselves—at the same time preparing for the inevitable future confrontation.

In addition to looking out for its own interests, Massachusetts rallied other colonies to action. In September 1774, Massachusetts sent delegates to the First Continental Congress held in Philadelphia, as did the other 12 colonies: Connecticut, Delaware, Georgia, Maryland, New Hampshire, New Jersey, New York, North Carolina, Pennsylvania, Rhode Island, South Carolina, and Virginia. Massachusetts' delegates were Thomas Cushing, Samuel Adams, Robert Treat Paine, James Bowdoin, and John Adams. The congress adopted the Suffolk Resolves, which demanded direct resistance to the Intolerable Acts and which were initially passed by Suffolk County delegates to Massachusetts' Provincial Congress. These delegates had first met in Dedham, then in Milton, to register a protest against the Coercive Acts. John Adams' *Declaration of Rights and Resolves* was also adopted enthusiastically by the First Continental Congress. This document articulated colonists' grievances against Britain but presented no new claims or disputes against the crown. Another boycott was established in which all colonies agreed not to import, export, or consume British goods.

Despite concerted action by all 13 colonies, British authorities—including King George III—believed Massachusetts to be the only colony showing signs of serious unrest. On the other hand, General Gage understood that Massachusetts was not alone in its resistance. In his position as royal governor and as a military commander of some experience, Gage recognized certain inevitabilities. Allied as one force, the colonies represented a formidable threat to Parliamentary authority. Gage knew militia were gathering and he also knew he had insufficient troops to suppress a colonial rebellion should one materialize.

Facing page: *The Liberty Tree, at the corner of Washington and Essex streets, was a giant and aged elm from which were hung likenesses of loathed Tories like the stamp collector. Patriots met under the Liberty Tree to plan the Revolution. The tree was thought to have been a seedling before Boston was settled by the Puritans in 1630 and was protected by a picket fence. That did not prevent the angry British from chopping it into 15 cords of firewood before they evacuated Boston. From* The London Illustrated News, *January 9, 1858*

Above: *This is a 1901 look at the North Bridge in Concord, an 1875 replica of the 1775 rustic bridge. In 1909 a cement bridge safe for the new automobiles was built, but today, a wooden replica again marks the historic place. In the distance is the Concord Minute Man statue by Daniel Chester French, commissioned by the town in 1875 for America's centennial celebration. From* New England Magazine, *Vol. XXV, September 1901*

Right: *In this engraving from a painting by Alonzo Chappel, the British troops retreat down Concord's main road while being harassed from both sides by groups of militia. British losses for the day totaled 73 killed and 174 wounded; the colonials suffered 49 men killed and 41 wounded. From Grafton,* The American Revolution: A Picture Sourcebook, *Dover, 1975*

Facing page: *General George Washington left Philadelphia on horseback on June 21, 1775, arriving at Cambridge on July 2 to assume command of the Continental Army. At six feet he was unusually tall for a man of his day and was an imposing figure. Upon his arrival he found his troops lacked arms, ammunition, and military stores. They were unruly, clearly not used to military discipline. It took him months of drilling to form his army, and months to bring order to the supply system. When the cannons arrived from Ticonderoga, the troops were ready. From Spencer and Lossing,* A Complete History of the United States, *Vol. I, 1878*

appointed brigadier generals in the American forces.

Thousands of American troops were already quartered in Cambridge, laying siege to Boston across the river. This siege lasted nearly 12 months before General Gage and his British troops finally were forced to leave the city in March of the following year, an exodus now celebrated in Boston as Evacuation Day. The inhabitants of Boston suffered greatly during this siege and the entire colony was relieved when the British departed. Their retreat was prompted in part by Henry Knox's ingenious strategy of aiming cannons at the British fortifications in Boston. Knox had gone to Fort Ticonderoga in New York in the middle of the winter to retrieve 55 pieces of captured artillery. It was due specifically to use of these cannons, shooting from the fortifications of Dorchester Heights, that colonists did not have to fight British troops on Massachusetts soil for the duration of the war. After March 1776 and the British evacuation of Boston, General Washington took the Continental Army to its war theater in New York.

Although there was almost no combat in Massachusetts, the War for Independence nevertheless had a great impact on the colony. Ship owners especially took advantage of wartime exigencies and many became rich from privateering. In practice, this meant raiding British ships—and Boston, as well as Salem and other smaller ports, was a center of operation for privateering until late in the war. By then, a British coastal blockade managed to put an end to this profitable illegal pastime. Captain Joseph Peabody of Salem was one of hundreds who made a fortune from privateering operations. Since Massachusetts no longer considered itself part of Britain, its ports were now technically open to foreign trading ships. It looked as if Great Britain's days of regulating trade in Massachusetts were over.

DECLARING INDEPENDENCE
By June 1776, John Adams of Braintree (now Quincy) and several others meeting in Virginia at the Second Continental

Congress helped draft an independence resolution. In July, the Declaration of Independence was submitted to the congress for approval. Boston's John Hancock, president of the congress, was first in signing the document written to help Americans identify as a unified group rather than as residents of colonies with separate grievances against the crown.

That Massachusetts had a grievance was unmistakable. John Adams, in his diary for March 1776, reasoned that resentment ". . . is a Passion, implanted by Nature for the Preservation of the Individual. Injury is the Object which excites it . . . ought, for his own Seccurity and Honur, and for the public good to punish those who injure him, unless they repent . . . It is the same with Communities. They ought to resent and punish."

PROMINENT INDIVIDUALS
John Adams' name is remembered because of his contributions to the Declaration of Independence, his close friendship with its main author, Thomas Jefferson, and his term as second president of the United States. But there are many others from Massachusetts whose courage and conviction before, during, and after the Revolution have kept them prominent in Americans' memories. Few names evoke such a vigorous image as Paul Revere.

Immortalized by the poet Longfellow nearly a century later, Revere was a man of great talent and inventiveness. An accomplished craftsman, he was well known for his abilities as a silversmith and a master engraver. Many of his silver spoons, cups, salvers, salt cellars, and other items can now be seen on display in the Museum of Fine Arts in Boston. Revere's portrait, painted by John Singleton Copley—a prominent Bostonian whose Loyalist sentiments caused him to flee Massachusetts for England in 1774—hangs as part of the same museum's collection of early American paintings. The portrait shows Revere

This engraving from a painting by M.A. Wageman shows the British boarding ships to evacuate Boston on March 17, 1776. Cannon barrels are being dumped off a wharf to prevent capture. Accompanied by Loyalist colonials, most of the British fled to Halifax, Nova Scotia. Today, Evacuation Day is a state holiday which just happens to coincide with St. Patrick's Day. From Grafton, The American Revolution: A Picture Sourcebook, *Dover, 1975*

holding a teapot and gazing intently, but benignly, out of the canvas. It is easy to imagine him flinging himself onto the back of a horse, preparing to send the alarm throughout Massachusetts that "the redcoats are coming." Revere embodies the quintessence of Massachusetts patriotism—self-confidence, independence, and a desire only to live in peace without interference from external authority.

Another Massachusetts native with a reputation for independence is Deborah Sampson. Hers is among the more interesting stories of the period and concerns her role as a soldier in the Continental Army. Born in Plympton, near Plymouth, on December 17, 1760, Sampson enlisted in the army at age 22 by disguising herself as a man. Under the

name Robert Shurtleff, she fought in the 4th Massachusetts Regiment. Wounded in a battle near Tarrytown, New York, Sampson was hospitalized and her deception was discovered. She was discharged from the army in 1783. Since she had actually been enlisted, Sampson-alias-Shurtleff was eligible for, and received, a military pension, the first woman in the nation to do so. In the years following her army adventures she married, had several children, and sometimes lectured publicly about her many experiences. Sampson died at the age of 66 in 1827.

Another unusual woman associated with early Massachusetts history is Phillis Wheatley. Born in Africa, she was sold in 1761 to a prosperous Boston family, who educated her and treated her as a

The Town House, built in Boston in 1711, is an early example of brick architecture. Built as a government center for Boston and the Province of Massachusetts, it housed courtrooms and a merchants' exchange. The Boston Massacre took place in front of the structure in 1770 when British troops were housed inside. The lion and unicorn, British symbols, were removed during the Revolution, and the Declaration of Independence was read to the people from the balcony. After the Revolution the building was used as a state house, a city hall, and a post office. Known today as the Old State House, it is the headquarters of the Bostonian Society with its library and museum, and the British lion and unicorn again stand on the stepped gables. From A Souvenir of Massachusetts Legislators, 1904

Paul Revere (1735-1818) set himself up as a gold- and silversmith in Boston in 1758, but he also did copper-plate engraving. Among his prints were a view of the Boston Massacre and the design for Massachusetts' first paper currency. After his ride as special messenger for the Committee of Safety in 1775, he became a major and lieutenant colonel of a regiment of artillery. He returned to metalsmithing after the war and built a bell and cannon foundry. In 1801 he established a large, and possibly the first, copper-rolling works, at Canton. Oil portrait by John Singleton Copley, circa 1768-1770. Courtesy, Museum of Fine Arts, Boston. Gift of Joseph W., William B., and Edward H.R. Revere.

Phillis Wheatley (circa 1753-1784) was born in Africa, kidnapped, and sold at a slave auction in Boston to a family named Wheatley. Phillis learned English with remarkable speed, and, although she never attended a formal school, she also learned Greek. She became a sensation in Boston in the 1760s because of her excellent poetry. In failing health, Phillis Wheatley was taken to England in 1773 by the Wheatley son, where she charmed the nobility. Her first bound volume of poems was published in London in 1773 with a copper plate engraving of her from which this engraving was made. From Duyckinck and Duyckinck, Cyclopedia of American Literature, Vol. I, Part 2, 1866

John Hancock (1737-1793) was a Boston merchant who inherited a fortune at age 27 and then went into politics. He was the first to sign the Declaration of Independence, and then became a militia commander during the war that followed. Hancock was elected governor of Massachusetts, serving from 1780 to 1785 and from 1787 until his death. From Winsor, The Memorial History of Boston, 1630-1880, *Vol. IV, 1883*

family member. She developed a talent for writing and became the first black woman poet in America. Her verse having been widely published beginning in 1770, she traveled to Britain in 1773 with a member of the Wheatley family where she was a guest of the Countess of Huntingdon. She received her freedom and married a free black man in 1778 but suffered severe reverses of fortune and, despite her skills, was barely able to support her family. In 1784, she died in

complete poverty. Only in subsequent years was interest rekindled in this remarkable woman's poetry, and today she is recognized for the iron will and incredible talent she displayed throughout her life.

John Hancock's name is instantly recognized by most Americans and has become a byword for signatures since his own was the first to appear on the Declaration of Independence. Although known today principally as a statesman,

Hancock was first a Boston merchant. Later Hancock, as president of the Provincial Congress in Massachusetts, issued calls for naval recruits in the year following the revolution's outbreak. He had hoped to be named commander-in-chief of the Continental Army, but that honor went to the more experienced George Washington. After Hancock was elected governor of Massachusetts, stories circulated concerning his lack of courtesy toward Washington. When the president visited Massachusetts after his election, it was said that an imperious and pompous Hancock still held a grudge against the first chief executive for the role he played in the War for Independence.

Samuel Adams (cousin of John Adams, America's second president) was one of the most outspoken of the Sons of Liberty. He took great pleasure in exciting the emotions of his fellow colonists, and some of the more moderate-minded considered his impassioned speeches and intemperate demands a liability. A driving force behind the nonimportation agreements and known as the "Great Agitator," Adams acted as a catalyst for interactions between Britain and the colonies. Without his determination, many attempts at obtaining justice would have achieved less prominence. Adams, a signer of the Declaration of Independence, was lieutenant governor under John Hancock in 1789 and was himself elected governor of Massachusetts in 1794.

No less a patriot than Samuel Adams, Mercy Otis Warren was known in pre-revolutionary times for writing political satire. Born in 1728, she authored both poems and plays. After she married James Warren in 1754, their home became a gathering place for patriots like the Adamses. Warren's outspoken writing was published in the *Massachusetts Spy* beginning in 1772, and her attacks on British authority continued for several years. Her brother James, a member of the Sons of Liberty, also attacked the British and supported colonial demands for repeal of several

acts of Parliament. Although the family lost its political prestige and power by the 1780s owing to its conservatism, Warren continued to write about political issues. Her major work was a three-volume history of the American revolution, published in 1805. Warren died in 1814 at her home in Plymouth.

These individuals and the efforts to which they devoted their lives are representative of thousands of Massachusetts residents who contributed to the colony's growth. Even those in remote areas—or those like Mercy Otis Warren and Phillis Wheatley who were subject to the gender and race discrimination of the era—left a rich legacy.

American patriot Mercy Otis Warren (1728-1814) was the sister of James Otis and the wife of James Warren. After writing poems, plays, and political satire for many years, Warren began in 1772 to attack the British in writings published in the Massachusetts Spy. *Her major work was a three-volume history of the American Revolution, published in 1805. From Ellet,* The Women of the Revolution, *Vol. I, 1818. Courtesy, The Jones Library, Inc., Amherst*

ECONOMIC AND POLITICAL FERMENT (1780-1814)

★　　★　　★　　★　　★　　★　　★　　★　　★

On August 19, 1812, the U.S.S. Constitution, *now preserved at Charlestown Navy Yard, vanquished the English frigate* Guerriere *in a 25-minute battle off Cape Race that wrecked the* Guerriere *but did so little damage to the* Constitution *that it was then called "Old Ironsides." The British lost 79 men, the Americans 14. When the* Constitution *sailed into Boston with its prisoners it received a grand welcome. It had made a new reputation for the young navy, challenging and bettering the proud British who had ruled the seas since the Spanish Armada. Engraved by James D. Smillie from a drawing by Alonzo Chappel. From Spencer and Lossing,* The Complete History of the United States, *Vol. III, 1878*

The economic chaos that ensued in the United States after the War for Independence had far-reaching effects on the formation of a federal government. In Massachusetts, virtually every resident experienced the postwar upheaval. While the revolution had freed North American colonies from a tyrannical British rule, it had also eliminated the commercial ties providing support for colonial prosperity.

New state governments, including Massachusetts', failed to meet their citizens' needs during this time of fiscal uncertainty and political change. Despite passage of a state constitution in 1780, in the Bay State there was little evidence that elected officials had either the will or the ability to govern wisely. And the crises resulting from poor decision-making had a profound effect on both state and national policy formation in the later years of the eighteenth century.

The new national government was defined by the Articles of Confederation, adopted by the Second Continental Congress in 1777 and ratified by the states in 1781. The articles deferred much authority to the individual state governments, as stated most clearly in Article 2:

Each state retains its sovereignty, freedom and independence, and every power, jurisdiction, and right, which is not by this confederation expressly delegated the United States . . .

Due to this power, the confederation could only suggest ways in which states could act collectively. Moreover, some very real fiscal problems resulted from the states' unwillingness to pay Congress monies needed for maintaining a federal government. In particular, refusal to fund back pay for soldiers in the Continental Army wreaked havoc at the local level. In all of the states in the confederation, soldiers returned home to farms and villages and wanted the money owed to them.

Federalist Caleb Strong (1745-1819) from Northampton was a state representative and county attorney when he was a delegate to the Massachusetts Constitutional Convention of 1779. He went on to become state senator and the Massachusetts representative to the U.S. Constitutional Convention of 1787. He was a senator from Massachusetts from 1789 to 1796, and was then elected governor from 1800 to 1807 and again from 1812 to 1816. Print by G. Stuart Pinx and J. B. Longacre. Courtesy, Forbes Library

had taken part in the uprising. While subject to certain restrictions in holding public office or voting, they would not otherwise be severely punished.

Leaders of the rebellion, and others from outside Massachusetts who had assisted in the attempted take-over of Springfield arsenal, were to be tried on charges of treason against the state. This decision caused an uproar. Many, even those who had actually opposed the rebel cause, were concerned that such measures would provoke further discord. It seemed to many elected officials that punishment of those responsible should be more temperate. Therefore, in 1787, the legislature reconsidered ways of dealing with the men not covered by the terms of the Disqualifying Act.

In April 1787, a new election spelled political defeat for many officials seeking severe penalties against participants in Shays' Rebellion. John Hancock was elected governor, succeeding James Bowdoin. But of 222 members of the House of Representatives, only 62 were reelected. Similarly, out of 24 senators, only 11 were returned to office. It was clear the public wanted a change of policy and this time peaceful, legal means were used to effect that change.

Many new officeholders were men who had openly supported, or actually taken part in, either the pre-uprising conventions or the rebellion itself. The new legislators repealed the Disqualifying Act and pardoned all participants—including Daniel Shays, who received his pardon in June 1788. He spent his remaining years in New York State and died there in 1825.

In the aftermath of Shays' Rebellion, the state legislature amended many laws dealing with taxes and payment of debt. It also fashioned a more responsive, flexible, yet strong, state government.

CONSTITUTIONAL CONVENTION

In May 1787, the Constitutional Convention met in Philadelphia to consider ways to formalize a federal government with credibility and utility. Among Massachusetts delegates whose presence at the Con-

The USS Constitution, "Old Ironsides," is a 204-foot frigate that first sailed in 1797. She became famous by defeating four British frigates in the War of 1812. In the 1830s Oliver Wendell Holmes' poem saved her from being scrapped. She was then used for training and restored in 1927. After being fully refurbished in July 1997, she was taken from her berth at the Charlestown Navy Yard in Boston up to Marblehead for a celebration. She is shown here at full sail July 20th, for the first time since 1881, at Marblehead Harbor. Photo by Janet Stearns. Courtesy, USS Constitution Museum, Boston

Right: *When phrenology (the study of the contours of the human head) was first introduced in Boston in the early 1830s, some of the most influential scientific leaders embraced it as a wonderful tool for reforming society. They thought it would scientifically allow men and women to determine, by the shape of the head, what careers their children should pursue. One could, supposedly, determine who would grow up to be a criminal, and who would be over-strained by too much study. Education reformers like Horace Mann believed in phrenology at first. Phrenologists even promised to help people choose the perfect mate—a compatible head. It was sexist (men had larger heads) and racist (fair skinned people were preferable). By the 1860s phrenology was dismissed by most people as unscientific after all. However, some people still believe. From a home medical book published in 1901*

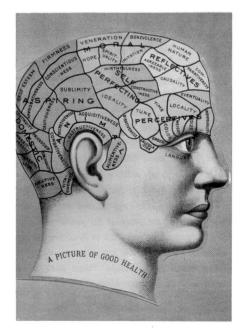

This mill complex in Lowell, now the Wannalancit Office and Technology Center on Northern Canal, was once a busy textile mill. Originally built in 1832 as the Suffolk Manufacturing Company when Lowell was a new experimental mill town, the buildings were rebuilt in 1862 and restored in 1983. Photo by Justine Hill

Sarah Elizabeth Ball, age 2, was painted circa 1838 by itinerant folk artist Erastus Salisbury Field. Miss Ball was the daughter of South Hadley minister Mason Ball and his wife, Orinda, who were also painted by the now-famous Erastus Field. Field, from Leverett, who went to New York City in 1824 to study with Samuel F.B. Morse. In his career as a portrait painter, Field traveled primarily in central and western Massachusetts, as well as Connecticut. His paintings of folksy people and scenes now hang in prestigious museums and galleries all over the nation. Courtesy, Mount Holyoke College Art Museum, South Hadley, Massachusetts

Trinity Row, in Wesleyan Grove on Martha's Vineyard, began in 1835 as a summertime Methodist camp meeting. The first year, there was a shed and nine large tents; by 1858 there were 320 tents and a few cottages. It is estimated that 12,000 people attended camp meetings there in 1857. By that time there were large boarding and lodging tents for guests, who slept on straw bedding. An 1866 New York Times article described the brightly painted cottages as the prettiest feature of Wesleyan Grove. Photo by John H. Martin

stitutional Convention guaranteed a pragmatic, all-encompassing document was Rufus King, later U.S. minister to Great Britain.

As with virtually all issues of the period, those surrounding the proposed federal Constitution provoked considerable debate. Among those who spoke out against the proposed Constitution was Mercy Otis Warren of Plymouth. A strong voice of dissent during the years preceding the War for Independence, she now attacked—from an anti-Federalist standpoint—various provisions of the pending Constitution.

In reference to a standing army, Warren cautioned that such military bodies had been "the nursery of vice and the bane of liberty from the Roman legions . . . to the planting of the British . . . in the capitals of America." Warren's caveat extended to the powers of the Supreme Court, the fallability of the electoral college system, congressional salaries, and the "dangerously blended" powers of the executive and legislative branches of government.

The anti-Federalist position, while not as strong as that which it opposed, claimed victory. For despite passage of a national Constitution binding all states into one government, the Bill of Rights, adopted December 15, 1791, addresses individual and state freedoms. These amendments to the Constitution exist in large part because of efforts like those made by Mercy Otis Warren. The first 10 amendments to the Constitution were passed in response to pressure from many Massachusetts delegates and others who feared a strong central government.

While Shays' Rebellion was small, it was an incident that prompted Constitutional Convention delegates to think carefully about federal response to future rebellions. Accordingly, Congress was empowered to call out state militia to "suppress insurrections." In this way, Daniel Shays and the others in Massachusetts who agitated for redress of their grievances helped effect lasting change in the way the nation's government was shaped and codified.

GROWTH UNDER "A MORE PERFECT UNION"

By 1788, despite dissenting opinions, the new constitution of the United States of America had been ratified by nine states. Massachusetts was the sixth state formally to support the constitution, voting "yes" on February 6, 1788. In the spring of 1789, George Washington was elected the nation's first president and Massachusetts native John Adams, who had received 34 electoral college votes, was named vice president. Adams would become the new nation's second president when Washington—besieged by ill health and advancing age—gave his farewell address

Eli Whitney (1765-1825) was born in Westboro, worked his way through Yale, and became a teacher in Georgia. By April 1793 he had built a machine, the cotton gin, that could take the seeds out of cotton. In 1798 Whitney obtained a government contract for manufacturing firearms and developed a manufacturing system utilizing interchangeable parts. He established a factory near New Haven which made him wealthy. From Cirker, Dictionary of American Portraits, *Dover, 1967*

The launching of the ship Fame *in Salem Harbor, 1802, was painted in oils by George Ropes and here turned into an engraving for* Harper's *magazine in 1886. At its height in the early 1800s, Salem's port was a strong rival to Boston Harbor in the international trade. From* Harper's New Monthly Magazine, *Vol. LXXIII, September 1886*

During the Federal period Massachusetts craftsmen executed some fine furniture. This semi-circular chest of drawers made by Thomas Seymour in 1808 was constructed of mahogany and satinwood in a highly patterned veneer and inlay technique with cast ornamental brass and paint. Courtesy, Museum of Fine Arts, Boston. From the M. and M. Karolik Collection of 18th Century American Arts

key to prosperity and were willing to take the risks involved. That they did this so often and in such impressive numbers is a testimony to the unmistakable allure of Asian markets.

When the China trade opened fully, Massachusetts reaped undreamed-of benefits. Local sailing ships skippered by shrewd entrepreneurs were quick to establish commercial ties with other nations. In August 1784, the *Empress of China,* a 360-ton vessel, left for Canton with a cargo of export ginseng. This plant, valued as an aphrodisiac and prolonger of life by the Chinese, grew in North America as well as in the Orient. Enterprising Massachusetts businessmen such as Boston-born Samuel Shaw knew an investment in ginseng exports was a sure bet—and he reaped a tidy fortune through this trade.

In Salem, the merchantman *Grand Turk* sailed for China in 1795. One hundred years after its divisive witchcraft trials, Salem was thriving and prosperous.

When the *Grand Turk* returned from the East loaded with silks, porcelains, and tea, 34 captains of other ships left from Salem on similar voyages in search of equally fine—and saleable—cargoes. But they soon discovered that by trading in what are now known as the Hawaiian Islands, profits would exceed those accruing from trade with China alone. The Pacific trade routes were traveled extensively and regularly by Massachusetts ships throughout the last years of the eighteenth and the early years of the nineteenth century.

FRUITS OF STABILITY

In 1796, Salem's Chestnut Street had begun to reflect the prosperity and stability of its inhabitants. Most fine homes in this neighborhood were designed and con-

John Adams (1735-1826) was a lawyer, political science scholar, writer, wartime diplomat to England, vice president to George Washington, and then president. He was one of the authors of the Declaration of Independence and of the Massachusetts Constitution on which the U.S. Constitution was based. Ironically, both Adams and Thomas Jefferson died exactly 50 years after the 1776 Declaration of Independence, on the Fourth of July, 1826. From Spencer and Lossing, A Complete History of the United States, *Vol. I, 1878*

structed by Samuel McIntire, responsible for some of the most beautiful examples of Federal architecture in New England. Among those exemplary Salem houses are the Pierce-Nichols House (1792), the Cook-Oliver House (1804), Hamilton Hall (1805), and the Pickering-Shreve-Little House (1816). These homes are visible, lasting monuments to the lucrative shipping trade that blossomed at the turn of the century.

The wealth pouring into Newburyport resulted there, as it did in Salem, in lavish architecture, much of which was crafted by ships' carpenters. A visitor to Newburyport in 1800 noted that the homes there, "taken collectively, make a better appearance than those of any other town in New England ... upon the whole, few places, probably, in the world, furnish more means of a delightful residence than Newburyport."

International shipping and trade made Salem the main brokerage center for a number of exotic items, including pepper. The United States traded some 7.5 million pounds of this spice in 1805. Clever investors, many of whom were based in Salem, had wisely purchased the entire Sumatran pepper crop for resale that year. Earlier sales figures for this essential cooking ingredient and preservative indicate that in 1791 the United States had reexported only about 500 pounds of pepper.

Even without recourse to Oriental trade, some communities in Massachusetts established themselves via maritime exploits, principally in the form of shipbuilding, fishing, and whaling. By 1800, the region around the Merrimack River north of Boston grew richer as thousands of tons of sail, rope, iron, and fittings were manufactured for the many vessels launched there each year. Haverhill had several shipyards, as did Amesbury, Salisbury, and Newburyport. By 1806, the latter town had 60 ships involved in fisheries, which concentrated on the Labrador fishing banks. Others were active in the Caribbean trade, which resulted in a proliferation of distilleries for whiskey and rum in the region.

It is not surprising that Massachusetts grew economically stable thanks to contributions from its harbor cities. The state's coastline, totaling about 750 miles, offered opportunities at every inlet, from Cape Ann to Cape Cod to New Bedford, and to the islands of Nantucket and Martha's Vineyard.

POLITICS AND THE ECONOMY

The political climate that encouraged economic expansion in the late eighteenth and early nineteenth centuries was the combined result of a number of factors. In addition to changes in its local economy stemming from the United States' foreign relations, Massachusetts successfully weathered many political storms that blew across the new nation in the late 1700s. Civil conflict was not restricted to disgruntled ex-soldiers demanding back military wages. Federalists and Republicans came into direct confrontation both within the state's boundaries and in the nation's capital—the Federalist position supported most often by those with strong commercial interests. Farmers with large landholdings looked for stable markets for their agricultural surpluses and were inclined to support Federalist causes and a strong central government. And the split that inevitably widened into two distinct political parties catapulted John Adams to the presidency in 1796.

Adams served competently until 1800, helping guide the nation through a variety of touchy political situations. Among the more challenging was the XYZ Affair. In 1798, when France refused to receive the American minister, President Adams sent a negotiating team to establish friendlier relations. Using go-betweens, however, the French foreign minister demanded a bribe from the Americans. These go-betweens were identified only as X, Y, and Z, and when the American public learned of this charade of diplomacy, feelings ran high against France. Some Federalists, including Alexander Hamilton, demanded that President Adams declare war on France since the French navy recently had been attacking American

Boston Common, Beacon Street, and the State House are depicted about 1811. The Federal style brick homes included, on the left, the 1804 house of John Phillips. On the far right stands the 1804 Armory House. In 1858 the London Illustrated News *noted that "The great charm of the scenery of Boston is its 'Common' or Park—a piece of ground covering about forty acres, and open on one side to the Charles River." Watercolor by Andrew Ritchie from a sketch by J.R. Smith. From Winsor,* The Memorial History of Boston, 1630-1880, *Vol. IV, 1883*

merchant ships. Adams refused, although strong anti-French sentiment did continue.

During Adams' Federalist administration, passage of the Alien and Sedition acts in 1798 reflected continuing federal attempts both to limit foreign influence and to control growing Republican sentiment in the country.

The Alien Act extended the length of residency required of immigrants wanting to become citizens. These immigrant voters, reasoned the Federalists, posed a threat to the stable U.S. government which had been so painstakingly created. The act also gave the president power to expel enemy aliens in time of "declared war." The Sedition Act called for fines or imprisonment of individuals who opposed "any measures . . . of the government of the United States." This opposition included anti-government sentiment published in newspapers—effectively stifling those who spoke out against the Federalist administration. While some in Massachusetts and the nation applauded Adams' conservative

and repressive actions, others saw him as a betrayer of personal liberties.

These and other issues caused public consternation and promoted unrest and disruption. Adams seemed not to care, however. While he was president of the United States, he never worked at developing his popularity. In fact, there were those who absolutely detested him. But he was an able man and had many Massachusetts supporters. His cabinet included Samuel Dexter, U.S. secretary of war in 1800, who became secretary of the treasury under Jefferson in 1801 before Albert Gallatin replaced him later that year.

The power of the Republicans grew nationwide, however, and in 1800 Adams relinquished the presidency to an ardent Republican, Thomas Jefferson, his old compatriot. The 10-year Federalist monopoly was over, and after that the Republicans maintained the upper hand.

This shift in administrations spelled great changes for Massachusetts. The state's economy was directly affected by the change in presidential administration,

since much maritime activity on which the state so heavily depended during these years was touched by decisions of the new Republican president. Under Jefferson, a shipping embargo in 1807 precipitated yet another period of depressed prices. The Embargo Act of 1807 was a response to several years of harassment—often of Massachusetts ships and sailors—by the British fleet. The British harassment policy was a response to the United States' shipping of goods to France and its possessions at a time when war raged between the two European countries. Profits accruing to the U.S. from such trade were more than

the beleaguered British were willing to tolerate. In addition, the British navy was in need of sailors and impressment of American sailors was often the quickest, most effective solution to Britain's perennial shortage of manpower.

Under its maritime laws, the British navy felt it was unlawful to capture American ships carrying cargo to and from French possessions. But to Massachusetts sailors, the risk of being captured—or running the resultant embargo with its federally imposed fine—was worth the probable profits. It is estimated that the United States enjoyed a substantial increase in the

Beacon Hill was the highest of the three hills in Boston. The hill was gradually reduced, necessitating the moving of the Bulfinch column. The famous dome on the State House was not gold until much later in the 1800s. Drawn from an 1855 chromolithograph of an 1811-1812 sketch by J.R. Smith. From Winsor, The Memorial History of Boston, 1630-1880, *Vol. IV, 1883*

The Gerrymander was a sala-mander-shaped beast seen in a realignment of Essex County towns into a new voting district. It was called a Gerrymander for Governor Elbridge Gerry whose Democratic legislature made the change to benefit their party in 1812. The new voting district created an unfair voting bloc and was returned to its former configuration in 1813 after this Gilbert Smart cartoon was published in the Boston Gazette. *Elbridge Gerry went on to be vice president under James Madison. From* Winsor, The Memorial History of Boston, *Vol. III, 1881*

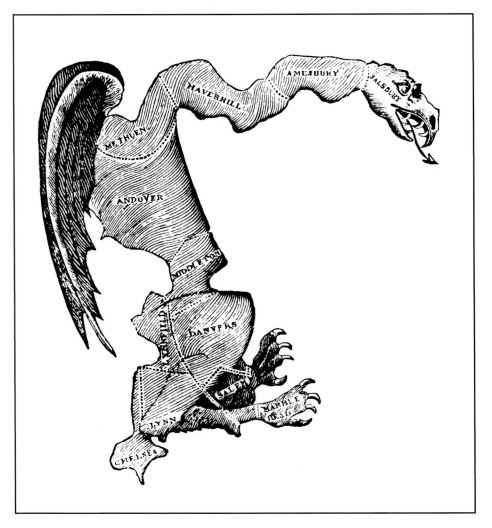

value of reexported products during this time. Trade figures for the period show that in 1803, the state brought in $13 million. By 1806, that number had increased to $60 million. And by 1807, the year the Embargo Act was signed into law by President Jefferson, the Massachusetts fleet was making $15 million in profits on freight charges alone. It is hardly surprising that the Embargo Act was extremely unpopular in the Bay State. One Massachusetts senator calculated that if, despite the blockade of its harbors, a single Massachusetts ship could get by the U.S. Navy, that ship would make a profit far outweighing any fines incurred by such illegal actions.

Despite frequent attempts to circumvent the Embargo Act, it spelled disaster for the nation's economy. In 1807, national exports totaled about $108 million. By the

following year, exports had fallen to $22 million. Similarly, imports went from $138 million in 1807 to $57 million in 1808. For coastal communities in Massachusetts, there was little incentive to punish individuals who defied the embargo—since trade carried on by those ships was often the only thing that kept an area alive economically.

Massachusetts rallied to the defense of its maritime activities. In Gloucester, an angry mob destroyed a U.S. revenue cutter sent to guard the harbor and watch for smuggling operations. The situation echoed those of the pre-revolutionary era and some feared an outbreak of violence nationwide if the Embargo Act was not repealed. By the end of Jefferson's term of office this repeal occurred. The Embargo Act was replaced with the less sweeping Non-Intercourse Act, which only prohibbited trade with Great Britain and France. But it was also unpopular and difficult to enforce and did little to protect American ships and sailors from seizure by British navy vessels. President James Madison finally settled the situation by permitting trade with both European countries, and the Massachusetts economy boomed once more, albeit briefly. The War of 1812 loomed on the horizon, presenting another serious threat to maritime activity up and down the nation's coast.

WAR OF 1812

Although precipitated by a number of factors, the War of 1812 was caused chiefly by Britain's stubborn maritime policies. Westward expansion in the United States during the first decade of the nineteenth century promoted trade and contributed to a mounting sense of indignation against Great Britain. Expansion demanded increased trade opportunities with many nations. These were opportunities the British navy interfered with at every turn.

Tension between the two nations grew. Although some supported war and called it inevitable, many were worried that the United States lacked the naval strength to fight the British fleet. When war was finally declared on June 28, 1812, the U.S. Navy was greatly underfinanced and many Americans despaired of the country's ability to overcome British naval supremacy. But means by which the Americans could expand their limited naval capacity were quickly implemented. Privateering became an official part of the American war effort. Merchantmen such as the *America,* which called Salem home port, were thus responsible for capturing more than 1,200 British ships. The *America* claimed more than $1 million in seized British prizes. Privateers probably contributed more to the ultimate success of the United States in the War of 1812 than any other single factor.

By 1813, the British had blockaded New England ports and caused continuous panic among coastal communities. When the war neared its end in December 1814,

public sentiment against the conflict had reached an all-time high. Federalists, always anxious to go against the Jeffersonian Republicans, refused to support the war effort and would not agree to provide militia to fight in the federal forces. This dissent would not be silenced and New England merchants were among the most outspoken critics of the war. In early December, these critics met in the Hartford Convention, a body assembled to discuss ways in which individual states could protect themselves from federal demands.

The focal point at the Hartford Convention was the U.S. Constitution. Timothy Pickering of Salem was among those Federalist extremists who advocated solutions that included secession from the Union. Finally, in February 1815, before the group could do any substantial damage to federal unity, the Treaty of Ghent was announced in Boston, ending the War of 1812. The Massachusetts Federalists were reduced to ineffectual grumbling and criticism and merchants were relieved that they could now resume an honest foreign trade. And of course, cessation of the conflict meant resuming relations with Great Britain and France—and an increase in economic rewards for the entire nation.

Timothy Pickering (1745-1829) was an active patriot from Salem who wrote, among other pamphlets, "An Easy Plan of Discipline for the Militia," which was much used in the Revolution. He fought in the war himself, and later founded the United States Military Academy at West Point. He was U.S. secretary of state from 1795 to 1800, and U.S. senator in 1803. From Cirker, Dictionary of American Portraits, *Dover, 1967*

THE INDUSTRIAL AGE AND CURRENTS OF REFORM (1814-1861)

★　　★　　★　　★　　★　　★　　★　　★　　★

The first five decades of the nineteenth century brought to Massachusetts, as to other northern states, unprecedented opportunity for industrial growth. Employment figures for manufacturing in the United States increased from 75,000 in 1810 to 1,200,000 in 1850. The years from 1840 to 1850 saw an increase of more than 100 percent in all industrial output in the country. An extensive variety of products were made in Massachusetts, and very early in the century its factories were leaders in producing everything from boots, buttons, and iron, to hats, knives, rope, and wool and cotton textiles.

To support this growing industrial output, the state's factories needed more and more workers. This ever-present need for unskilled and semi-skilled labor gradually transformed Massachusetts' population. The state went from being a predominantly agricultural society of independent farmers to one increasingly dependent on manufacturing. Soon the native-born work force was insufficient, and particularly after 1850 immigrant labor became an integral part of the labor force. Once virtually nonexistent, women factory workers became a familiar sight by the 1830s in Massachusetts, particularly in the mill towns north of Boston—Lowell, Lawrence, and Haverhill. Children also were employed in the factories, but a gathering outcry against such practices brought about some legislative regulations and limitations of child labor in Massachusetts as early as 1842. Similar laws concerning women workers did not appear on the books until after the Civil War.

While those rooted in tradition mourned the passing of the agrarian age, others believed Massachusetts' future stability and prominence depended on a solid manufacturing base. Therefore, industrialists, philanthropists, and entrepreneurs encouraged and facilitated

Whale oil lamps were common in Massachusetts before petroleum was discovered in this country in the mid-1800s. This fine molded and engraved glass lamp is from the Eliphalet Kingman family of North Bridgewater, now Brockton. Probably made about 1830, the lamp also has unusual double pewter wick tubes. Photo by Randy Chase. From a private collection

Bedford boasted 350 whaling vessels, more than any other whaling community in the world. Its population of 4,000 people in 1820 had increased to nearly 12,000 by 1840, when it was the fifth most active shipping port in the United States. The life and activity of this bustling whaling port inspired one of America's finest nineteenth century novelists, Herman Melville, to write a book which is among the greatest of all sea stories.

Much of what we know today of nineteenth-century Massachusetts sailors and whaling is due to Melville's inspired writing. He drew on personal experience of life at sea, for he had signed on to a whaling ship in 1839. Leaving from New York, he spent most of the next four years at sea. As Melville described so eloquently, American whalers sailed into every ocean and sea of the world. The Pacific, the Indian Ocean, and the Northern Atlantic all yielded their treasures of oil, whalebone, and other whale by-products. In 1851, Melville wrote in *Moby Dick* about Massachusetts whalers, observing that their vessels were "penetrating even through Bering's Strait, and into the remotest secret drawers and lockers of the world."

THE SHIPPING TRADE

Several impressive secondary industries were the direct result of successful maritime activity in Massachusetts. Among the most important was rope-making. In 1820, a total ship tonnage of about 21,000 shipped sugar, iron, and hemp between Boston, Havana, and Russia. The latter nation provided hemp from the Baltic region, which in New England was transformed into rope used for riggings on sailing ships. Even anchor cable, 120 fathoms in length, was made of hemp before the widespread manufacture of chain cable in later years.

Cordage was critical to the Bay State's economy, and one of its more important manufacturing firms was the Plymouth Cordage Company. Located in the community where the first permanent

between two and four years. In 1841, estimates set the average cost of outfitting a whaling ship for such a voyage at $20,100—half of which was the value of the vessel itself. One whaler, the ship *Lagoda,* made six voyages between 1841 and 1869, and returned an average profit of 98 percent for each trip.

But in spite of the island's success, Nantucket's early successes in whaling were overshadowed by that of the New Bedford whalers. New Bedford had the advantage of both a spacious, deep mainland harbor (in contrast to Nantucket Island's somewhat shallower waters) and access to railroads. The latter sped up distribution and sale of whaling products and helped create a solid niche in the region's economy. By 1847, New

Massachusetts settlement sprang up, it undoubtedly owed some of its success to that hardy group of Pilgrims who called the New World home. In 1824, when the Plymouth Cordage Company was established by Bourne Spooner, John Russell, and Caleb Loring, there was little at the factory site except for an ancient gristmill. A year later, in 1825, the owner of the brig *Massasoit* purchased 324 pounds of rope for $32.40. By 1837, the company had upped its capacity for production, but still made little more than 400 tons of hemp rope per year. Soon, however, manila rope was introduced and by the late 1860s was used on all American ships. Prior to the heyday of clipper ships Plymouth Cordage Company had employed fewer than 100 people, but by 1860 there were 140 on the payroll.

Advancing maritime technology—which cut down on the number of weeks in travel time—helped to expand the local, as well as the state, economy. As Lowell profited from its mills, so Plymouth benefited from the success of the ropemaking business, and everyone, from owners to stock boys, saw their fortunes increase. One young man who entered the company as an office boy at age 15 in 1859 earned three dollars a week. By 1867, he was an accountant earning $1,400 a year. His experience was repeated all over the state in a variety of industries, as by mid-century the national economy continued to expand.

CANALS FOR TRANSPORTATION

Manufactured goods demanded adequate means of transportation to various markets, but this was by no means unique to the nineteenth century. In Massachusetts, construction of the Post Road to New York had seemed a perfect solution to colonial transport problems in the late seventeenth and early eighteenth centuries. By 1808, the United States secretary of the treasury, Albert Gallatin, had devised a new plan to cope with the nation's transportation needs: a federally

funded system of turnpikes to connect the East Coast with the Mississippi River. Just two years before, Congress had given its approval to conduct surveys on which this National (or Cumberland) Road was to be based. Part of the overall plan described in Gallatin's extensive "Report on Roads and Canals" included a scheme to construct inland waterways as well as highways and turnpikes.

Supporters argued that federal funding for transportation was critical. John Quincy Adams, a native son of Mas-

John Quincy Adams (1767-1848) was the son of diplomat and Federalist president John Adams and Abigail (Smith) Adams. He had a long career as a diplomat, starting at age 14, and as a politician. He was a senator from Massachusetts, secretary of state under James Monroe, the sixth president of the United States (1825-1829), and after that was returned to Congress by his south shore constituents. From Spencer and Lossing, A Complete History of the United States, 1878

sachusetts elected to the U.S. presidency in 1824, also agreed with this idea. A system of canals and highways could link different areas of the nation and contribute to general prosperity. However, Adams' strengths did not rest in powers of persuasion or cordial relations with political enemies, so he found it difficult to gain necessary congressional backing to support projects like a transportation system. Some of the era's most influential senators and congressmen, however, agreed with Adams' ideas about federal monies for communications links. In the northeast, by 1821, only $1.3 million had been spent on canal-building by public and private agencies. That figure rose quickly in just two decades, and by 1841 $8.8 million had been spent on transportation projects. In Massachusetts, canal building, although not backed heavily by state or federal funds, became a favored project in several areas. But no Bay State canal ever reached the degree of national promi-

nence claimed by the Erie Canal, built between 1817 and 1825. Wages paid to laborers working on the Erie Canal after its completion give an idea of its importance to the region's economy. In 1828, the common laborer there earned 71 cents a day. By 1861 that daily wage had risen to one dollar.

Several artificial waterways served important economic functions in limited areas of Massachusetts during the first half of the nineteenth century. The Middlesex Canal owed a great deal to improved granite-cutting techniques that helped speed up large building projects. These techniques also ensured greater precision when constructing canal locks, previously made of wood. The Middlesex Canal itself boasted 16 locks, stretching from Chelmsford to Boston. Completed in 1808, the canal provided easy transport from the Merrimack to the Charles River and was utilized extensively by various textile and shoe mills in the region north of Boston.

Charlestown, on the north rim of Boston Harbor, was drawn by John Warner Barber in the late 1830s from Copps Hill burying ground in Boston. An unfinished Bunker Hill monument on Breed's Hill is in the center, while the Charlestown Navy Yard, established in 1798, is on the right. Charlestown and the Charles River were named for King Charles I of England who was in power when the town was incorporated in 1635. From Barber, History and Antiquities of Every Town in Massachusetts, *1839*

The Middlesex Canal was built entirely without federal money. While the Massachusetts state government was not generous with support for canal building, it did provide a small grant of land for construction of connecting waterways north of the Merrimack River. For the most part, however, Bay State canal projects were privately funded affairs.

The very first of those canals in the Lowell area was the Pawtucket Canal, built in 1796 to circumnavigate Pawtucket Falls on the Merrimack River. This canal was designed to provide a viable route for rafts carrying timber and other wood products to shipping facilities at Newburyport on the coast. When Nathan Appleton, a major partner in the Merrimack Manufacturing Company,

Gridley Bryant built a horse-drawn railway in 1825 from Quincy's quarries to the Neponset River. Including branches, the railway was only four miles long, with stone ties and wooden rails at first; later, it even had stone rails. The railway made the granite age of architecture possible in Boston, encouraging the Greek Revival style. Although an early steam locomotive was already in use in England, and soon in America, the Granite Railway flourished for 40 years. The most difficult task for horse and driver was to hold the load of granite as it made the 84-foot drop from the quarry in just 315 feet of distance. From Winsor, The Memorial History of Boston, 1630-1880, *Vol. IV, 1883*

viewed the Pawtucket Canal—a rudimentary arrangement with wooden locks—he was impressed with the site's possibilities: "We . . . scanned the capabilities of the place, and the remark was made that some of us might live to see the place contain twenty thousand inhabitants." Appleton's prediction was well-founded, and the manufacturing concerns located in Lowell ultimately made private investors wealthy.

Despite the fact that it was enlarged and modernized in 1822, the Pawtucket Canal was soon supplanted by the Middlesex and other canals as the preferred transport route for raw materials and finished goods. In addition, the area's complex canal system included the Merrimack, the Lowell, the Western, Eastern, Hamilton, Lawrence, and Northern canals—all part of a system known as the Lowell Canals.

The eastern part of the state was not alone in canal-building. An inland waterway connecting Northampton, in western Massachusetts, with New Haven,

Mount Auburn Cemetery in Cambridge, begun in the 1820s, was intended to be a pleasant park-cemetery, unlike the gloomy churchyard cemeteries of colonial New England. Motifs on gravestones were now more cheerful; there were fewer death's heads and more angels. Religion was changing and cemeteries began to reflect the newer concepts, becoming less utilitarian and more pleasant places to visit. From Gleason's Pictorial Drawing Room Companion, *October 7, 1854*

on the Connecticut coast, was begun in 1825. The Farmington Canal, completed in 1835, turned into a financial disaster. One historian referred to it as the nation's "longest and feeblest" canal, since it was 78 miles long but produced virtually no income. Although the Farmington Canal was intended to aid economic development of the Connecticut River Valley by bringing goods to the port of New Haven, it could not sustain the necessary traffic. Despite support from private sources and from Connecticut banks, a lack of public money, coupled with the area's terrain, made the Farmington Canal an impossible dream.

Nor could the Blackstone Canal, built in the 1820s to connect Worcester with Providence, Rhode Island, compete with less-costly railroads that soon provided area factories with an efficient, dependable means of transport for raw materials and finished goods. The Blackstone Canal—with 45 miles completed by 1828—received some support from the Rhode Island state bank, but it only remained in operation for two decades. Like the Middlesex and the Farmington canals, the Blackstone's brief

existence was a testimony to the ingenuity of Massachusetts entrepreneurs and builders and to the precarious economic climate in which they operated. None of these inland waterways could be sustained as viable business ventures, and all ultimately failed in the face of burgeoning railroad development.

Another transportation project initially receiving at least some public support within Massachusetts' boundaries was a canal to reach westward to the Hudson River. In 1825, an engineer named Loammi Baldwin, Jr., completed a report on a canal to pass through the state's western region. In addition, its promoters asserted that it could tunnel under Hoosac Mountain, near Adams in the northwestern corner of Massachusetts. Although this project seemed preposterous at first, initial interest in this canal would later shift to a railroad connection through the same region. Unfortunately, this idea, too, proved costly, over-ambitious, and under-capitalized.

YANKEE INGENUITY AND ECONOMIC EXPANSION

Massachusetts' population and economy

grew in the early nineteenth century as a result of many entrepreneurial impulses. The Quincy granite works also contributed greatly to the permanence of the state's expansion.

During building of the Middlesex Canal, workers discovered that by drilling holes in the granite and splitting it along a line made by these holes, they could produce evenly hewn granite blocks. Very soon, granite became the preferred building material for many structures throughout the nation. In 1818, the city of Savannah, Georgia, ordered $25,000 worth of granite blocks for a church. Massachusetts architect Samuel Willard, who designed and superintended construction of the Bunker Hill monument commemorating an early battle in the War for Independence, chose Quincy granite as the preferred material for the monument. Willard also invented a wide range of machinery for quarrying and moving large blocks of the grey stone, devices instrumental in expanding the market for granite to a considerable degree. Willard noted that, due to construction of the Bunker Hill monument and the attendant publicity, "A business has grown . . . since the work commenced, and in a space of a few miles, amounting . . . to $3,000,000 which would not otherwise have been done at these quarries, and of which the work on the obelisk is but about one-thirtieth part."

By mid-century, granite was being used everywhere as a primary building material. Schools, churches, town halls, and courthouses were constructed of this hard stone. Among the more famous buildings constructed predominantly of Massachusetts granite during the period were the Astor House in New York and the Tremont and Customs houses in Boston. Mount Auburn Cemetery in Cambridge grew in prominence because of Jacob Bigelow's interest in the use of granite for driveways, portals, and stone markers. By the end of the 1800s, more than 60 million granite paving blocks were produced each year in New

England—the majority of them from Bay State quarries.

Interest in the further development of industry and manufacturing, coupled with a desire to use various New England resources, resulted in more comfortable lifestyles and the establishment of numerous personal fortunes. This expansion was paralleled by support for banking ventures. In 1791 the Bank of the United States had been established amid much controversy, and federal banks soon set the stage for state-chartered banks. In the last nine years of the eighteenth century, 29 state banks were set up in the northeast from New York City to Nantucket.

In Massachusetts, acceptance of state-chartered corporations meant that more manufacturing companies would spring up, as capital for investment was easier to obtain. In 1809 the Massachusetts legislature passed a law establishing rules for incorporation since there were so many individual requests to do so. As a result, by 1837 incorporation legislation appeared on the books in many states. In addition to the growth in corporate legislation, the business community received support between 1819 and 1824 from the U.S. Supreme Court under Chief Justice John Marshall. During this time, Supreme Court decisions on bankruptcy and taxes paved

Entrepreneur Frederic Tudor (1783-1864) was called the "Ice King" because he made his fortune by shipping Boston-area pond ice to tropical ports all over the world. In 1856 he sent 146,000 tons of cut ice in 363 cargoes to 53 places, including China. His business was an important factor in international trading and employed many people. It was said that he had ingeniously turned ice, a Yankee liability, into an asset. Courtesy, Graduate School of Business, Harvard University. From Cirker, Dictionary of American Portraits, *Dover, 1967*

the way for the pro-business legal climate so necessary to new companies during the first half of the nineteenth century.

A good example of the ingenuity common to Massachusetts politicians, entrepreneurs, inventors, and businessmen is represented by the successes of Daniel Webster, Frederic Tudor, Nathaniel Wyeth, and Francis Cabot Lowell. Although not a Massachusetts native, Webster later represented the state in the U.S. Senate and was an eloquent spokesman for pro-Union sentiment during antebellum years.

Bostonian Frederic Tudor began an ice business in 1806. At first derided for his unusual idea, he worked for 15 years to make the company successful, providing ice for chilling beverages in tropical climates and for storage of perishables. Tudor was one of many thousands of Americans during these years whose business interests helped promote a culinary fashion that remains today, since his early efforts bolstered the popularity of ice cream as a dessert. After months of exhaustive experimentation, Tudor designed an efficient ice house with a unique construction that cut down loss through melting to less than 8 percent a season in the tropical regions of the Caribbean. In 1824 Tudor teamed with Cambridge-born Nathaniel Wyeth, and the latter soon invented a way to harvest ice from New England ponds. By 1825 the two had reduced the expense of cutting ice to 10 cents a ton. Although they soon after dissolved their business

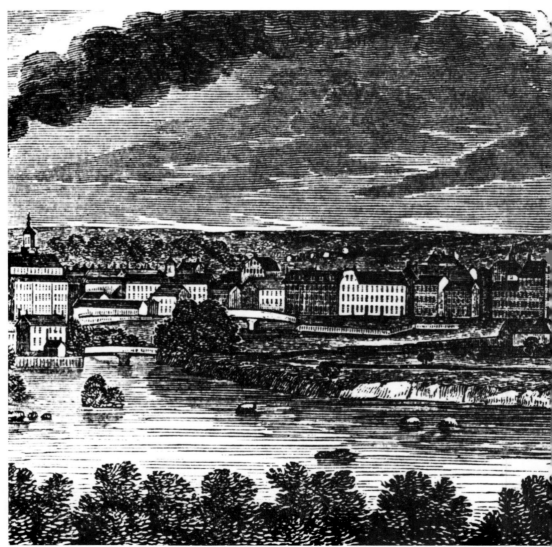

partnership, Tudor and Wyeth continued independently to reap large profits in the ice business.

Wyeth was successful in developing an ice cutter which he later used to free a Cunard ship frozen into Boston Harbor one winter. He also went on a westward expedition to Oregon and established Fort Hall on the California and Oregon trail. By the early 1830s, Tudor was shipping ice to locales like India and Persia, and would later ship to more than 50 destinations worldwide. Like some latter-day alchemists, the Yankee genius of Frederic Tudor and Nathaniel Wyeth turned ice—in monotonous abundance during long Massachusetts winters—into gold.

Massachusetts native Francis Cabot

Lowell was responsible for an even more significant transformation, having to do with the growth of factory communities. Lowell, sometimes called the "Father of American Cotton Manufacture," was determined not to duplicate the cramped, poverty-stricken living conditions of English factory centers.

In 1813, Lowell founded the Boston Manufacturing Company in the town of Waltham, just west of Boston, the first American factory to produce cotton textiles in one building. Soon, Lowell and his partners—other shrewd investors such as Nathan Appleton—were planning an enormous company town to the north in the small village of Chelmsford. The Merrimack and Concord rivers were among the natural resources available to

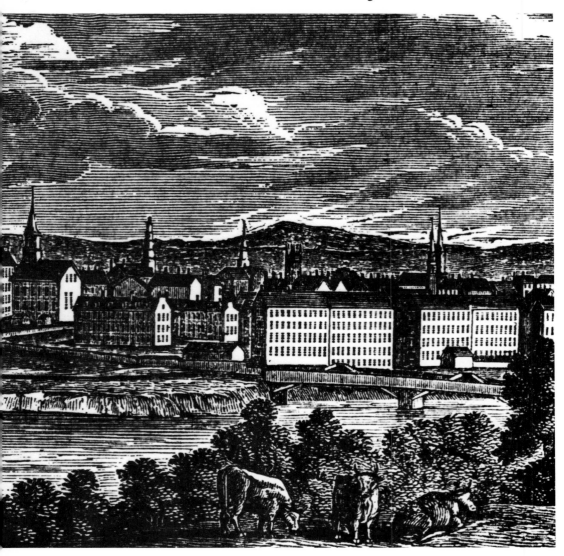

Lowell in the late 1830s is depicted by John Warner Barber from the Dracut, or north, side of the Merrimack River, with the Concord River entering the Merrimack on the left. Natural waterways were soon augmented by canals in Lowell, which was the fastest growing community in New England at this time, increasing from 2,500 residents in 1826 to 33,000 in 1850. Barber noted that there were 10 houses of public worhsip in Lowell, one of them Catholic, showing that a good number of Irish immigrants were already there by 1839. From Barber, History and Antiquities of Every Town in Massachusetts, *1839*

Designed by State House architect Charles Bulfinch, Massachusetts General Hospital was built in 1818 and opened in 1821. It was constructed of Chelmsford granite and was considered a model of architecture in its day. Ether was first demonstrated as a general anesthetic here in 1846. From Gillon, Early Illustrations and Views of American Architecture, *Dover, 1971*

fuel Lowell's Merrimack Manufacturing Company, and locks and canals built there helped establish the region's virtually unlimited potential. Although Francis Cabot Lowell died in 1817, his ideas were implemented by his partners, who built an enormous complex of textile mills, company-owned housing, stores, churches, and other facilities.

On March 1, 1826, the community of Lowell was incorporated and at that point had a population of about 2,500. Due to the rapid success of the Merrimack Manufacturing Company, however, the population quickly increased. Ten years later, Lowell had 18,000 inhabitants, and by 1856, 12,000 looms there produced cotton and wool textiles. Some 36 million pounds of cotton and 5 million pounds of wool were woven into more than 100 million

yards of cloth at Lowell during these years. The city's success was phenomenal and proved the utopian hypothesis of Francis Cabot Lowell and his partners. At least until the economic recession and increasing labor activity of the 1840s, Lowell appeared to have avoided the harsh excesses frustrating industrial centers in Great Britain. Massachusetts residents could point with justifiable pride to Lowell, the second largest city in the state, as the biggest and most productive cotton textile center in the nation.

Added to the factories themselves was the innovation of waterpower. The successful use of canals in Lowell foreshadowed the later success of railroads in transporting goods and materials from source to marketplace. As one historian noted,

Left: *Reformer Lucy Stone (1818-1893) was born in West Brookfield and graduated from Oberlin College. She lectured widely about slavery and women's lack of legal rights. In 1850 she headed the first national women's rights conference, which was held in Worcester. In 1855, when this picture was taken, she married Dr. Henry Blackwell, but shocked all by keeping her maiden name. Stone and Blackwell noted that in 1855 the husband was in total legal custody of the wife and her material goods and earnings. She could not make a will, inherit property, sue or be sued, and if her husband died first, the wife inherited a much smaller interest in the husband's property than he would of hers had she died first. In short, the wife was treated legally as if she were a child, lunatic, or mentally retarded person. From Mary Thacher Higginson,* Thomas Wentworth Higginson: The Story of His Life, *1914*

Above: *Susan B. Anthony (1820-1906), antislavery and women's rights worker, was born in Adams, but by the age of six her family had moved to New York State where she resided for most of her life when not on the lecture circuit. She is shown here, in a black dress with lace on the front, at the 1897 summer reunion of her Anthony, Reed, Richardson, and Lapham relatives at her Grandfather Anthony's farm in Adams. She always considered herself a proud New Englander as she stumped back and forth across the country for more than 50 years in the cause of women's rights. From Harper,* The Life and Work of Susan B. Anthony, *1898*

The Lowell Canal System was one of the most impressive engineering achievements of nineteenth century America . . . the power canals which carried water to each major mill complex in the city were the product of engineering expertise and years of difficult labor. Water power was the source of Lowell's prosperity and Lowell was the pacesetter for a young industrial nation.

Not all was ideal, however. Lowell may have been a pacesetting city, but it ultimately proved profitable only for mill owners. Wages paid to those working in

Lowell's mills seem low by today's standards and were, in fact, only barely adequate at the time. The average male worker earned between $4.50 and $12 for a 72-hour work week and women were paid between $2.25 and $4 a week for the same work. The industrial complex at Lowell was a model of manufacturing innovation and later the area would be a major attraction for waves of immigrants to the United States. But in the beginning, the mills were filled with native workers and none of the laborers—native-born or immigrant—found the streets paved with gold.

In the 1820s and 1830s, the specter of inflation and debt threatened towns and cities across the nation. One of the several fiscal questions of the day concerned a protective tariff on manufactured items and raw materials. New Englanders—and Massachusetts residents in particular—opposed the Tariff of Abominations, as it was called. In 1828, just as John Quincy Adams was leaving the U.S. presidency, the tariff passed into law despite attempts by New England politicians to amend it. As the presidential administration changed and Andrew Jackson assumed office, Massachusetts followed the national trend toward reform.

The era known for "Jacksonian Democracy" instilled in Americans a spirit of improvement and a desire to make life better. Accompanying this were many innovations in industrial development that marked the period. In fact, reform and technological advancement seemed to go hand in hand, each creating situations that could be aided, to some degree, by the other's attention.

Some of the more significant changes during this period were in areas of social and educational reform. Throughout the United States in the early nineteenth century, a number of different reform movements motivated people to attempt improvement in public education, care of the insane, women's rights, working conditions (especially for children), and care and education of the deaf and blind.

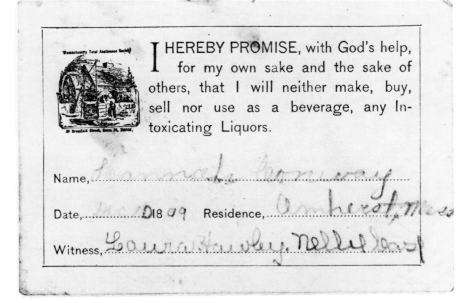

I HEREBY PROMISE, with God's help, for my own sake and the sake of others, that I will neither make, buy, sell nor use as a beverage, any Intoxicating Liquors.

Name,

Date, 18 Residence,

Witness,

Many prominent figures in these areas were natives of Massachusetts.

CURRENTS OF REFORM

Some reformers in the first half of the nineteenth century forever changed the way Americans perceived and treated workers, women, the handicapped, and the nation's youth. A few of these reformers traveled worldwide to deliver their messages. Margaret Fuller, a prominent transcendentalist and writer and one of the ablest critics in America, worked for social reform. Samuel Gridley Howe organized the Perkins Institute for the Blind in Boston in 1832, later becoming an influential abolitionist. In 1831, journalist and reformer William Lloyd Garrison, another abolitionist, moved to Boston and established the famous antislavery journal, *The Liberator*. In 1833, he founded the American Anti-Slavery Society. In 1834, Elizabeth Peabody and Bronson Alcott established a school based on new methods of teaching and handling children. Susan B. Anthony and Lucy Stone, two of the best-known early feminist theorists, were both born in Massachusetts, as was Mary Mason Lyon, founder of Mount Holyoke College—an educational institution that was among the first of its kind for women.

One of the most tireless reformers was Dorothea Dix. She almost single-handedly brought to public attention the plight of the insane. A former teacher, in 1841 she was involved in volunteer work at the House of Correction near Boston. She soon persuaded important state legislators and others active in reform to help her launch a crusade to change conditions in Massachusetts prisons. Men like Charles Sumner, Samuel Gridley Howe, Horace Mann, and many more joined Dix in her campaign to change the evaluation and treatment of the insane in public institutions.

Dix's work took her to virtually every jail and prison in the state, where she recorded the conditions and needs of inmates. What she saw in those

institutions led her to protest the "present state of Insane Persons confined within this Commonwealth in cages, closets, cellars, stalls, pens! Chained, naked, beaten with rods, and lashed into obedience!" By 1845, she had prepared detailed documentation of her findings. Almost immediately after reading Dix's report, the state legislature passed a law enhancing facilities of the Worcester insane asylum, legislation which became a model for that passed in other states.

Horace Mann's interest in education led him to establish the system on which all public schooling in the United States is now based. Mann, a lawyer and state legislator, helped found Massachusetts' first state board of education, serving as its first secretary and as a member of the board for 11 years between 1837 and 1848. According to Mann, "Education . . . is the great equalizer of the conditions of men—the balance-wheel of the social machinery . . . it does better than to disarm the poor of their hostility towards the rich; it prevents being poor." Because of Mann's energetic promotion of free public education, his standards for public schools were gradually adopted nationwide.

Religion also enjoyed a renewed enthusiasm among numerous Massachusetts residents in the 1800s. Some of the evangelical fervor associated with the

Horace Mann (1796-1858) was a lawyer, state representative, state senator, congressman to Washington, founder of the first American lunatic asylum, antislavery worker, and temperance and women's rights advocate, but he is usually remembered for his 11-year stint as secretary to the newly formed Massachusetts Board of Education, beginning in 1837. He worked against great opposition to make Massachusetts a model of modern educational reform. Mann improved the individual schools, lengthened the school terms which were often as short as eight weeks per year, began teacher training schools at a time when teachers were often college students on vacation or high school graduates at best, and tried to ensure a free public education to many more children than were then being educated. He declined the governorship in 1852 and went to Ohio to be president of Antioch College, where he died in 1859. From Mann, Life of Horace Mann by his Wife, *1865*

Right: *Fidelia Fiske (1816-1864), from Shelburne Falls, was educated at Mount Holyoke Female Seminary with the class of 1842. She was caught up in the religious fervor of the time and dedicated her life to teaching and missionary work. A Congregationlist, she was the first unmarried woman ever to go abroad as a missionary. In 1843 she began a girls' school in Persia, living with the students, learning their language, and teaching them their lessons. For 16 years, despite cholera and typhoid epidemics, opposition from factions in Persia, and vast cultural differences, she worked to better the lives of young women who were sometimes taken from her for wealthy men's harems. After returning to Massachusetts, she taught at Mount Holyoke and lectured about her mission. Courtesy, Mount Holyoke College Library/Archives*

Facing page: *Ralph Waldo Emerson (1803-1882), poet and philosopher, was a Harvard graduate who left the Unitarian ministry to make his living as a writer and lecturer in the 1830s when that profession was new and unusual. He lived 50 of his years in Concord. This gifted speaker and thinker protested the materialism he saw changing his world with the advent of the industrial revolution. "Things are in the saddle,/ And ride mankind," he said. He felt people should find their true selves in nature: "Adopt the pace of nature; her secret is patience." From* New England Magazine, *Vol. XV, 1895*

Great Awakening in the past century simmered in New England and elsewhere until the 1820s and 1830s, when it once more burst into prominence. The Second Great Awakening, as it is sometimes called, drew on the efforts of many from Massachusetts, including William Miller and John Murray. The religiosity and ardor of this period spilled over into and directly influenced other reform movements, particularly women's rights, temperance, and abolition.

TRANSCENDENTALISM

Transcendentalists who flourished during the first half of the nineteenth century undoubtedly received the most lasting fame and had the most critical influence on American literature and philosophy at that time. Transcendentalists believed that

God is inherent in man and nature and that individual intuition is the highest source of knowledge. Their belief led to an emphasis on individualism, self-reliance, and rejection of traditional authority. Their acknowledged leader was Ralph Waldo Emerson of Concord, but the movement attracted many other writers and thinkers including Nathaniel Hawthorne, Henry David Thoreau, Margaret Fuller, Bronson Alcott, and George Ripley. In 1841, the latter founded Brook Farm in West Roxbury, a few miles from Boston. Based on cooperative living, the community expected each member to take part in manual labor in order to make the group self-sufficient. Brook Farm was established to further the philosophy these men and women espoused and provide a congenial setting for their intellectual efforts.

Many of Emerson's contemporaries were skeptical of his ideas and thought little of the transcendentalists. Emerson himself never lived at Brook Farm, confining his affiliation there to occasional visits. Other visitors included Dr.

Oliver Wendell Holmes, Margaret Fuller, and the Reverend William Ellery Channing, who made frequent pilgrimages to Brook Farm during its short life (the experiment survived only until 1847). All of these visitors came to study and absorb the transcendental view of the world.

George Ripley's interest in establishing a community in which he and others could ponder life's mysteries is evident in his words to Emerson in this letter of 1840, the year before the founding of Brook Farm: "I wish to see a society of educated friends, working, thinking, and living together, with no strife, except that of each to contribute the most to the benefit of all." The almost evangelical tone of his message is similar to many of those written by Ripley's colleagues as well. Indeed, the entire period was one

Dr. Oliver Wendell Holmes (1809-1894) became famous for patriotric poems such as "Old Ironsides," which helped to save the old U.S.S. Constitution from being demolished. His real vocation, however, was medicine, which he taught at Dartmouth and Harvard. His summers were spent in the Berkshires at Pittsfield, where he wrote novels and poems as well as hymns. Here, Holmes at age 80 sits in his study on Beacon Street in Boston. From New England Magazine, *October 1889*

of intellectual, moral, as well as industrial, evangelism—much of it having its inception in Massachusetts.

Unlike some attempts at communal living, Ripley's bore fruit for a few years. When he and 15 others moved to Brook Farm, Hawthorne was on a committee for direction of agriculture, and he later affectionately satirized the entire experiment in *The Blithedale Romance.* For about four years the members of this utopian venture enjoyed a combination of industry, agriculture, education, and philosophy. In 1844, however, outside influences caused major revisions in the articles of association drawn up by the original members. The change spelled a swift and complete downfall of Brook Farm as a transcendentalist haven, and by 1847 the property was up for sale. Nevertheless, Brook Farm tested the practicality of Ripley's ideas and provided fertile ground for literary expression. It had been, according to Orestes Brownson, another trascendentalist, "half a charming adventure, half a solemn experiment."

LITERARY ACCOMPLISHMENTS

Certain other developments characterized the intellectual reform sweeping the state and the nation during these years. Nearly two centuries had passed since the *Bay Psalm Book* was published in Cambridge, and now Boston became noted for its diverse publishing establishments. The *North American Review,* founded in 1815 by William Tudor—brother of Frederic Tudor of ice-trade fame— became the foremost magazine of its type in the nation. Tudor, the first editor, encouraged the publication's high standards, and as a result the *North American Review* was the preferred forum for most, if not all, important writers and poets of the period—many of whom were from Massachusetts.

The *North American Review* was joined in the early decades of the nineteenth century by Ticknor &

EMILY DICKINSON (1830-1886)

Emily Dickinson has now achieved respect as one of the finest poets in the English language, yet only ten of the almost 1,800 poems and one letter of her 1,046 are known to have been published during her own lifetime, all anonymously. We probably have less than half of her writing due to heavy censorship by her family.

Dickinson today has a devoted following of a surprisingly wide range of people from all over the world who feel she speaks to them. Her poems and letters are now translated into most languages, and the play, *The Belle of Amherst*, has been produced on stages all over the world from New York to Tokyo to Moscow.

A gifted woman, Dickinson had an ability to write with force, using a concentrated style of writing. She tackled such universal ideas as anxiety, fear, doubt, loss, sickness, the hell of the Civil War, and death. She also wrote passionately about love, pride, humor, the joy of nature and the seasons, and the ecstasy of just being alive. Her poems can often be read on many levels—explaining her appeal to so many types of people. For example, the bee and flower in her garden that she describes may be also read as being about her lover (the mysterious and unknown Master figure) and Emily: "The flower must not blame the bee/ That seeketh his felicity/ Too often at her door...."

Emily Dickinson was an eighth generation American. Both of her parents were descendants of English Puritan settlers, and her parents still practiced a strict Calvinist-Congregational faith in what was, in Emily's youth, a very small town of like-minded people. Dickinson went to neighborhood schools and Amherst Academy where she was remembered as a witty and creative writer of essays. She studied such subjects as Latin, Greek, botany, geology, and English and attended the three-year Mount

Emily Dickinson is shown here in a 1986 wood engraving. This image was for a centennial of her death and based on the only photograph of her thought to exist. The original photograph was an 1847 daguerreotype taken when she was only sixteen years old. Wood engraving by Barry Moser, Pennyroyal Press, Hatfield

Holyoke Female Seminary in nearby South Hadley. While at Mount Holyoke she could never profess her faith in a Congregationalist God as President Mary Lyon wished, and young Emily never officially joined the church of her family. Her poems and letters show that she had read the Bible and knew it well, but she wrestled with her faith in a new era of science and evolved a more Emersonian style of thought for herself.

Living near Amherst College, where her father was treasurer and her brother was in the class of 1850, she met and dated bright young men who gave her encouragement as a writer. She played the piano for groups of friends, skated, went on horseback rides, and sleigh rides,

The Dickinson Homestead was the home of Emily Dickinson for all but 15 years of her life. Built in 1813 for her grandparents, and painted yellow in her day, it is still an imposing federal-style brick home. On the high end of Main Street in Amherst it was the birthplace of Emily Dickinson, the haven where she wrote most of her now famous poems and letters, and the place in which she died in 1886. Photo by John H. Martin

sometimes alone with a young man. One Amherst College student gave her Ralph Waldo Emerson's writing.

In 1856 Dickinson's brother Austin, who had graduated from Harvard Law School, married Susan Gilbert, already a good friend of Emily's. Austin and Sue built a house next door, and Sister Sue was a positive, strong influence and an appreciative audience for Dickinson's early work.

Dickinson traveled easily by train to Springfield and Boston as a young woman. Her father was a State Representive, then a State Senator and on the Governor's Council. For two years he went to Washington, D. C., as a Representative from his district. Emily and her sister visited him there in 1855, and stayed in Philadelphia on their way home. In 1864 and again 1865 Emily Dickinson lived in Cambridge with her cousins for months at a time in order to have eye treatment in Boston. However, after Emily was in her mid-30s, about late 1865, she stopped traveling; she even stopped leaving her family property, and she became "The Myth" to her own neighbors. The mystery remains, and there are entire books which now speculate on why she chose to stay at home, wear white dresses most of the time, and see only selected visitors for the rest of her life.

The years that she wrote the most (and the best) poetry were just *before* this withdrawal from society, during the early years of the Civil War, 1861, 1862 and 1863, when she wrote sometimes nearly 300 poems a year. After she withdrew, there were at times fewer than 15 poems a year. Most people feel that she had been in love with a married man, a man who left the area.

Dickinson, even after she withdrew, continued her letter writing, letters that were cleverly often humorously written and that show her amazing ability to describe her life well. Her letters also give a wonderful look at the mid 1800s in Massachusetts.

Emily Dickinson died at age 55 from what modern medical experts think was high blood pressure. Four years after her death, Roberts Brothers in Boston published the first small book of her poetry, and it was a smashing success. More editions followed, and then her letters were collected and published. Her fame grew, and her audience continues to grow as evidenced by the thousands of people each year, often traveling from great distances, who visit her home and grave in Amherst.

— Ruth Owen Jones

Company (1833) and Little, Brown (1837), both Boston-based publishing houses of excellent reputation. The power behind these efforts came partly from a nucleus of expertise in Massachusetts that included historians George Bancroft of Worcester, Francis Parkman of Boston, Jared Sparks, numerous Adamses, as well as the transcendentalists Ralph Waldo Emerson, Bronson Alcott, and Henry David Thoreau. In addition, the novelist Nathaniel Hawthorne and poets Henry Wadsworth Longfellow, Emily Dickinson, and Walt Whitman contributed to the flowering of American literature in the early- to mid-nineteenth century. Massachusetts was a spawning ground for creative endeavors at that time, and the works of these individuals proved the success and endurance of that innovative zeal.

There was no one location where this literary flowering seemed to be centered. Yet, Bronson Alcott and his daughter Louisa May Alcott, whose stories for young people have delighted generations of readers, lived in Concord, as did many other writers, including Emerson, Thoreau, and, for a brief time, Hawthorne. Herman Melville, born in New York City, lived for a time at a house named "Arrowhead" in the Berkshires and wrote his classic tale *Moby Dick* there. In another generation or two, many writers and poets would flock to western Massachusetts, where the quiet hills and rural scenery provoked vivid, sensitive imagery. Emily Dickinson—a native of Amherst—was content to spend her entire life in her family home in that western Massachusetts town. A virtual recluse, Dickinson, born in 1830, saw only a few of her poems published in her lifetime. Her work was discovered after her death in 1886, and she has been recognized subsequently as one of America's greatest poets.

Unlike Dickinson, who lived a life bounded by Yankee convention, Edgar Allen Poe embodied daring and unrest in his writings as well as in his daily living. He wrote macabre tales and produced fascinating, convoluted verse dealing with sorrow, mystery, and horror. A native of

THE CIVIL WAR AND THE GILDED AGE (1861-1890)

★　★　★　★　★　★　★　★　★

The American Civil War was not a single-issue conflict between two geo-graphic regions about slavery. It was, rather, a bundle of disputes that ranged from states' rights to protective tariffs, from land policy to slavery. Affecting virtually every U.S. citizen, no matter how far removed from the actual fighting, the Civil War began at Fort Sumter, South Carolina, on April 12, 1861.

Residents of Massachusetts may have been spared the trauma of Civil War battles within their state's boundaries, but its citizens were by no means immune to the upheaval and tragedy of war. In fact, Massachusetts soldiers were the very first to die in Civil War-related fighting, even before large-scale battles began.

An understanding of the full effects of the horror and waste this civil conflict engendered best proceeds after consid-ering the factors that led the country to war. From the very beginning, the United States grappled with the slavery issue. Delegates to the Constitutional Con-vention in Philadelphia in the 1780s argued about whether slaves should be counted as citizens. Resolution of this issue would determine a state's share of federal taxes. As could be expected, different opinions concerning inclusion of slaves in this head count came from northern and southern convention delegates. As early as the late 1600s, vastly different economies in North and South had emerged, and these differences caused constitution delegates in the 1780s to clash. Chief among their disputes, slavery presented a major stumbling block. The North wanted slaves counted as citizens for tax purposes, but the South wanted slaves excluded from the tally. Inconsistently, the South demanded slaves to be counted when state representation in the House was to be determined—even though slaves could not vote. Finally, the "three-fifths

Born in Newburyport, William Lloyd Garrison (1805-1879) started the radical abolitionist paper, The Liberator, in Boston in 1831. By calling for immediate emancipation of all slaves Garrison made enemies in the South, where a price was offered for his capture, and, reportedly, a higher price if he was brought in dead. But he was also despised by a large group in Boston who, in 1835, dragged him through the streets with a rope around his neck. From Winsor, The Memorial History of Boston, *Vol. III, 1881*

compromise" was reached, which stated that three-fifths of "other Persons," that is, slaves, be counted for both purposes: taxes and representation. As far as the slavery controversy was concerned, the convention ended with agreement that importation of slaves should not be forbidden before 1808. This was the first in a number of compromises hammered out between North and South during several decades before the Civil War.

Slavery was not the only issue of dispute between North and South. Trade was also a difficulty, particularly since

southern states disliked export taxes. These taxes, they argued, would affect southern states most extensively since their goods (largely cotton) were for foreign export. The North was concerned only marginally with this issue since much of the manufacture in the northern states was for the domestic market and thus would not be affected as severely by export taxes.

By the beginning of the nineteenth century, southern life and culture had evolved as distinctly different from that in the North. The South was primarily agricultural, the North increasingly dependent on factories and mills. Cotton was an important crop—both to the South which grew it and the North which processed it. This had become even more true since the 1793 invention of the cotton gin, which allowed for faster processing of raw cotton fiber. Northern mills depended on cotton for textile manufacture, and both regions enjoyed increasing prosperity due to the success of cotton production and export. Both sides had an interest in keeping conflict to a minimum, but both sides

were destined to fail in their attempts to preserve peace. The agricultural way of life that made cheap cotton cultivation possible was predicated on slavery. And the abolitionists of the North were determined to put an end to the enslavement of other humans.

THE PECULIAR INSTITUTION

Southern cotton production resulted both in overwhelming economic reliance on the crop and on ever greater reliance on slaves for its cultivation and harvest. In 1800, there were about 90,000 slaves in the United States. By 1860, the eve of the Civil War, there were at least four million slaves at work on plantations all across the South. Because of slaves' efforts, cotton production increased steadily. The "peculiar institution," as one historian has called it, gave the South its unmistakable and inimitable culture, and gave the North justification for its charges of the moral degradation of slave labor. Questions surrounding the institution of slavery and the culture it supported helped build the foundation on which the Civil War was ultimately based. Abo-

lition of slavery became a rallying point for opponents of the entire southern way of life.

Abolitionists in Massachusetts were numerous, and none was more famous or more effective than William Lloyd Garrison. He was founder, in 1833, of the American Anti-Slavery Society, and his magazine, *The Liberator*, became reformers' main vehicle for popularizing the antislavery cause nationwide. Abolitionists such as Garrison were vehement in their opposition to slavery and adamant in their attempts to outlaw slavery both in theory and in practice.

"I am in earnest. I will not equivocate—I will not excuse—I will not retreat a single inch—and I WILL BE HEARD!" Garrison left little doubt about his position or his sincerity. His emphatic, forceful prose motivated thousands to stand behind the abolitionist cause, and as the nineteenth century wore on, his views carried more and more weight in states across the North.

By the second decade of the nineteenth century it was clear that the political and economic unity of the North

The Liberator was founded by William Lloyd Garrison because he had found, on a speaking tour of New England, " . . . prejudice more stubborn, apathy more frozen, than among the slave owners themselves." He wanted immediate emancipation: "On this subject, I do not wish to think or speak or write, with moderation . . . [would you] tell the mother to gradually extricate her babe from the fire into which it has fallen?" The masthead of the paper shows a slave auction in view of the nation's capitol, an embarrassment to many in a land where all men were, supposedly, created equal. Garrison published his incendiary paper until after the Civil War when his cause was finally won; a bronze statue was later erected in Boston in his memory. From New England Magazine, December 1890

Samuel Bowles (1826-1878) was the capable editor of the Springfield Republican, *which he developed from a weekly into a world-class daily in the mid-1800s. A provincial paper, it was national and even international in scope and was read widely outside of its geographic area. Bowles was a Republican when the new party was born in 1856; the paper had been the* Republican *since 1824. He denounced slavery and its spread to the West, and editorialized against the hanging of John Brown. After the Civil War he continued his reformatory zeal in attacking political and financial corruption characteristic of the new era. From Everts,* History of the Connecticut Valley in Massachusetts, *Vol. II, 1879*

was greatly dependent on industrial production that often involved southern cotton. Furthermore, southern cotton was the crop that determined the relative economic success of the United States in the world market. As several historians have noted, northern industrial cities such as Lowell depended on continuing shipments of raw cotton from the South. Cotton was very much "king," even in the North. In many northern mill communities abolitionist activity was therefore unpopular, as it represented a threat to the economy. An abolitionist newspaper, *The Middlesex Standard,* was edited in Lowell from 1844 to 1845 by John Greenleaf Whittier, but was unable to sustain itself for more than a few

months. The pro-South/pro-cotton bias of many mill owners and most workers prevented the abolitionists from becoming powerful in this area before 1860. In other Massachusetts cities, however, there was criticism of the connection between "the lords of the loom and the lords of the lash," as mill and slave owners were described. A related article in the *Springfield Republican* noted that "prosperity . . . has frequently stood in the way of very necessary reforms."

The South had virtually none of the factories characterizing cities such as Lowell, Lawrence, and Waltham. The entire southern identity was predicated economically and culturally on its dependence on cotton cultivation and slavery. Unlike the North, which had a diverse economy based on agriculture *and* industrial production, the South was totally dependent on one crop.

The two regions—along with the ever-increasing western portion of the country—were affected simultaneously (but often in opposite ways) by various issues. Free trade versus protective tariffs divided them, with New England almost always favoring some protective tariff. National banking likewise affected the North and South differently, as did land policy. But no issue was more divisive, more persistent in its ability to cause conflict among elected officials and private citizens alike, than slavery.

Importation of slaves to the U.S. ceased in 1808. Although slave smuggling continued after 1808, it was seen only as part of the larger issue of slavery. Smuggling was not, in itself, an overriding concern of most abolitionists. In fact, between 1840 and 1860, the U.S. Navy captured only 50 ships attempting to smuggle this pitiable human cargo. Most abolitionist efforts focused on complete eradication of slavery from the nation. In 1819, there were 22 states in the Union evenly divided between those permitting slave ownership and those that were "free." Free and slave states continued to join the Union in balanced

Sojourner Truth (1790?-1883), an escaped Michigan slave, came to Massachusetts between 1842 and 1846 and lived for a time in a utopian community with abolitionist sentiments in the Florence section of Northampton. In such a community everyone was expected to help with the work, and Truth took it upon herself to do the laundry, as depicted in this 1867 drawing by Charles C. Burleigh. She became famous in the years before the Civil War for her moving antislavery lectures and efforts to free her fellow blacks. Photo by Ecclestein. Courtesy, Northampton Historical Society

numbers, and it looked as if slavery would continue as a way of life, at least in the southern states, for decades to come.

The year 1820 proved critical to future disputes over slavery. That year, the nation's growing rift was clearly illuminated. Many observers publicly stated that, unless the North and the South could find ways of eliminating their grievances, future conflict of a more serious and debilitating nature was inevitable.

Missouri was admitted to the Union in 1820 as a slave state along with Maine. The latter was previously a part of Massachusetts and was admitted as a free state. This enabled maintenance of the balance of free and slave states, and the Missouri Compromise, as the events of these state admissions were known, underscored the importance of a bal-

Right: *Charles Sumner (1816-1874) was a young Boston lawyer when he became caught up in the antislavery movement of the 1830s. He wrote against slavery in the South—it had been unlawful in Massachusetts since the Revolution—and became especially vocal after 1850 and the passage of the Fugitive Slave Law, which meant that northerners must return escaped slaves. He was elected to the U.S. Senate, where his fiery speeches irritated southern leaders. In retaliation for one speech, the cousin of the slandered southerner in question beat Sumner with a cane until he lay senseless on the Senate floor. His seat was left vacant and his attack became the focus of outrage from the North, while southern leaders upheld the attack as deserved. From Stearns,* Cambridge Sketches, *1905*

as a northern man, but as an American. I speak today for the preservation of the Union. Hear me for my cause."

Webster's opponents were not moved. Senator John C. Calhoun, old and ill, spoke only as a South Carolinian: "I cannot agree that this Union cannot be dissolved. Am I to understand that no degree of oppression, no outrage, no broken faith, can produce the destruction of this Union? The Union *can* be broken."

As the decade unfolded, increasing numbers of incidents involved pro-slavery and antislavery groups. Economic issues attending slavery could not be overlooked, and as the nation entered the 1860s, many counseled against future compromise. Some predicted accurately that the gathering clouds of dissent meant only one thing: the storms of war.

Senator Charles Sumner of Massachusetts stated his feelings in a letter to a friend in 1857. A staunch advocate of abolition, Sumner said the practice of slavery "degrades our country and prevents its example from being all-conquering." As the 1860s wore on, Sumner became an ultra-radical Republican known for his support of total freedom and full civil rights for all black Americans. He also became an arch foe of southerners who demanded states' rights.

Shortly after the attack on Fort Sumter, South Carolina, the Massachusetts militia was activated and led to Washington, D.C. On its way to the nation's capital the Sixth Massachusetts Regiment commanded by General Benjamin Franklin Butler passed through Baltimore, where it was set upon by angry, pro-Confederate rioters. The mob attacked the Bay State troops on April 19, 1861, killing four soldiers and causing the deaths of nine civilians. These casualties occurred 86 years to the day after the War for Independence had begun with the battles of Lexington and Concord in 1775. Although General Butler was not directly involved at Baltimore, having arrived in Washington, D.C., he became associated historically with this engagement that preceded the more devastating encounters between North and South later in the war.

The Sixth Massachusetts Regiment was quartered in the Senate chamber when it reached Washington. President Lincoln personally welcomed this first fighting unit as it set up its temporary headquarters in the Senate. It was joined in strategic defense of the city by the Fourth Massachusetts Regiment, based at Fort Monroe, Virginia.

Within a few weeks of the Baltimore event military victims of the clash were buried in their native soil in Massachusetts. The soldiers—the first Civil War fatalities, for the bombardment of Fort Sumter had killed no one—were Sumner H. Needham of Lawrence, Luther C. Ladd and Addison O. Whitney of Lowell, and Charles A. Taylor, whose residence was unknown.

General Butler, of Lowell, was one of a handful of Massachusetts natives whose connection with the military granted a prominence he might otherwise not have enjoyed. Butler's activities during the Civil War were both notorious and notable. A lawyer, he had twice run unsuccessfully for governor before the war, but later was elected to that office in 1882. Butler was a Republican congressman during the postwar years, and he ran for president of the United States in 1884 on the Anti-Monopoly and Greenback tickets. He was perhaps best known for his behavior during the occupation of New Orleans.

In May 1862, just after becoming military governor of that Louisiana city, General Butler issued a document to its citizens, a decree known as General Order Number 28, or the "Woman Order." In it, Butler made clear his uncompromising position toward the conquered city and its proud residents. The text of Order Number 28 reads in part, "As the officers and soldiers of the United States have been subjected to repeated insults from the women (calling themselves ladies) of New Orleans . . . when any female shall . . . show contempt for the United States, she shall be regarded as a woman of the town plying her avocation."

It was due in part to this ill-mannered and unnecessary directive that President Lincoln removed Butler from command in December 1862. Butler's disregard for convention and lack of tact in dealing with the inhabitants of New Orleans was long remembered as another example of Yankee bad manners. In Butler's defense, it is true that none of his military successes are recalled when Order Number 28 is cited as an example of his incompetence as a military leader.

Another famous Massachusetts native

Below: *On December 11, 1862, Massachusetts and Michigan volunteer troops cross the Rappahannock River toward Stafford Heights, Virginia, in an effort to drive off Confederate sharpshooters who are aiming at the soldiers assembling prefabricated bridge sections. The result of this battle was 300 Union men killed, and possibly more than that number of Confederate dead, as the North took possession of the riverfront, finishing the bridge for future assaults. From Mottelay and Campbell-Copeland,* Frank Leslie's Illustrations: The Soldier in Our Civil War, *Vol. II, 1900*

made a major contribution toward the Union war effort: Brigadier General Joseph Hooker. A native of Hadley, Hooker graduated from West Point and was named brigadier general of volunteer troops in the Washington, D.C. region between August and October 1861.

A tall, blue-eyed man described by a contemporary as "the handsomest soldier I ever laid eyes on," Hooker was named the fourth head of the Army of the Potomac in 1862. He held this post for six months but resigned from his command a few days before the battle of Gettysburg and was replaced by George Meade.

As the war dragged on, President Lincoln put out a call for additional militia from all states. Among those who answered that call was the 54th "Colored" Regiment from Massachusetts, under the command of Colonel Robert Gould Shaw, a white officer. The poet Henry Wadsworth Longfellow, observing this regiment of black soldiers drilling in the streets of Boston, commented that it was an "imposing sight, with something wild and strange about it, like a dream." Shaw and his regiment were memorialized by a Saint-Gaudens sculpture now on the Boston Common. The 54th Regiment was one of many black regiments fighting for the Union during the Civil War. An intense desire to rid the nation of slavery was a common bond among all Union soldiers, black and white, and there was a total of 53,000 black enlistees from free states

such as Massachusetts.

While the Civil War fighting raged out of state, much war-related activity occurred in Massachusetts. Massachusetts was joined early in its efforts to preserve the Union by 17 other nonslave states— Maine, New Hampshire, Vermont, Rhode Island, Connecticut, New York, New Jersey, Pennsylvania, Ohio, Indiana, Illinois, Wisconsin, Iowa, Minnesota, Kansas, Oregon, and California. The western part of Virginia had opposed that state's secession from the Union, and with its almost total absence of slavery the region had separated from the state. West Virginia was admitted to the Union as a state in 1863. Four border slave states— Kentucky, Delaware, Missouri, and Maryland—also remained loyal to the Union.

Massachusetts, the site of the initial battles of the War for Independence almost a century before, was saved from the destruction and ravages of the Civil War experienced by the southern states.

However, Bay State soldiers enlisted and died in large numbers to save the Union. Massachusetts suffered 13,942 casualties during the war out of a total state enlistment of 122,781 white troops, 3,966 black troops, and 19,983 sailors.

Battles in which Massachusetts regiments participated ranged from Antietam to Fredericksburg, Cold Harbor to Malvern Hill, and Gettysburg to Appomattox Courthouse.

Throughout the hard, lonely months of fighting and waiting for battles to begin, Yankee soldiers comforted themselves with stories of home and songs of sweethearts, bravery, and patriotic pride. Among these songs was the *Battle Hymn of the Republic,* written by Massachusetts native Julia Ward Howe. She composed the words in the early weeks of war while her husband, Dr. Samuel Gridley Howe, was inspecting Bay State troops in the nation's capital. It was a haunting hymn that soon came to represent all the Union army stood for.

The Civil War experience probably had one positive result in the improved efficiency of local fire companies. Here the Pontoonsuc Engine Company shows off in Pittsfield in December 1867. Courtesy, The Berkshire Atheneum

WAR MANUFACTURE AND WAR PROFIT

During the war, manufacture of firearms was centered chiefly in New England, which supplied regiments such as the Sixth Massachusetts, the 54th, and others. Smith & Wesson of Springfield was, next to Colt Firearms in Connecticut, the foremost manufacturer of revolvers. Most of these saw little use during actual battle, however, as their range was too limited. Only after the Civil War did Smith & Wesson develop revolvers in a caliber high enough to be useful in large-scale combat. But Smith & Wesson undoubtedly benefited from the lessons learned during the many battles fought. That weapons manufacture, founded by Horace Smith and Daniel B. Wesson in 1853, along with the Springfield Armory (maker of the "Springfield" rifle), made this western Massachusetts city prominent in arms manufacture right through to the twentieth century. In Chicopee, north of Springfield, Savage Arms began producing major armaments for the United States military in 1864. However unpleasant their business, it is clear that

Like many mill sites on rivers in Massachusetts, this one has a varied history. In 1810 it was a woolen mill in the Cabotville section of Holyoke. During the Civil War military leather goods were manufactured here, and it was part of the separate town of Chicopee by then. In the 1870s, known as the Gaylord Manufacturing Company, it produced iron, especially for locks, and ornamental swords for the post-Civil War customer. From Everts, History of the Connecticut Valley in Massachusetts, *Vol. II, 1879*

arms manufacturers of Massachusetts and surrounding areas gained a great deal from the suffering of the country as a whole.

Massachusetts was not new to innovation, either in arms manufacture or in other entrepreneurial areas. For more than two centuries, the state had been home to a number of inventive geniuses, and despite interruptions of the Civil War the state's cities and towns continued to be spawning grounds for new ideas in manufacture, agriculture, science, and education.

The town of Sterling, north of Worcester in central Massachusetts, was home to tailor Ebenezer Butterick, inventor of the first standardized paper patterns for shirts, suits, dresses, etc. Butterick's 1859 invention was a sweeping success that grew into the large company now known as Butterick Patterns. Sterling was also the home of two brothers, Silas and Lucian Stuart, who devised a way to mass-produce sewing machine needles. Nearby Spencer was home to Elias Howe, inventor of the home sewing machine, which was patented in 1846.

An anti-Catholic mob of hundreds burned the Charlestown convent of St. Ursula on the night of August 11, 1834. Fire companies responded to the alarm, but did very little to douse the flames. The ruins were left for many years, a stark reminder of the mob's violence. From Winsor, The Memorial History of Boston, 1630-1880, *Vol. III, 1881*

IMMIGRATION AND XENOPHOBIA

After the Civil War ended, Massachusetts—like other states across the war-weary nation—was affected by the inevitable chaos occurring with a shift to a peacetime economy. Returning soldiers needed work, and immigrant labor was gradually increasing in number. In Boston, the population grew at a steady pace following the Civil War. By 1880, there were 1,783,000 people in Massachusetts of whom 362,839 lived in the state capital. In 1890, Boston's population had grown to 448,477. The entire population of the United States stood at 50,155,783 in 1880—much of it clustered along the Atlantic seaboard in the Northeast.

The state population in the decades following the Civil War is of continuing interest to historians. Among the most obvious changes in Massachusetts' demography during these years was an increase in non-native-born citizens. Although immigrants were common prior to 1860, the state's population expanded tremendously after 1870 as French Canadians, Scandinavians, Eastern Europeans, and some Asians joined the thousands of Bay State factory and agricultural workers in cities like Boston, Springfield, Worcester, and Pittsfield.

For example, in 1875, 60,000 foreign-born Irish called Boston home, and by the end of the 1890s the Irish represented about 35 percent of the city's entire population. By the final decade of the nineteenth century, the influx of Irish had abated slightly, only to be replaced by a wave of Jews, Italians, Poles, and others from Eastern Europe.

The pattern was the same, whether it was Boston, New York, or Chicago. Immigrants worked hard, putting in long hours at factories or on farms. Women and children joined husbands, fathers, and brothers in sweatshop factories, pooling their wages into a meager total per family. All were determined that Massachusetts should live up to the promise it held out to them: freedom and a new way of life, a release from oppression, hunger, and fear.

Despite their high hopes, many immigrants found life was not easy in the United States. Before the Civil War, a nativist influence in the Massachusetts state government tolerated anti-foreign, anti-Catholic sentiments, provoking a considerable number of confrontations between native-born Americans and immigrants. Riots involving foreigners, who were usually Roman Catholic, and native-born Massachusetts residents, who were often Protestant, were all too frequent. In 1834, a Roman Catholic convent in Charlestown was burned to the ground. Such incidents and other manifestations of a growing nativist influence had, by the post-Civil War era, proved that native-born citizens feared losing their jobs and were outraged by religious practices contrasting so obviously with their own. But immigrants to Massachusetts were tenacious. They did not succumb to intimidation and threats of harm, as their desires for comfort, a steady living, and a safe life matched those of the native-born. Somehow, the two groups maintained an uneasy coexistence, and in many communities they learned to work side by side for the good life they all hoped for.

Newburyport, north of Boston, saw an influx of Irish Catholics during the middle to late decades of the 1800s, and Lawrence became heavily Roman Catholic

during the same period. In 1881, an Irish Catholic became mayor of that city, the first non-Protestant elected to office there. Southbridge saw an influx of French-Canadian immigrant labor that soon transformed the community, a phenomenon as much the result of active recruiting on the part of manufacturers as it was a result of chance immigration.

This immigrant wave was the second of three such surges of foreigners who sought a new beginning in America. The first wave, between 1820 and 1860, brought mostly Germans and other Northern Europeans to Massachusetts. Most were Protestants, but already some groups of Roman Catholic immigrants had settled in the Bay State. The second immigrant wave arrived between 1860 and 1890 and comprised about 15 million people, as compared to 5 million in the earlier group. Boston was the nation's second-largest port of entry in 1880—58,000 immigrants arrived there in one year. Of the city's total population in 1880, 54 percent were Massachusetts-born, 32 percent were foreign-born, and

This cartoon in the Boston Sunday Globe *in 1886 reveals the fear generated by "anarchist" immigrants from Hungary and Poland, as well as the fact that most of these immigrants were attracted to America by the availability of jobs—jobs that were provided because they would work for less than those already here. The caption reads: "Uncle Sam: 'Who are these fellows? Why are they coming here?' Mr. Contractor: 'I sent to Hungary and Poland for them. They come cheaper than the natives or the decent immigrants.' Uncle Sam: 'Yes, but they are bomb-throwers. Who's going to pay the police and military bills?' Mr. Contractor: 'That's your lookout. My duty is simply to buy my labor in the cheapest market.'" From the* Boston Sunday Globe, *May 16, 1886*

The pride of Fitchburg was its magnificent railroad station, which handled Boston-to-Albany passengers and most of the east-west, west-east traffic in the 1870s and 1880s. From Jewett, History of Worcester County, *Vol. I, 1879*

the rest were born elsewhere in the United States.

This changed ratio of foreign-born to native-born meant that change in the social fabric of towns and cities was inevitable. Furthermore, relations between workers and employers were changing. Labor union activism was perceived as a direct result of immigrant labor. It represented foreign influence on a democratic, capitalist society. By the 1880s, when labor union activism in Massachusetts and elsewhere provoked demonstrations and riots, newspapers pounced on these incidents as proof that something terrible was happening. The effect of such reporting increased nativism and xenophobia and caused more suspicion and hatred among Massachusetts residents who were different from each other.

One facet of mutual distrust was the growing favor parochial schools held with Roman Catholic parents. Such schools, set apart from the public schools that native-born children attended, were seen by the native-born as threatening imminent takeover by Rome. In Boston, a minister with well-developed nativist leanings—the Reverend Justin Fulton —spoke to enthusiastic crowds of fearful residents who worried that the pope was going to usurp all parental (and governmental) power in the United States. It was a time of almost unrelieved suspicion and antagonism, inevitable to a certain degree, but these impulses existed alongside other, more constructive ones that helped build the Bay State into a stronger, more flexible and welcoming

No. 24 B.

1892. Corrected to June 6. 1892.

Official Time-Table

OF THE

Boston & Albany

RAILROAD COMPANY.

Subject to Change and Corrections without Notice.

This Time-Table shows the times at which trains may be expected to arrive at, and depart from, the several stations; but their arrival or departure at the times stated is not guaranteed, nor does the Company hold itself responsible for any delay, or any consequences arising therefrom.

* ——— INCIVILITY. ——— *

Passengers are respectfully requested to report to the General Superintendent any instance of incivility on the part of employes of this Company. While it is the aim of the Company to redress just grievances, it is suggested that courtesy is equally commendable, whether practised by the railroad employe or the passenger.

H. T. GALLUP,   A. S. HANSON,
Gen'l Superintendent,   *Gen'l Pass'r Agent,*
SPRINGFIELD.   BOSTON.

R. A. SUPPLY CO., BOSTON.   1556

Railroad tickets from the 1890s were often specific about behavior aboard the trains. Incivility was not to be tolerated. Courtesy, The Walter C. and Sarah H. Jones Collection

environment for all citizens, immigrant or native-born.

RAILROADS AND LABOR MOVEMENTS

Railroads were one development that helped provide a leavening agent. After 1860, more and more rail activity occurred throughout the United States. Before the Civil War, only a limited amount of railroad lines were available, about 65 percent of them in the Northeast. Massachusetts had committed nearly $7.2 million to railroad promotion by the time of the Civil War. But despite its promise, railroads had only limited usefulness, as the existing mass of track—some 35,000 miles total throughout the nation—was made up of small, local lines using different track gauges. Soon after the Civil War, 10,000 miles of new track was hammered into place—most of it in standard gauge. This resulted in an enormous railroad network connecting all areas of the country. This development continued, and by the 1890s, tracks in the United States represented one-third of the entire railroad mileage in the world.

A postwar burst of industrial activity was concurrent with general railroad expansion but lasted little more than a decade. In 1873, a series of economic depressions affected virtually every part of the nation, hitting especially hard in Massachusetts factories, prompting wholesale layoffs and a drop in textile workers' wages for those lucky enough to

THE HOOSAC TUNNEL

Amid the bustle of early nineteenth-century American life, a constant clamor for new technologies produced revolutionary items like the cotton gin and the sewing machine. Eventually, these two inventions would help boost the textile output of Massachusetts, placing the state in the forefront of northern industrial economies. Other inventions were designed to further various interests in the Bay State and elsewhere. Some were successful, like the revolver, the steel plow, and the process of vulcanizing rubber. Others have long been forgotten. Among innovations that helped transform America was dynamite, the product of years of research by Swedish scientist Alfred Nobel. Dynamite led directly to a project of some importance in western Massachusetts: the Hoosac Tunnel.

This engineering marvel of the 1800s, located near North Adams, was the brainchild of Alvah Crocker. A prosperous Fitchburg industrialist, Crocker hoped to tap into the lucrative shipping trade of the Erie Canal. But in order for Crocker's mills in Fitchburg to access the Erie Canal, it was necessary to devise a quick, relatively inexpensive means of transport across western Massachusetts. There the craggy, uneven terrain made overland transportation costly and time-consuming and construction of a canal impossible.

Crocker's solution was a tunnel. Construction of this tunnel was begun in 1851 and its ultimate purpose would be to speed up rail shipment of goods and materials to and from Fitchburg.

Hoosac Mountain was the natural stone barrier through which Crocker's engineers would drill. Crocker's expectation was that this tunnel would take three years to build. But after 10 years,

using steam drills and black powder, workers had only gone about one-third of the way through the mountain rock.

Nobel's invention—dynamite—was a major contributor toward hastening the project. And Alvah Crocker's willingness to invest in new technologies brought compressed air drills and remote control detonators to the site. The Hoosac Tunnel was thus integral to the development of industrial America. Without this Massachusetts mill owner's desire to increase his productivity, many of the skills and procedures developed during the building of the Hoosac Tunnel may have been longer in coming.

Crocker's desire to complete the tunnel within three years was unrealistic at best. The Hoosac Tunnel was 24 years in the making and was a project that claimed the lives of 195 miners between 1851 and 1875. The opening at the eastern end of the tunnel carries the inscription "1875," and bears only a mute testimony to those nearly 200 workers who spent many hard, fruitless hours tunneling through the solid facade of Hoosac Mountain. And along with Crocker's need to complete the project within a handful of years was his expectation that the tunnel would result in increased profits for his Fitchburg mills. Ultimately, Crocker was proven wrong about this as well. Over the 24 years that it took to build, the Hoosac Tunnel cost $14 million and was never able to develop Crocker's mills into the most important economic factor in Massachusetts.

The entrance to the 25,031-foot tunnel is still visible, tucked away in the overgrowth on the side of Hoosac Mountain. Nowhere to be seen are the two million tons of rock, removed during

excavation. Neither is it possible to view easily the 20 million bricks used to line the inside arches of the tunnel for nearly five miles. But the now-obsolete tunnel remains a monument to the miners, engineers, and common laborers who devoted their working lives to its completion. The vitality of these men represented the economic vigor surging through the state and the nation throughout the nineteenth century. It was this vigor that paved the way for even greater industrial and technological innovations in the twentieth century.

In an article titled "Feats of Railway Engineering," Scribner's Magazine *in July 1888 ran this picture of a tunnel construction technique that was pioneered during the building of the Hoosac Tunnel. Wood framing was used to line the tunnel as it was bored out, while rock and debris were removed by shovel and cart.*

★   ★   ★   ★   ★   ★   ★

In 1880, the city of Boston celebrated the 250th anniversary of its founding. In this scene, a replica of the first printing press in America rolls by on a float past the newly unveiled statue of Puritan founder John Winthrop, the first governor of Massachusetts Bay Colony. Winthrop, sculpted in "ancient garb," holds the colony charter in one hand and the Bible in the other. On the pedestal with him is the stump of a tree with a rope attached, symbolizing the fastening of the boat from which he had just disembarked. A duplicate statue was presented in Washington, D.C., at the Capitol. From Harper's Weekly, *October 9, 1880*

evangelist Dwight L. Moody's interest in religious education led him to found the Northfield Seminary in 1879. Moody, a Northfield native, had moved to Boston shortly before his 20th birthday. In 1856, after experiencing a religious conversion, he moved to Chicago where he began his evangelical work with orphaned children and with the poor. Moody garnered support from rich and influential people like Cyrus McCormick and George Armour. Moody was president of the YMCA in Chicago and a few years later preached in England, campaigning for converts and telling people that eternal life was theirs.

The Northfield Seminary, a school for young women, was mirrored in 1881 by a similar institution for young men, the Mount Hermon School, also in Northfield. The schools merged in 1971 and are now known as the Northfield Mount Hermon School, a coeducational, college preparatory school of high quality and

fine reputation.

Other new educational institutions of the period include Smith College in Northampton, founded in 1875 through the generosity of Sophia Smith, a native of nearby Hatfield. Smith College was designed to promote the development of "the intelligent gentlewoman," and was well regarded as soon as it opened. Similarly, Wellesley College, founded in 1870, and Radcliffe College, founded in 1879, contributed to Massachusetts' prominence in post-secondary education of women. Mount Holyoke College had been founded in 1837 and was, like the others, part of a larger, national trend. Post-secondary education for women was new, and some institutions dedicated to this goal existed outside of New England. In Massachusetts, however, women of the late nineteenth century found a wide variety of educational opportunities.

In 1862, the United States Congress passed the Morrill Land Grant Act,

WILLIAM SMITH CLARK (1826-1886)

William Smith Clark may be the most famous American in Japan. His statue overlooks Sapporo, on the island of Hokkaido, and his face and parting advice to Japanese youth, "Boys, be ambitious!" are emblazoned on tee shirts, coffee mugs, and packages of cookies today. Japanese visitors still come to Amherst to visit Clark's grave and his memorial garden, while the University of Hokkaido and the University of Massachusetts at Amherst continue to have a strong relationship as sister Universities.

Clark may be considered the father of both schools. After becoming the first Amherst College graduate to study in Europe and to earn a Ph.D., Clark returned to Amherst teaching chemistry, botany, at the same time also serving as a state representative, and a colonel in the Civil War. He helped found Massachusetts Agricultural College, now the University of Massachusetts at Amherst, and became its third president, teaching botany, building greenhouses, and directing the students in scientific indoor and outdoor planting.

Mass. Aggie was so successful that the Japanese government, fearing Russian ambitions on its remote northern island, asked Clark to replicate his school on Hokkaido. Clark spent 1876 and 1877 building the Sapporo Agricultural College (now the Hokkaido Imperial University), teaching botany and chemistry, and introducing milk cows, sheep, and American-style barns. Legend has it that the young men Clark had inspired crowded around their dashing and spirited president, escorting him to the ship that would carry him home to Massachusetts. Clark turned on his horse and issued a farewell challenge, "Boys, be ambitious!"

Many of Clark's students went on to greatness in Japan, and Hokkaido became a secure and stable part of Japan. Clark planted seeds in Japan, and in Massachusetts. Having introduced American crops and livestock to Japan, Clark brought Japanese plants back to Massachusetts, which today can be found in Boston's Arnold Arboretum and in Amherst. The two universities he founded, half a world apart, the University of Hokkaido and the University of Massachusetts, continue to inspire their graduates to be ambitious.

— Ruth Owen Jones

William Smith Clark as he looked in 1876. From Scribner's Magazine, Vol. 12, October 1876

PRESIDENT CLARK.

URBANIZATION AND LABOR UNREST (1890-1914)

★　★　★　★　★　★　★　★　★

This photo of a Boston three-decker was used in a state report on immigrants and their housing and the "problems" of Americanizing the newcomers. From Report of the Commission on Immigration on the Problem of Immigration in Massachusetts, *1914*

During the last half of the nineteenth century, political turmoil and disorganization marked election activities in the United States. In Massachusetts this upheaval both paralleled and reflected changes in Bay State social fabric. The Democrats were in the minority. There were no Democratic congressmen from Massachusetts until 1876, so strong was Republican sentiment in the state.

Among leading Republican party members were Henry Cabot Lodge of Boston and George Frisbie Hoar of Worcester, the latter a follower of the outspoken Massachusetts antislavery advocate, Senator Charles Sumner. Hoar was also an ardent abolitionist, and was best known for his role as chief author of the Sherman Antitrust Act of 1890. At a time when imperialism ruled the nation's foreign policy, Hoar was one of the few politicians who did not support the U.S. effort to conquer the Philippines during the Spanish-American War.

Although many in Massachusetts agreed with Hoar's anti-imperialist views, he and his supporters were in the minority.

Imperialism held sway in the United States in 1895 when Cuba, off the coast of Florida, was in rebellion. All over the United States newspapers carried stories of struggles between Cuban rebels and the island's Spanish government. The situation seemed in some ways to replicate the story of the colonists' bid for self-government and freedom from British rule 120 years earlier. In Massachusetts, the battles of Lexington and Concord in 1775 appeared to be historic blueprints for Cuban action in 1895. Those whose interests warranted it called for U.S. intervention and aid on behalf of Cuban rebels fighting what was termed an undesirable government. Senator Henry Cabot Lodge was one of those most eager for the United States to get involved in the Cuban rebellion.

After several unsuccessful bids for

Mary Baker Eddy (1821-1910) from New Hampshire founded the Christian Science Church in Boston in 1879. In 1892, when this photograph was taken, the First Church of Christ Scientist in its present form was begun in Boston. Mrs. Eddy had written the religion's textbook, Science and Health with a Key to the Scriptures, *in 1875, and one of her final achievements was the founding of the widely respected newspaper,* The Christian Science Monitor, *in 1908. Courtesy, The First Church of Christ Scientist and the Mary Baker Eddy Library for the Betterment of Humanity, Inc.*

public office, Lodge had been elected to Congress in 1886. He thereafter enjoyed a prominent position in the Republican party for almost 40 years. In 1893, he became a United States senator—with a decidedly pro-imperialist position concerning the brewing Spanish-American conflict. Lodge was also an ardent proponent of immigration restrictions, and his activities on behalf of native-born Americans—and against the nation's immigrant population—were enthusiastically supported by many like-minded conservatives. Perhaps most important of all, Lodge was a friend of Theodore Roosevelt. Lodge, an instructor at Harvard University when Roosevelt was an undergraduate, was to be the progressive president's staunchest Mas-

sachusetts supporter in the early years of the twentieth century.

In 1898, Lodge saw his hopes realized for military action against the Cuban government. On February 15, 1898, the U.S. battleship *Maine* was blown up in Havana Harbor. More than 250 U.S. naval personnel were killed in the attack, the origins of which were never definitely determined, although Spanish complicity was suspected. U.S. public opinion was aroused and pro-war sentiments grew. The *Maine* incident's effect on the nation was electrifying. The pro-war faction—with Henry Cabot Lodge at its head—demanded instant and thorough vindication of the terrible "act of dirty treachery," as the *Maine's* destruction was called by Theodore Roosevelt, who at that time was assistant U.S. secretary of the navy. By April 1898, President William McKinley reluctantly persuaded Congress that armed force in Cuba was the best way to stave off future difficulties with Spain. The warmongers were thrilled. Most people in Massachusetts and elsewhere supported the president's action as the only possible response to the *Maine* incident.

For most Massachusetts citizens, the declaration of war meant little, but it did provoke excitement and flurries of preparatory activity as several units of the military looked forward to mobilization. "Remember the *Maine*" was the rallying cry heard all across the state and the nation, as soldiers assembled prior to departure for the Cuban war theater.

About 20,000 Bay State soldiers took active part in the Spanish-American War. The Sixth Massachusetts Regiment, an infantry unit, was called to duty once more. This regiment, remembered for its early role in the Civil War, asked for and received permission to travel through Baltimore on its way to Cuba, retracing its route of nearly four decades before. This time the Sixth was greeted warmly by residents of the city who cheered the gallant Bay State soldiers on their way south.

Although the Sixth Massachusetts did

not see action during its short tour of duty in Cuba and Puerto Rico, the Second Massachusetts Infantry was part of the legendary battle of San Juan Hill on July 1, 1898. The Ninth Massachusetts Infantry was also sent to Cuba, and during 18 days at the scene of battle there, it lost 177 men.

Hostilities in Cuba ended when an armistice was signed in August 1898. The war officially concluded with the signing of the Treaty of Paris on December 10, when Cuba was freed but placed under U.S. jurisdiction. Meanwhile, an outbreak of military activity in the Philippine Islands introduced another phase in the conflict with Spain. First, annexation by the United States prompted a Philippine revolt, and occupation of the islands by U.S. troops provoked a war lasting three years. President Theodore Roosevelt eventually

proclaimed an end to the Philippine insurrection on July 4, 1902.

SOCIAL REFORM

The nation turned hopeful eyes on the future, and many leaders in the late nineteenth and early twentieth centuries were known as zealous reformers. They hoped to improve everything from urban slums and public education to race relations and labor conditions. Between 1880 and 1920, there was an air of optimism that seemed to promise big improvements in many areas. In Massachusetts, there was an early effort which reflected the nationwide settlement-house movement. At Boston's Andover House, just as at the more famous Hull House in Chicago, social workers dedicated their energies to upgrading the lives of neighborhood people. Many of these social workers

W.E.B. Du Bois (1869-1963) is at front left in this photograph of people active in the Niagara Movement in 1907 in Boston. Du Bois is considered by some to be the father of the black-power movement, which later tried to blend civil rights integration with the more militant black nationalism. Courtesy, Special Collections and Archives, Library, University of Massachusetts at Amherst

The mill houses in rural areas differed from those in the city, as shown in this circa 1900 photo of a mother and her children outside their modest home near a brick factory in the Leeds section of Northampton. Courtesy, Northampton Historical Society

often were graduates of Massachusetts women's colleges such as Smith, Mount Holyoke, Wellesley, and Radcliffe, as well as of coeducational institutions. These women were highly motivated, well-educated, and eager to take an active role in the reform of American society.

These reformers hoped to salvage urban dwellers from poverty and ignorance, but the urban poor represented only a small percentage of Massachusetts' total population. For the most part, Bay State residents had until now lived in smaller cities and towns where opportunities for aiding the less fortunate were generally limited. Between 1880 and 1920, however, the population increase in Massachusetts began to take place in cities rather than in the rural areas.

Many of those living in Massachusetts in the late nineteenth century were factory workers whose jobs were continually threatened by a major decline in the textile and other manufacturing industries. Reformers were for the most part unable to alter economic conditions creating recessions and depressions. Nor were they able to amend the social conditions surrounding the very real racial segregation that existed in northern, as well as southern, states at this time.

American blacks enjoyed little in the way of social or political progress. Some black leaders tried to effect change, however. Among them was William Edward Burghardt Du Bois. Born in 1868 in Great Barrington in western Massachusetts, he received a Ph.D. from Harvard University and became a spokesperson for black citizens who desired equality, an integrated society, and fair treatment. Du Bois was a cofounder of the committee which later became the National Association for the Advancement of Colored People. Formation of the NAACP marked a break between Du Bois, an integrationist, and Booker T. Washington. Washington preached self-sufficiency and segregation, promoting establishment of a black community operating separately from the white world, a community which would nevertheless be maintained without a radical departure from middle-class norms.

Du Bois was for the most part disappointed in his efforts to promote sweeping reforms for blacks in America and elsewhere. He spent the last two years of his life in Africa and died in 1963 after years of hard work. Du Bois' papers are maintained in a special collection at the library of the University of Massachusetts, Amherst. A memorial park is located on the site of Du Bois' childhood home in Great Barrington in the Berkshires.

Blacks were not alone in their struggle for integration. Massachusetts was changing and immigration was chiefly responsible for the new, and some said stronger, social fabric. Although nativists such as Henry Cabot Lodge were loathe to admit it, immigrant labor and the cultural pluralism resulting from a mix of nationalities across the state produced a more vital, vigorous population.

By the middle of the nineteenth century, Roman Catholic immigrants made up fully one-fifth of the Massachusetts population, most of them of Irish descent. The election of an Irish Catholic mayor, John Breen, in Lawrence in 1881, was symbolic of the gradual transformation of public opinion toward immigrants. Boston saw another Irish-born Roman Catholic, Hugh O'Brien, elected mayor in 1884. By 1885, the formerly antagonistic relationship between native-born Yankees and foreign-borns, such as O'Brien and Breen, had changed. In Boston, Thomas Gargan, an Irish lawyer, was chosen that same year by the Democrats to give the traditional Independence Day oration. Following the acceptance of Gargan, native-born and Irish Catholic speakers alternated as Fourth of July speakers each year thereafter.

Another Irish immigrant and Fenian nationalist who had fought for Irish independence from England, John Boyle O'Reilly, became prominent in Boston as editor of the *Pilot*, a widely read Roman Catholic newspaper. O'Reilly found acceptance throughout the ranks of Massachusetts literati, and in 1889 some of his poetry was read at the rededication of Plymouth Rock.

Many women worked long days on their feet in paper mills like this one in Holyoke, circa 1900. The photographer labeled this image "In the Rag Room." The census of 1900 counted 2,805,346 people in the state, 329,033 of them women in "gainful occupations." Of these women, only about 12 percent were married. This count of working women did not include the thousands of women who worked on farms or in family-owned businesses, since they did not get paid wages. Photo by Clifton Johnson. Courtesy, The Clifton Johnson Collection, The Jones Library, Inc., Amherst

LABOR REFORM

Political upheaval went hand in hand with labor struggles, and both marked the late nineteenth and early twentieth centuries in Massachusetts. A critical factor in the state's industrial decline rested in the fact that textile mills were no longer lucrative, low-cost operations. During the heyday of the early industrial revolution wages were low, but labor costs continually increased after 1830.

During the depression of 1873, many factory workers left Massachusetts. Those who stayed looked for ways to obtain real bargaining power and guarantee job security. Their success in this search was only moderate. In 1893, about 15,000 mill workers in Lawrence were out of work, and all the mills in the city shut down. By 1909, prosperity had slowly regained a foothold, and the average weekly wage for most male workers hovered around nine dollars. For women, earnings were slightly lower, averaging eight dollars a week. By 1911, all workers in Lawrence were limited to a 54-hour work week as a result of new state legislation governing the number of hours that women and children could work. Some maintained that this protective legislation was needed, but others—including many of the workers

themselves—demanded further changes. Their complaints fell on deaf ears, for there was little labor organizing occurring then. The enormous mill complexes—American Woolen Company's Wood Mill, the Arlington Mills, and the Pacific Mills—remained peaceful and seemingly placid industrial centers without overt labor dissent. But this did not last.

By the beginning of 1912, mill workers in Lawrence expressed their dissatisfaction over working conditions. The 54-hour work week had brought a decrease in wages that most families could ill afford to absorb, and laborers were finally speaking out.

On January 12, 1912, at the Wood textile mill, angry workers, many of them immigrants, burst into a frustrated rampage, destroying machinery, telling co-workers to quit, and defying police sent in to quell the disorder. On Monday, January 15, about 8,000 striking mill workers picketed the Wood mills and several other Lawrence factories, preventing other workers from going to their jobs. The International Workers of the World (IWW), whose members had organized the strike, called for help, both financial and otherwise, for striking workers and their families. By Wednesday of that week, 10,000 striking

New England Magazine *described the 1912 Lawrence strike as "a small Civil War." As many as 15,000 strikers took part; many are seen here, marching down the snowy streets of Lawrence. From* New England Magazine, *March 1912*

workers gathered to listen to the radical views of union agitators Big Bill Haywood, Elizabeth Gurley Flynn, and the Socialist poet Arturo Giovanitti. Two weeks later more strikers mobbed the streets, and headlines in the *New York Times* read "Real Labor War Now in Lawrence." One striker was killed and a police officer was stabbed. Giovanitti was arrested for inciting trouble, and the children of many striking textile workers were evacuated from the city in order to secure their safety.

Several weeks after the main out-breaks of violence, mill owners, anxious to get factories back into production, offered pay increases of nearly one dollar a week to most workers in hopes of encouraging their return. Almost all the textile workers agreed to the terms of the concessions offered, much to the owners' relief. They had worried what further disruptions in their production might do to the already tenuous economic balance.

The year 1912 was pivotal in terms of ultimate settlement of labor disputes,

although the rift between immigrant workers and police took years to mend. The old division between native-borns and immigrants, including Italians, Irish, Poles, and Franco-Americans, was less apparent as union organization became mutually important to these ethnically diverse groups. Union membership in Massachusetts went from 4,000 to 17,000 in one year, giving workers the strength to make subsequent demands.

After the 1912 strike was over, immigrant workers began to leave Lawrence. In 1920, they represented only 42 percent of the population, while in 1910, they had made up nearly half. This shift took place without a corresponding increase in the general population of the city. By the eve of World War I, immigrants in Lawrence had begun to identify more closely with native-born Americans rather than with their own ethnic roots. Liberty bond drives yielded several million dollars from the for-eign-born during World War I, and immigrants and their sons enlisted in the

An early streetcar line was run by the Holyoke Street Railway Company, whose South Hadley-to-Sunderland route was staffed in 1901 by John Haskins and Fred Garey. Some streetcars had passenger and driver's seats that turned around at the end of the line. The car was then driven "backwards" on the return trip, with the driver in the rear of the car. Courtesy, The Baxter Eastman Collection

Nantasket Beach was newly commercialized and popular in 1882 when Harper's Weekly featured it on its cover with a caption that began "What Coney Island is to New York, Nantasket Beach is to Boston—the great popular summer resort for the masses, easy of access, crowded, noisy, bustling, and democratic, with some corners devoted to the elite . . . ." Nantasket could be quickly reached from Boston on the steamer or the Old Colony railroad, and most people could afford the fare. From Harper's Weekly, August 19, 1882

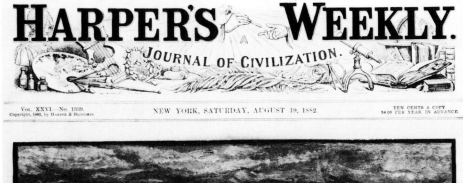

military, died for their new country, and were memorialized by their survivors, native-born and foreign together. It appeared by the second decade of the twentieth century that the previous friction and unrest between the two groups had largely abated.

TRANSPORTATION

The Boston Post Road in the seventeenth century had been the major artery in and out of several cities. Then, it traversed the Commonwealth on its way to New York State, but now, in the early twentieth century, there were other means of transportation. Eastern Massachusetts residents could select one of several as yet rudimentary but viable methods of getting from place to place. Most exciting was the advent of the automobile. Few had access to this new conveyance, but those who did were able to travel much farther and more frequently. Among the first manufacturers of this new mode of transportation were Charles and Frank Duryea, credited with building the first really successful gasoline automobile, in

Springfield in 1893. In 1896, they made the first auto sale in the United States, kicking off what was to become one of the nation's largest, most important industries. Eventually the brothers went their separate ways, and in 1900, Frank Duryea opened a factory named the Stevens-Duryea Company, located in Chicopee Falls.

Common to more residents of Massachuetts was a different, yet still fairly innovative, form of transportation: the streetcar. At first it was drawn by horses, but by 1900, streetcars in many urban areas had been electrified. In 1891, there were 245 miles of trolley track in Boston alone. All over the greater Boston area, from the North Shore to the South, and westward with ever-expanding regularity, the streetcar unified the region. In 1850, there had been a three-mile streetcar radius in Boston; by the turn of the century, that radius exceeded 10 miles.

One of the early streetcar promoters was Stephen Dudley Field, a resident of Stockbridge. His interest in electricity was

Lake Pleasant, a village of Montague, was a summer camp meeting place for spiritualists—those who believe that the dead communicate with the living. Tiny lots for tents around a common were soon used for cottages, and the cottages grew and grew on the same small lots. The July 8, 1888, edition of the Boston Globe *noted that beautiful summer places, "models of architectural design," were being built at Lake Pleasant. As the belief in spiritualism declined over the years, so did the beauty of the Lake Pleasant community. Another spiratualist mecca was located at Silver Lake in Plympton. From a circa 1908 postcard*

provoked at an early age by an uncle, Cyrus W. Field, who was responsible for the laying of the first submarine telegraph cable between the United States and Europe. The younger Field worked with dynamos, experimenting with ways to employ them in streetcar operation. His work was critical to the evolution of the modern rapid transit system common to Boston today, and thanks to Field, the electric streetcar soon replaced the horse-drawn variety. According to one historian, the electric streetcar moved twice as fast as the horse-drawn vehicle and tripled the street-railway's passenger capacity.

Early in the 1900s, the inhabitants of southeastern Massachusetts marveled at an engineering feat which many had long sought. On July 29, 1914, engineers opened the Cape Cod Canal, started five years earlier in 1909. Symbolic of many technological advances that had their inception in the Commonwealth during the twentieth century, the project actually had been discussed seriously a century earlier. The canal was a shining example of the type of advance that benefited thousands while boosting the state's commercial abilities. The waterway connects Cape Cod Bay with Buzzards Bay south of the Cape. Discussion concerning building a canal had begun in

1697, but not until the early 1800s did widespread interest in the project grow. State and federal authorities brought up the topic for consideration several times, but canal construction did not get under way until the twentieth century.

There were various reasons for building this type of canal in this location. Among the most pressing were considerations of safety for both lives and property. Between 1875 and 1903, nearly 700 vessels were lost in the waters off the Cape, and 105 lives were lost in these shipwrecks as well.

In June 1899, the Boston, Cape Cod and New York Canal Company signed a construction contract. On June 22, 1909, the first shovel of earth was turned and work began in earnest. By the end of the year, 200 workers had been engaged and by 1912, 750 men were employed on the project in various capacities. They worked 10-hour days for between $1.50 and $2.00 an hour. When it was completed, the canal eliminated the need for ships from New York and points south of New England to navigate treacherous shallow waters off Provincetown in order to access Boston Harbor and points north. Completion of the canal meant Barnstable County was now technically an island. In 1935, the Bourne Bridge was constructed, con-

At the turn of the century a cleaner Charles River was popular with canoeists. This picture from a circa 1906 postcard may have been taken at the Forest Grove area in the Waltham section of the river.

necting Cape Cod with the mainland. In later years, this bridge was supplemented by the Sagamore Bridge. Both received increasingly heavy usage as Cape Cod became a popular vacation spot following World War II.

TIME FOR LEISURE

Thanks to innovations such as the automobile and the streetcar, cities from Boston to Pittsfield extended their boundaries. From Boston, people could now travel to other locations to enjoy leisure activities. The entire North Shore area, from Beverly to Salisbury, changed into an important playground for both rich and poor in the late nineteenth century. By the early twentieth century, the South Shore had also become popular. Resorts such as Nantasket Beach, Revere Beach, and Lincoln Park, near New Bedford, all were populated heavily during summer months by pleasure-seeking people from all over eastern Massachusetts and beyond.

Another spot that grew in popularity as a summer resort was Martha's Vineyard. Originally, it was a Methodist meeting ground for religious revivals, but was discovered by "ordinary" vacationers and became an exclusive summer destination. Its only means of surface access is by ferryboat, as is that of Nantucket, the island to the east of Martha's Vineyard. Both had relied earlier on fishing and whaling as main sources of income, but by the twentieth century, this maritime economy was replaced forever by tourism.

The growing number of talented foreign-born and native-born residents of Massachusetts, combined with improved transportation networks and an increase in leisure time, meant that new institutions would continue to grow and acknowledge culturally-diverse factors. Wealthy, well-educated citizens of eastern Massachusetts rejoiced in 1881 in the formation of the Boston Symphony Orchestra. Henry Lee Higginson, a wealthy Boston Brahmin, donated money and put in considerable time and effort to establish the symphony, of which some musicians were trained at the New England Conservatory of Music, established in 1867. Others, however, came from the increasing ranks of artistically gifted immigrants. In 1900, construction of Symphony Hall, the future home of the Boston Symphony, was begun at a location off Huntington Avenue in the city's Back Bay.

Less sedate pastimes included baseball, which grew in popularity as the Boston

Dr. James Naismith of Springfield invented the game of basketball in this gymnasium in the school for Christian Workers in December 1891. He hung a peach basket on each end on the area below the overhead running track. Eighteen players took part in the first games played here. Courtesy, The Naismith Memorial Basketball Hall of Fame, Springfield

179

In 1899 the new South Station was the largest railroad station in the world, according to an article in the New York Sun. This circa 1911 postcard shows the exterior; the interior was noted for its complicated turntables for the engines that stationed there.

Baseball Club, active since 1871, became the delight of hundreds of avid fans. Similarly, boxing had aficionados who grew ecstatic when Boston-born John L. Sullivan became national boxing champion in 1882. Conversely, they despaired when he lost the title in 1892. A new sport, basketball, had been invented in Springfield in 1891 by James A. Naismith. He was an instructor at the YMCA College in Springfield (now Springfield College), and devised the game as a way of ensuring his student athletes would stay in good physical condition during the winter months.

Naismith's ingenious idea consisted of attaching overhead peach baskets to the walls on opposite sides of the gym and then having opposing teams try to throw soccerballs through the baskets. His game basically remains the same today as it was when invented nearly 100 years ago, although there have been important upgradings of equipment.

ART AND ARCHITECTURE

Statewide interest in culture resulted in the establishment of a number of important museums by 1900. The largest and most generously endowed was the Museum of Fine Arts in Boston. Founded in 1870 at Copley Square, it was moved in 1909 to its present site on Huntington Avenue in a building designed by Guy Lowell. The museum faced the Fenway, part of the "Emerald Necklace" designed by the famous urban planner and landscape architect, Frederick Law Olmsted. His idea of connecting important residential and commercial areas of Boston resulted in the lovely strip of parks that begins at Boston's Public Gardens and ends at the Fenway, near Isabella Stewart Gardner's former home.

Just as the period 1790 to 1830 produced architectural gems in residences throughout the state, in 1900 similarly grand architectural displays were in

vogue. Constructed in part as a result of the economic boom enjoyed by important industrialists (so aptly described in William Dean Howells' *The Rise of Silas Lapham*, these homes reflect the affluence of the age.

In Worcester, the Salisbury Building marked the beginning of that city's apartment-house boom. Three-decker homes were popular at this time also, springing up especially in middle-class or working-class neighborhoods where families did not have the income to sustain large, single-family dwellings but still had pretensions to middle-class lifestyles. Chicopee also sported many new homes in the 1890s and early 1900s, most of them ornately designed and decorated with gingerbread trim, many with mansard roofs. Again, much of this urban, and later suburban, growth was made possible by expanded transportation networks enabling people to live farther away from their workplaces. Boston's first skyscraper, the Ames Building, located near the Old State-house, also dates from this period.

A loose assemblage of Impressionists, the group of painters known as the Boston School, came to enjoy world renown. This is somewhat remarkable, considering that many of them drew on inner resources fueled by the beauty and tranquility of the same region—Massachusetts. The Boston School included Frank Benson, Joseph DeCamp, Childe Hassam, Philip Hale, his wife Lilian Westcott Hale, William Paxton, his wife Elizabeth Paxton, and Edmund Tarbell. Many had studied in Paris or other European cities, yet returned to paint scenes and individuals in Massachusetts, thereby immortalizing the region of their birth. The legacy these artists left is one that represents Massachusetts during one of its most interesting periods of growth and change.

By 1900, Massachusetts' population had grown to 2.5 million people, most of whom lived in urban centers. Vestiges of rural life remained throughout the state, however, particularly in smaller

communities to the west of Worcester. Like few other states, Massachusetts successfully clung to both the charm of an agrarian past and the challenge of brisk, industrial lifestyles. This pluralism was in part represented by the distinct divisions still remaining between native-born and immigrant. It was clear that in factory cities like Lawrence this division often meant trouble, for fear and uncertainty provoked by cultural differences erupted into violence. Underneath the facade of progress, both groups clung to the known. Labor agitators, political splinter groups, and most of all, the horror that World War I brought to the entire nation, were as much a part of Massachusetts' experience in the first two decades of the twentieth century as had been the patriotic fervor of the 1760s and 1770s in the Bay State.

America's premier landscape architect, Frederick Law Olmsted, is probably most famous for his design of Central Park in New York City, but he did commissions across the country. By 1881 he was living in Brookline, which was to become his home and office headquarters and is now a National Historic Site. In Massachusetts his work includes the Emerald Necklace park system in Boston and numerous other contracts. Olmsted's social and design principles are as appropriate today as in the 1800s, and his work is enjoying a revival of appreciation. An inventory of his commissions was made by the Massachusetts Association of Olmsted Parks, a pilot meant to be a model for other states. From Cirker, Dictionary of American Portraits, Dover, 1967

struction of battleships occurred at Quincy's Fore River Shipyard. Many small but critical items were also provided by Bay State industries, among them, shoes, boots, uniforms, pistol belts, and incendiary cartridges. This intense effort was a boon to the economy while it lasted, but later caused major portions of Massachusetts industry to grind to a halt after the Armistice. Portions of the state's economy were then left in a precarious position, and many able workers were unemployed.

THE STATE ECONOMY AFFECTED

Changes in the nation's economy due to wartime were reflected in the increase in union membership rolls. In 1916, before the United States entered the war, there were about two million members in the American Federation of Labor (A. F. of L.), but by 1920 that figure had grown

to 3.26 million. War manufacture also provoked federal government involvement in economic production. Centralized bureaus such as the War Industries Board monitored coordination of war goods manufacture, and the National War Labor Board helped negotiate settlements between employers and workers. Most often, the board favored the union position. Federal control was clearly necessary during wartime, but after the Armistice was signed and soldiers returned to civilian life and work, government involvement in business and industry was no longer necessary.

During World War I, shoe and textile factories in Massachusetts had experienced a burst of activity. Production demands of wartime provided comfortably for workers during wartime and augured well for the future. In addition, war-related shipbuilding created many new jobs in the state. But the economic prosperity reigning in Massachusetts throughout the war diminished following the Armistice. Postwar recession spelled economic downturn in Massachusetts, and meant a decline in manufacturing production and employment statewide. Still, in 1919, the state's factories were producing $4 billion in products compared to only $109 million in farm income. There were about 700,000 industrial workers in Massachusetts by this time—almost six times the number of farm workers. By 1920, some factories were closing down since defense-related production was no longer required. Even so, that year Massachusetts produced 6.4 percent of all U.S. manufactured goods. However, it was increasingly common for big investors to move plants to other parts of the country, where better risks for capital investment were located. This combination of factors meant layoffs and factory shutdowns across Massachusetts. Added to the inevitable postwar decline, yet another issue caused difficulty throughout the state. An increase in labor union activity across Massachusetts meant greater demands for higher wages among those workers who had kept their jobs.

Some recalled the textile factory strikes of 1912 during the Boston police strike of 1919. During this incident Calvin Coolidge, a somewhat obscure Republican from Northampton, achieved national prominence and respect through his terse, direct approach to the strike. As Massachusetts' governor, Coolidge demanded that striking police officers return to their jobs, which they did after an interlude of only two days. The fortunate Coolidge was credited with efficient handling of a potentially dangerous situation. He went on to win the Republican nomination for vice president in 1920, largely on the strength of his performance during the strike.

A DECADE OF CONTROVERSY

Massachusetts residents looked to the future with ambivalence. Changes of every type in every area of life were inevitable. Some embraced these changes willingly; others attempted to forestall them through various legislative means. Some legislation of this period was propelled by attitudes and ideologies that were questionable at best. The 1920s were of pivotal importance for the United States. A more sophisticated

Calvin Coolidge (1872-1933) was born in Vermont, but graduated from Amherst College and became a lawyer in Northampton. After holding various civil offices there he became a Massachusetts representative in 1907. From 1910 to 1911 he was mayor of Northampton, then went back to Boston as a state senator. Coolidge was lieutenant governor from 1915 to 1919, then governor from 1919 to 1921 when he became vice president under Warren Harding. When Harding died in 1923 Coolidge became president, and he was reelected in 1924. The Coolidges retired to a modest home in Northampton, where he died in 1933. Here Coolidge and his wife, Grace, enter their car circa 1928 when they retired from the White House to Northampton. Courtesy, Northampton Historical Society

Right: *Imagine this Roaring 20s flapper with a broad red ribbon around her cloche hat, bright red lips, and a red collar. Then imagine her inviting you to meet her at the fair, as advertised on this 29-inch-diameter tire cover on the back of a Model A Ford sedan. The Three County Fair (Hampshire, Hampden, and Franklin counties) is the longest continuously running fair in the country. It was founded in 1818 by such men as Judge Joseph Lyman and Noah Webster. The early fairs, held after harvest season, offered premiums for the best bull, milk cow, oxen, sheep, cheese, knitted mittens, handwoven diaper fabric, and sheeting. Breeding stock and new seed varieties were bought and sold or swapped; important advances in agricultural techniques were shared. The first fairs also held oratory competitions featuring the more vocal of the civic leaders. Photo by Kathryn Stadler. Courtesy, The Collection of Walter C. and Sarah H. Jones, gift of Albert Omasta of Hatfield*

Facing page, top: *The appointed state commission on immigration in 1914 reported to the legislature that immigrant living conditions were unacceptable. This picture from the report showed a room, probably in Worcester, in which 10 Turkish people slept in day and night shifts. The commission declared such overcrowding bad for health and morals. They noted that only a small percentage of immigrants were women—94 percent of Turkish immigrants in 1911 to 1913 were male. The commission recommended that housing laws be enforced but it had no ideas on how to alleviate the Turkish men's general forlornness. Having no normal social relations, the men's lives were open to temptation and vice. From* Report of the Commission on Immigration on the Problem of Immigration in Massachusetts, *1914*

Facing page, bottom: *The 1914 Commission on Immigration report included this picture of immigrant men in a construction workers' shanty near Boston, where the extension of the steam and electric railroad was in progress. The report noted that 80 percent of the workers were foreign-born, mostly from Italy but also from Portugal, Poland, Greece, and Russia. The men were required to live in camps even if their homes were nearby. Sometimes they were billeted in old box cars or sheds of corrugated iron. Bags of straw served as mattresses, laid on platforms the length of the building. The report was critical of the fact that water was often hard to acquire, so that men with standards of cleanliness soon lost them. From* Report of the Commission on Immigration on the Problem of Immigration in Massachusetts, *1914*

culture, combined with new technologies and an upward trend in the nation's economic picture, now contrasted sharply with the Victorian-era mores and manners of the previous century. The population was growing rapidly: from 1900 to 1910, the number of people in the United States grew by 21 percent. Demographic shifts, from a mostly rural settlement pattern to one where more than 50 percent of U.S. homes were in cities or towns with more than 2,500 inhabitants, signaled both the end of a lifestyle and the beginning of a new age. In 1920, the U.S. census showed that 94.8 percent of Massachusetts residents lived in urban areas. Perhaps even more significant was the fact that in 1920, for the first time, people who worked in some type of industrial job outnumbered those in agricultural jobs by five to four.

Immigrants continued to swell the ranks of the state's population, and the implications of this continuing wave of

John Francis Fitzgerald, "Honey Fitz" (1863-1950), the son of Irish immigrant parents, was a newspaper publisher, insurance broker, banker, and a leading Boston Democrat in the most rowdy era of American politics. He began in the Common Council in 1892, was a state senator in 1893-1894, was a United States representative from 1895 to 1901 and again for six months in 1919, was mayor of Boston from 1906 to 1907 and from 1910 to 1914, and was an unsuccessful candidate for governor in 1922. Prominent as he was in politics, Fitzgerald is best known to today's voters as the father of Rose Fitzgerald Kennedy and grandfather and great-grandfather to the Kennedy candidates. From Boston Statistics Department, The Municipal Register for 1910, *1911*

foreign immigration worried many state and federal officials. Their concern was fueled by a nationwide nativistic impulse that emphasized the perceived virtues of the native-born and the disadvantages of welcoming more immigrants into the United States. This attitude resulted in federal immigration restriction laws in 1921 and 1924. Among the most vociferous supporters of this legislation was Massachusetts senator Henry Cabot Lodge.

In Massachusetts, changes in demography due to foreigners were quite apparent. The nation's heaviest concentrations of immigrants were in the cities of Boston and New York, and the greatest population density for the nation overall was found in the Northeast. In 1920, several Massachusetts cities—among them Springfield, Worcester, Lynn, and Lowell—had populations of well over 100,000 people; Boston had 750,000 residents; 81.6 percent of the state's citizens lived in communities of at least 10,000 people; and 66 percent lived in cities of 25,000 or more. The fact that Massachusetts was becoming more urban, as well as absorbing ever larger numbers of foreign-born, was of great concern to a vocal majority of politically-influential individuals.

The largely Roman Catholic population in and around Boston continued to be a cause of friction. By 1920, only 31.9 percent of the Commonwealth's citizens were "native white of native parentage," according to census reports. Nearly 67 percent were either immigrants or offspring of foreigners.

Immigrants threatened what was, for the native-born in Massachusetts, a comfortable economic status quo. Staid Yankees of the region—white, Anglo-Saxon Protestant descendants of those who had settled Massachusetts in the seventeenth century—probably agreed with immigrants on a few things, however. The 1920s posed a threat to a seemingly safer, more secure time. Antiradical sentiment ran high and

reached a peak with the Sacco-Vanzetti case, which brought Massachusetts' politics into national prominence. Two Italian immigrants, Nicola Sacco and Bartolomeo Vanzetti, had been charged with robbing a shoe factory and murdering two employees there. The climate of the times carried a distinct note of hysteria against suspected anarchists and communists, and the Italians had little hope of a fair trial. As many of their supporters feared, the men were found guilty and executed. Their case prompted a wave of liberal-radical outrage expressed in a variety of ways, among them, a poem titled "Justice Denied in Massachusetts" by Edna St. Vincent Millay (who made her home in the Berkshire Mountains, just over the Massachusetts border in New York).

Changes in public morals and manners in the 1920s alarmed all but the most avant-garde thinkers. Together,

Due to overcrowded schools, young Syrian immigrant women were obliged to meet in a Boston kindergarten room when they attended classes to learn English. The women were taught such words as "millinery," "piece," "sale," "special," "bargain," "department," "change," and "gentlemen," probably in anticipation of their likely employment as salesgirls. From Report of the Commission on Immigration on the Problem of Immigration in Massachusetts, *1914*

both immigrant and native-born decried the daring explicitness of new novels, and the unashamed boldness of popular silent films and the newer "talking" pictures. They shuddered at the shocking freedom of behavior exhibited by the younger generation. In the eyes of many, smoking, drinking, and sexual activity equaled moral degradation. The nation's future

as a pacesetter in medicine and in a range of industrial technologies.

Certain trends that showed up early in Massachusetts would later affect the entire country. Among these was a growing tendency toward prohibiting alcoholic beverage consumption. As early as April 30, 1908, the city of Worcester voted to become "dry." This move made

Women and some men worked actively to get women the vote in Massachusetts from the early 1850s; by 1895 they were still petitioning the state legislature. This 1895 cartoon shows the fears some men seemed to have concerning women voting. The Nineteenth Amendment to the Constitution finally gave women that privilege in 1919. From the Boston Sunday Globe, *January 13, 1895*

seemed imperiled, and as a defense there were attempts to resist and limit change by more powerful citizens (usually native-born, although their numbers included some Irish-Catholic politicians in the Boston area who had grown increasingly influential, as exemplified by Boston mayor "Honey" Fitzgerald's success). Some efforts were successful, such as restrictions on foreign immigration. Any change, demographic or otherwise, carried with it the suggestion of crisis, and Americans who recalled the more genteel manners of the nineteenth century were aghast at the contemporary decline they now witnessed.

SHIFTING POLITICAL WINDS

Like most of the nation, Massachusetts enjoyed a variety of industrial innovations and technological advances during the initial decades of the twentieth century. The Bay State was a leader in education, particularly of women, as well

Worcester, at the heart of the Commonwealth, the largest dry city in the United States. Smaller communities would follow suit, foreshadowing passage of the Volstead Act in 1919. This federal legislation mandated prohibition nationwide and ultimately provoked such illegal activities as bootlegging (importing alcoholic beverages from outside the United States) and operation of clandestine stills and speakeasies for the production and serving of alcohol.

Across America, people either applauded or decried ratification in 1920 of another constitutional change: the Nineteenth Amendment to the Constitution, guaranteeing suffrage to women. The first presidential election in which women were eligible to vote catapulted Massachusetts politician Calvin Coolidge to the U.S. presidency. He had risen from small-town lawyer to popular state governor to inoffensive vice president. From there, it seemed inevitable that

Coolidge would become president. In 1923, after President Warren G. Harding's untimely death, Coolidge stepped with characteristic diffidence into the White House. And in 1924, Coolidge's 2-to-1 popular vote margin in the race against Democratic challenger John Davis ensured his victory. The nation's 30th president, Coolidge was the first Massachusetts president to be elected since John Quincy Adams.

TECHNOLOGICAL ADVANCES

Numerous new gadgets, machines, and novel technologies became popular and widespread during the 1920s. The automobile grew ever more popular, amateur photography became increasingly common, the marvel of the helicopter expanded the possibilities of the aviation industry, and use of electrical power in American homes and factories grew. In 1900, the nation's electrical output was only about six million

kilowatt-hours—one-twentieth of all the power used by factories in the United States. By 1927, two-thirds of industrial power in the nation was generated by electricity, and use was just under 120 million kilowatt-hours. A great many of these manufacturing facilities were located in New England, despite the pull-out by some large investors shortly after World War I. Power used in the area was generated by hydropower facilities situated along the region's powerful rivers.

Radio became more and more popular in the 1920s. At Medford, the first radio station in Massachusetts accessed the airwaves and began broadcasting in 1921. Six years later, in 1927, there were about 10 million radio sets in use throughout the nation. Despite public fascination with radio in the late 1920s, the popular topic of conversation in Massachusetts (and the nation) had little to do with airwaves—but a lot to

In 1916 women still could not vote, but these women celebrating Enfield's centennial dressed up like their mothers and grandmothers in parody of women's rights activists. From a 1916 postcard. Courtesy, Special Collections and Archives, Library, University of Massachusetts at Amherst

A supervisor poses circa 1903 in a 7½ x 13-foot steel pipe in Wayland during construction of the Weston Aqueduct. The new aqueduct had to go under railroads as well as roads and through a boulder clay ledge in its nearly mile-long route. At its peak, 125 men and 22 horses worked on the project. From Second Annual Report of the Metropolitan Water and Sewerage Board, *1903*

do with air.

Charles A. Lindbergh's 1927 nonstop transatlantic solo flight captured the imagination of millions of Americans, and the subsequent efforts of many less-publicized pilots caught the nation by storm. The idea that humans could actually fly had been tested and proven by the Wright brothers at Kitty Hawk, North Carolina, in 1903. After that, hundreds of people attempted to further the science of aviation by a variety of means. Among the most significant of these efforts were a series of experiments conducted in Worcester. The year before Lindbergh's famous flight, a virtually unknown researcher was bent on proving the viability of air and space exploration. Dr. Robert H. Goddard successfully fired a liquid-fueled rocket that achieved a height of 41 feet, and in so doing, ushered in the modern space era. Goddard was highly optimistic about the ramifications of his modest success. However, he was slightly inaccurate in a 1918 Smithsonian Institution report concerning future space exploration. In

his report, Goddard predicted the world would see human exploration of the moon's surface by the year 2000—a guess that was late by more than three decades.

Within 10 years of his original experiment, Goddard built and tested rockets that went 700 miles per hour, reached heights of 7,500 feet, and exceeded the speed of sound. However, not until the nation's defense needs expanded rapidly during World War II did Goddard's pioneering work with rocketry receive the credit—and the financial support—it deserved.

Statewide interest in science extended to areas of direct human benefit as well. Medicine, its study and practice, had been held in high regard in Massachusetts as far back as the seventeenth century. Boston in particular has a long tradition of excellence in medicine and has long been a center of the highest quality medical care and research. The history of formal support for medical practice in Massachusetts was highlighted in 1797 when Samuel Adams, one of the original

On May 19, 1938, the first mail plane to fly out of Pittsfield was captured on film by a photographer. The destination of the plane is unrecorded; perhaps it flew to Boston over the Old Post Road? Photo by Gravelle Pictorial News Service. Courtesy, The Berkshire Atheneum

Sons of Liberty, helped found the Massachusetts Medical Society. Well over a century later, in 1926, two Boston doctors, George R. Minot and William P. Murphy, developed a successful treatment of pernicious anemia. This condition had previously been fatal, but due to Minot and Murphy and their research, lives could now be saved. The pair, along with Dr. George H. Whipple, received the 1934 Nobel Prize for Medicine as a result of these findings.

In addition to these physicians, other doctors based in Boston during the 1920s and later deserve mention because of the comprehensive quality of their medical contributions. Neurosurgeon Harvey Williams Cushing was surgeon-in-chief at Peter Bent Brigham Hospital and professor of surgery at Harvard Medical School. He received a Pulitzer Prize in 1925 for a biography of the Canadian physician Sir William Osler. Cushing was also known for his work with the United States Army during World War I.

The well-known heart specialist, Paul Dudley White, began his career at Massachusetts General Hospital in Boston. Research in cardiovascular diseases led him to become attending physician during President Dwight D. Eisenhower's recovery from a heart attack in the 1950s. White, through his position as executive director of the National Advisory Council of the National Heart Institute, is credited with saving thousands of lives. Due to his efforts, the American public was educated about the causes and prevention of heart disease.

Individual physicians' contributions to research and medical treatment helped increase the quality of life for all Americans and made possible a longer life span. Some outstanding Boston-area medical institutions that grew up during the early twentieth century were critical to these individual contributions. Massachusetts General Hospital, which was founded in the early nineteenth century, was joined in the first few decades of the 1900s by Peter Bent Brigham Hospital, Beth Israel Hospital, the Floating Hospital, Children's and Infants Hospital, the Lahey Clinic, and Boston University Hospital. The reform efforts connected with these medical institutions represented positive forces at work in Massachusetts up through the 1920s.

circumstances as more and more businesses failed, and few people could rely on regular work hours or the security of a weekly paycheck.

ECONOMIC DISASTER

Despite his intentions, President Herbert Hoover (elected in 1928 and an ally of private industry) was unable to reverse the terrible economic slide. It was a descent that plunged the entire country into chaos. The handful of programs established during Hoover's administration, such as the Reconstruction Finance Corporation (RFC), helped only a few people. The president, true to his conservative economic theories, claimed that only voluntary self-help programs could be applied to the nation's problems, despite the reality of a 25 percent unemployment rate from coast to coast. There was little Hoover could do since he staunchly insisted that relief was *not* the business of the federal government. He was adamant that the private sector must rely on itself for support and

solutions. However, this national crisis ultimately spelled failure for the Republican administration, and by 1932 most Americans looked hopefully toward the next election as an opportunity to stave off future catastrophe.

The Democrats won an easy majority of congressional races almost everywhere in 1932. Unlike its voting record in previous presidential races, Massachusetts did not follow the lead of Connecticut, New Hampshire, and Vermont. Instead, the Bay State joined the rest of the nation and was among all but five states casting their electoral votes for Franklin D. Roosevelt. Roosevelt won 23 million popular votes while Hoover garnered only 15.8 million of those votes. The nation wanted a change, and within a few years the results of this change were clear in Massachusetts.

THE QUABBIN RESERVOIR

Construction of Quabbin Reservoir in the central part of Massachusetts was a project representing many decades of planning. In fact, as early as the first quarter of the nineteenth century officials in the eastern part of the state looked to the Swift River Valley as a potential source of drinking water for Boston's growing population.

Despite the political wheeling and dealing so inevitable in a project of this magnitude, a study group finally was formed in 1919. Its express goal was to seek a solution to Boston's water-supply problems. In 1926, legislation known as the Ware River Act formally created the Metropolitan District Water Supply Commission (MDWSC). This agency would study and make plans for building a dam, flooding the Swift River, and creating a reservoir. The name of the reservoir would be *Quabbin*, an Algonquin name meaning "well-watered place." Native American tribes living in this area of the Swift River Valley had been ruled by a sachem known as Nini-Quaben. It seemed natural to derive the name of the reservoir from this once-powerful ruler's name.

Because reservoir construction coincided with the high unemployment of the 1930s, the state-funded plan became one of the biggest public works projects in the state, offering jobs to large numbers of Bay State workers. This project ultimately resulted in a 38.6-square-mile reservoir in the state's central region to the west of Worcester. In order to carry out the project, it was necessary to expropriate great parcels of land. The entire towns of Dana, Enfield, Greenwich, and Prescott were bought up, their inhabitants moved, and their boundaries flooded. Since these communities—along with many in the Swift River Valley—were sparsely populated, such upheaval was not as far-reaching as it might seem. More importantly, for the flagging economy of the 1930s, construction projects of the magnitude of Quabbin meant jobs, income, and security. The work involved in moving people out and demolishing buildings was considerable, but it was dwarfed by the construction task itself. As part of the

Top: *Many local men were hired to clear the land and burn brush on the ground that would be covered with the Quabbin Reservoir's water. This photograph, taken on February 27, 1939, shows the magnitude of the job as an Oshkosh tractor drags a tree to the fire. Courtesy, Massachusetts Archives*

Above: *To clear the Swift River Valley, many houses, inns, stores, and churches were burned. Others were taken apart board by board and erected elsewhere, while some were disassembled for the lumber, windows, or mantels alone. But some homes or parts of homes could be towed; here, the Thayer house is moved from Greenwich on March 21, 1939. Courtesy, Massachusetts Archives*

The Chandler Place, the best located large home in Enfield, was kept by the state as the Enfield office until the last possible moment. This photograph was taken September 1, 1939, looking north to the cleared valley that would soon become an 18-mile-long reservoir, with the hills in the distance becoming islands. Courtesy, Massachusetts Archives

Quabbin project, the Winsor Dam was built to hold back the many tons of water that would engulf the land and create the state's largest man-made reservoir.

Engineers had determined early which areas would be flooded by the reservoir. By March 27, 1938, the MDWSC had filed necessary paperwork with the state to take 117 square miles of land by eminent domain. People were paid for their property, although for most the state's remuneration in no way made up for the total loss that they experienced. Everyone who lived within the marked areas was instructed to evacuate by July 1, 1938.

The actual flooding was not to begin until 1939, so the region's inhabitants left slowly. But as poignant as their departure seemed, they were not leaving behind a land of promise. The economy of the region had been deteriorating for decades, and for most people, relocation suggested an opportunity to begin again, in prosperity.

The move could not be effected merely by relocating people, however. Special legislation was needed in order to disincorporate the four towns to be flooded. In addition, towns had to hold

special meetings to finalize municipal affairs and dismantle their individual governmental structures. Special celebrations, as well, marked the demise of these tiny central Massachusetts communities. The most widely publicized was the Enfield Firemen's Ball, held on April 27, 1938. It was a social affair of memorable proportions, and several thousand people attended. Publicity surrounding the event was wide-ranging. For months, newspapers that had carried progress reports on reservoir construction now focused on this last, festive occasion. The *Springfield Union* described the ball in vivid terms: "Muffled sounds of sobbing were heard, hardened men were not ashamed to take out their handkerchiefs, and even children, attending the ball with their parents, broke into tears." It was a curious blend of celebration and funeral. From the perspective of the region's economy, the death of the four towns was inevitable—the Quabbin project merely hastened the process along—but for town residents, it was sorrowful.

In September 1938, the few buildings and municipal properties remaining in the four communities were auctioned off.

Late in the month, a hurricane swept through the empty towns—a final, vehement salute and farewell to the hundreds who had lived and struggled there for several centuries. After flooding started on August 14, 1939, the ghostly remains of abandoned towns remained visible for almost the entire seven years it took for Quabbin Reservoir to fill with water.

THE NEW DEAL

During the initial months of Franklin D. Roosevelt's administration, some important legislation was passed. Affecting all Americans, the set of bills was designed to provide comprehensive relief to farmers and to industry. Three major efforts of the early Roosevelt years—establishment of the National Recovery Administration (NRA), the Agricultural Adjustment Administration (AAA), and the Public Works Administration (PWA)—aimed at encouraging factory and agricultural production without

dismantling the concept of private industry.

Many disagreed with the president's policies. Some feared what extensive government intervention would do to the economy, while others felt that too little was being done. Controversy reigned, and in Massachusetts, as in other states, skeptics criticized Roosevelt while supporters argued on behalf of his programs. It was some years into the New Deal before Roosevelt's legislation had a major effect on the Massachusetts economy. Eventually, however, Bay State citizens benefited in a variety of ways from the Works Progress Administration (WPA), the Civilian Conservation Corps (CCC), and the Federal Emergency Relief Act (FERA).

The annual report of the Metropolitan District Commission for 1937 detailed the success of the CCC camp at the Great Blue Hills Reservation near Boston. The camp operated at Blue Hills until September of that year, although there

The least controversial and most popular of all the New Deal federal legislation was the Civilian Conservation Corps. In 1933 Franklin D. Roosevelt requested money for a peacetime army to work against the destruction of national resources. In time 50 camps of men were at work in Massachusetts, planting trees, building dams, fire towers, and bridges, and clearing beaches and campsites. This photo was taken at the Mount Greylock CCC camp in the Berkshires, where unemployed males between 18 and 25 were given jobs. Clothing and equipment were mostly World War I surplus, and the camp was run like a military camp. Courtesy, Massachusetts Department of Environmental Management, Division of Forests and Parks

were other CCC camps at other locations in the state. The 1937 report noted that the Blue Hills camp, which helped preserve and upgrade recreational facilities at Blue Hills, was a leader of "First Corps Area camps in general excellence and was flying the honor pennant as the best camp in New England when it ceased its operations" that year. This federally-funded corps of young male workers constructed roads, built a stone observation tower, sprayed extensively to control gypsy moths, completed construction of cross-country ski trails, and planted 15,000 pine and spruce seedlings. The report indicates that 22,000 work hours were spent on CCC work at the Blue Hills reservation that year.

The WPA funded employees in a variety of projects across the state. Together with a basic grant of $50,000

from the legislature, the WPA brought about $550,000 into the Commonwealth for a total of 22 new projects in 1937 alone, in addition to some projects carried over from previous years. These projects included landscaping, construction of MDC buildings, and continued work on public golf courses, tennis courts, and baseball diamonds. Other similar projects involved development of major waterfront recreation areas such as Nahant Beach and parks such as the Middlesex Fells Reservation.

MDC reports indicate that in 1938, 36,602 work hours were expended by the CCC across the state, some of which included work done after the infamous hurricane of that year. This disaster required extensive clean-up as well as repairs to roads and highways. The hurricane struck on September 21, felling

On January 23, 1938, one of the first snow-ski trains arrived from New York City at Pittsfield's South Street station, and the tourist ski industry in Massachusetts was launched. Photo by Gravelle Pictorial News Service. Courtesy, The Berkshire Atheneum

trees, flooding roads, farms, and towns, stranding hundreds of residents in their homes. Some Massachusetts residents lost their lives. The *Boston Globe*'s headlines the next day read, "11 Deaths in Line Storm, Roads Out," and "State's All-Time Rainfall Record for September Broken, 12.49 Inches." Nearly $1 million in state funds were required for the clean-up.

WORLD WAR II

Despite the hardship and tragedy of the Depression years, the country was secure and at peace. Rumblings of war in Europe provoked debate in the U.S., but throughout the 1930s the nation was able to remain detached. Massachusetts, along with the rest of the nation, was shocked into action, however, by the news of Japan's attack on Pearl Harbor on December 7, 1941. With that single, devastating strike, occurring at 8 a.m. local time, Pearl Harbor's Battleship Row—where the nation's most valuable naval vessels were moored—was in flames. Nearly 2,300 service personnel died, as well as 68 civilians.

The following day, President Roosevelt asked Congress to declare war. Despite several years of isolationist activities and major reluctance to become involved in global conflict, Americans rallied around the president. Few had any real reservations now, since the country had little choice but to fight back. In fact, most isolationists agreed that "that date ended isolationism for any realist," according to Senator Arthur H. Vandenberg (R-Michigan).

Demands placed on American industry during the war were diverse and complex. Recruitment of workers, expansion of facilities, conversion of old plants, and construction of new industrial sites, as well as problems imposed by wage and price ceilings and rationing of resources, meant that the home front needed to exercise ingenuity, caution, and a sense of unity far greater than they had shared for several decades.

Various factories throughout Massa-

Above: *The Richardson Trail in West Townsend's CCC Camp was built in 1937 in what is now the Townsend State Forest in the north-central section of the state. One camp in the Berkshires cleared a ski trail to boost the state's tourist industry. Courtesy, Massachusetts Department of Environmental Management, Division of Forests and Parks*

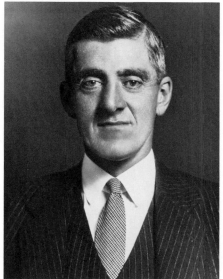

Above: *Leverett Saltonstall, born in 1892 in Chestnut Hill, earned his law degree from Harvard in 1917. He served as an alderman in Newton from 1920 to 1922, as Middlesex County assistant district attorney from 1921 to 1922, and in the Massachusetts House of Representatives from 1922 to 1937. This photograph was taken when he was speaker of the House. A Republican, he was elected governor in 1938, defeating James Michael Curley. Saltonstall then served three terms as governor and in 1944 was elected to the U.S. Senate, where he served until his retirement in 1967. Courtesy, Massachusetts Archives*

Right: *On March 22, 1942, Bobby Ford, 7, Malcolm Keeler, 9, and Paul Mathews, 4, piled up salvage to contribute to the war effort from Tyler Street in Pittsfield. Rubber and metal were especially needed for reuse, and every bit helped. Photo by Gravelle Pictorial News Service. Courtesy, The Berkshire Atheneum*

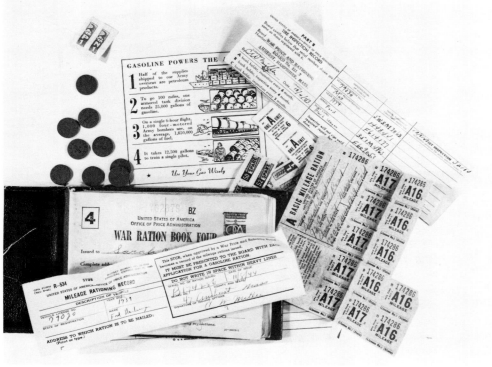

Left: *During World War II, certain consumer items were earmarked for the war effort, or were not available because raw materials from foreign countries were not easily obtained. Ration coins and coupons were distributed by the War Price and Rationing Board and were needed when purchasing a car, gasoline (farmers were given more coupons for vehicles and fuel), and for scarce consumer goods like butter, sugar, and coffee. Photo by Brenda Lilly. Courtesy, The Walter C. and Sarah H. Jones Collection*

chusetts were converted to defense production. In Worcester, Harrington and Richardson produced Reising submachine guns for the marines. Like the Springfield Armory, they also manufactured M1 rifles. At Savage Arms in Chicopee, hundreds of workers produced Thompson submachine guns. Raytheon produced a range of electronic equipment, including radar for use by the Air Force. A number of shipyards such as Fore River and Lawley's turned out naval vessels. At the Boston Naval Shipyard, ships came in for repairs and new vessels were outfitted. Smaller arms were important as well as large battleships and tanks, and Smith & Wesson in Springfield manufactured revolvers for the United States military as well as for the allies in Britain.

Ammunition, aircraft, heavy weapons and tanks, and ships poured out of American factories just a few months after Pearl Harbor. By 1943, twice as much freight was shipped by rail as had been transported in 1940, and three times as many passengers traveled via railroad. The latter increase was due to the fact that few automobiles, and even fewer replacement parts for existing cars, were available. In particular, rubber rationing meant that tires on cars would have to last for the duration of the war.

In Massachusetts, researchers at medical facilities worked to come up with solutions to problems that plagued doctors and nurses close to the battlefield. On May 3, 1944, two chemists at Harvard University, Doctors Robert B. Woodward and William E. Doering, announced that they had successfully produced synthetic quinine to alleviate suffering from malaria, among the most

Above, left: *Dorothy Luz of Pittsfield had been, for nine years, a supervisor at the Elmvale Worsted Company when World War II was declared. She joined the Red Cross Ambulance Corps motor unit, and when the WACs were organized, she was the first woman from Berkshire County to enlist. Photo by Gravelle Pictorial News Service. Courtesy, The Berkshire Atheneum*

Above, right: *Corporal John Collins of Pittsfield was a proud young marine on the Solomon Islands when he smiled for a photographer in 1942. He was killed in action later that year. Courtesy, The Berkshire Atheneum*

FRANCES PERKINS

Frances Perkins was born in Boston in April 1880, but moved to Worcester with her parents, Frederick and Susan (Bean) Perkins, when she was two. She was one of the few women in her class at Worcester Classical High, where she graduated in 1898, and then went on to study chemistry and physics at Mount Holyoke in South Hadley. President of her class at Mount Holyoke, she volunteered in settlement houses in the inner-city of Holyoke. Though her parents were conservative Republicans, this experience of working with very poor people transformed Frances Perkins into a very liberal Democrat, and her interest changed from science to social work. After teaching school for a few years in Worcester, she moved to Chicago and then New York City, continuing her settlement house work while earning a master's degree in economics and sociology from Columbia in 1910.

The horrific Triangle Shirtwaist Fire in 1911 inspired Perkins to work diligently toward industrial reform, and to secure the rights of working people. Though she married Paul Wilson in 1913, she continued her work for the rights of workers, and to better conditions for their families, doing so under her maiden name. The year after her daughter Susanna was born, in 1916, Perkins became the first female member of the New York State Industrial Commission. As a tireless advocate for working people, and as a committed social worker, Perkins developed a close relationship with Eleanor Roosevelt, and with New York governors Al Smith and Franklin D. Roosevelt. Governor Roosevelt appointed Perkins to head the Bureau of Mediation Arbitration, which oversaw labor disputes.

As Secretary of Labor for the entire 12 years of Franklin Roosevelt's presidency, Perkins led the fight for the New Deal. She protected the right of workers to organize into unions, set minimum wages and maximum working hours, and established the Labor Standards Bureau. For the first time, the United States government was on the side of working people. Perkins also helped to draft the Social Security Act, and implemented the Wagner Act's National Labor Relations Board to arbitrate labor disputes. Though the administration could not enact a national health insurance program, when Perkins left government in 1945 she had done more to better the lives of American workers than any other cabinet official.

As Franklin D. Roosevelt's Secretary of Labor, Frances Perkins (1880-1965) was the first woman to serve in a Presidential Cabinet. She is shown in a still frame from an early 1940s film at the Library of Congress.

troubling illnesses in the Pacific theater.

During the war, consumers found many common items unavailable, and they struggled with limited quantities of whatever *was* still produced for civilian consumption. Grocery shelves were stocked meagerly, if at all, with butter, sugar, and coffee. There was some attempt in 1943 to freeze prices on consumer goods, but this was not successful, as it was difficult to enforce a price freeze. New items entering the marketplace (such as margarine) did not fall within established price guidelines for standard items (butter).

Massachusetts provided a solid number of service personnel throughout the entire war—550,000 people either volunteered or were drafted into the military. Fort Devens in Ayer once again became an induction center, and at Otis Air Force Base on Cape Cod a military training center was established.

It was a challenge to decide how best to allocate human resources available during the war. In order to utilize talents most efficiently, the War Manpower Commission, set up in 1942, determined where workers were needed and how to divide their efforts among various industries and the military. This federal agency acted as a coordinator, not as a controller. This fact, plus the emergency nature of wartime, meant that few people reacted negatively to the commission, although there were some pockets of resistance to military service.

Most Americans contributed their time and efforts willingly. One of the most interesting phenomena on the home front was an increase in women workers, particularly in previously male-dominated jobs. Because of defense needs, women were hired to build planes, tanks, and battleships and to produce munitions—bullets, guns, and bombs. Throughout the nation, women expressed pleasure at the opportunity to earn substantial wages and to participate in a war effort that produced such tangible and gratifying results.

About 10,632,000 women were part

of the U.S. work force in 1930. Immediately after Pearl Harbor in 1941, defense plants began hiring women as replacements for military recruits who had left for the front. Actually, women had been entering the work force even earlier than that, for as it became clear to many that U.S. entry into the war was only a matter of time, factories began hiring more and more women. By 1940, there were 13,840,000 women employed outside the home. Four years later, at the height of the war, 18,449,000 women worked at a variety of factory and other industrial jobs. By the end of the war, that number had been reduced to 16,323,000, and the decline from the peak years continued as many women were laid off from war-related jobs or in order to open up jobs for returning GIs.

Above: *In the 1940s a chestnut tree blight struck Massachusetts full force. This man was obliged to cut down an enormous, but dead, chestnut tree on the Sumner lot in Leydon. The lumber from the tree might well have been used for postwar construction that answered the demands of the returned service people. Courtesy, The Walter C. and Sarah H. Jones Collection*

Facing page: *The battleship* Missouri *docked in Boston Harbor for a ceremony commemorating the surrender of Japan during the 1946 encampment of the Veterans of Foreign Wars. John F. Kennedy, soon to be a U.S. representative, was in charge of the local arrangements. Courtesy, John F. Kennedy Library*

Joseph P. Kennedy, Sr., was on the Post-War Rehabilitation Commission immediately after World War II to study the Commonwealth's economic position. This photograph is thought to have been taken at a black tie dinner meeting of that commission. To the left of Kennedy sits a young Massachusetts legislator named Thomas P. "Tip" O'Neill. Courtesy, The John F. Kennedy Library

Christian A. Herter (1895-1967), shown here about 1939 when he was speaker in the Massachusetts House of Representatives, was a 1915 Harvard graduate and had been an assistant to Herbert Hoover from 1915 to 1924, then editor of the Independent *from 1924 to 1928. He was elected to the Massachusetts House in 1938, where he served until 1943 when he was elected to the U.S. House of Representatives. A Republican, he was a congressman for Massachusetts until 1952 when he returned to Boston to become governor from 1953 to 1957. In 1959 he was appointed secretary of state under President Eisenhower. From 1961 to 1962 he was chairman of the U.S. Citizens Committee on NATO. Courtesy, Massachusetts Archives*

POSTWAR ADJUSTMENTS

Most people in the United States believed the war would end in allied victory. But there were concerns over what U.S. soldiers would do when they returned from the battlefields. Massachusetts attempted to forestall any serious assimilation difficulties by advance planning. In 1943, the state legislature established a Post-War Rehabilitation Commission to investigate and make recommendations concerning the state economy. As a result of its work, the

commission published a report in 1945 detailing its findings and explaining where the economy's most pressing needs were. Particular attention was paid to agriculture—still an important part of the economy in this predominantly industrial state. Housing, urban redevelopment, and industrial development were also discussed by the commission. It was clear that Massachusetts would suffer if these economic factors were not addressed with consideration of the large numbers of returning soldiers and the shift to peacetime production.

Recommendations of the Post-War Commission said it was critical to provide for the employment, housing, and hospitalization needs of former military personnel. The reality for returning soldiers held both promise and challenge. Throughout the nation, housing was at a premium. GIs were anxious to take advantage of benefits offering them a college education in return for their military service. During the postwar years, colleges and universities in Massachusetts would see a marked increase in freshman enrollment based on the benefits of the GI Bill of Rights. In Amherst, the University of Massachusetts was just one of many

Menemsha Port, Chilmark, Martha's Vineyard.
Photo by Richard W. Wilkie

An aerial view of the quiet town of Petersham in central Massachusetts is seen with its common and churches. Photo by Richard W. Wilkie

Above: *Faneuil Hall with its grasshopper weathervane is seen behind the popular Quincy Market. Photo by Justine Hill*

Facing page: *The cast iron gates of Smith College in Northampton in winter. Photo by Jim Gipe, Pivotmedia, Florence, Massachusetts*

Above: *In Rockport Harbor on Cape Ann this fisherman's shack is known as* Motif #1 *and is the town's most photographed and painted landmark. In fact, it is perhaps the favorite artists' subject on the entire East Coast. During the blizzard of 1978 the shack was destroyed, but through funds raised by town citizens it was soon restored. Photo by Justine Hill*

Facing page: *Chatham, Cape Cod. A beach fence with flowers. Photo by Justine Hill*

Above: "The Illumination," a historic tradition for graduation at Smith College, Northampton. Photo by Jim Gipe, Pivotmedia, Florence, Massachusetts

Facing page: Autumn (top) and winter (bottom) views over the Connecticut River valley from Mount Sugerloaf in Sunderland south toward Northampton and the distant Holyoke Range. Photos by Richard W. Wilkie

Above: *The State House, Beacon Hill, Boston.*
Photo by Richard W. Wilkie

Facing page*: The seasonal Swan Boats in the*
Public Garden next to Boston Common are
a tradition begun in 1877.   They were
inspired by an opera in which the hero
crosses the lake pulled by a swan.   Photo
by Justine Hill

Above: *Nantucket Town, Nantucket Island. Photo by Justine Hill*

Facing page: *Nobska Point Light, Woods Hole on Cape Cod is the home of the commander of the Woods Hole Coast Guard Base. Photo by Justine Hill*

Above: *The pond in autumn at Mount Holyoke College, South Hadley.   Photo by Jim Gipe, Pivotmedia, Florence, Massachusetts*

Facing page: *Fishing at Menemsha Beach, Martha's Vineyard.   Photo by Richard W. Wilkie*

The John F. Kennedy Library and Museum commands an ocean view at Columbia Point in the Dorchester section of Boston. Designed by I.M. Pei and built with donated funds, the building was donated to the U.S. government and opened its doors in October 1979. As a presidential library it is now part of the National Archives and belongs to the people of the United States. Photo by Justine Hill

institutions across the nation with enrollments suddenly loaded with former military personnel now seeking an education.

DEFINING THE NEW ECONOMY

As the nation resumed peacetime production efforts, many regions were anxious to examine relations between labor and management. The crisis of the 1930s had made leaders of both groups wary, and New Deal legislation had changed the face of union organization with passage of major bills such as the National Labor Relations Act, also known as the Wagner Act.

In Massachusetts, Governor Robert F. Bradford appointed a special labor-management committee to study the effects of marketplace trends on the state's economy and to make suggestions about how best to handle the relationship between union leaders and industry spokespersons. Nine persons representing top industry and labor interests made up the committee. In their March 1947 report to the governor they stressed several points: the state was advised to make legislative provision for facilitating collective bargaining procedures, and was urged to "set up a new and stronger service of conciliation and arbitration." Amendments to "bring into balance" the State Labor Relations Act and ways in which to mediate labor-management disputes were also recommended.

In his response to the report, delivered to the state House of Representatives and the Senate, Governor Bradford encouraged adherence to the committee's recommendations. In his words, "This is the first time in industrial history that so comprehensive a subject has been so conscientiously studied . . . by representatives of every group affected. Moulded . . . into legislation, the Massachusetts plan can become a modern Magna Carta for labor and industry."

Elected and appointed officials in Massachusetts recognized, as did labor and management leaders, how the

immediate postwar years could bring recession and even another economic depression. At this time, many industries—particularly textile works—moved to warmer climates, predominantly in what is now termed the "Sunbelt." This exodus was the result of lower wages and greater tax benefits to industry in the South. The attempts of the Bay State labor-management committee indicate one way in which future planning was intended to stave off any further drain of industrial activity and help build the state into an economic giant in the Northeast. Several decades later, Massachusetts had proven that this

In the summer of 1966, before the student uprisings, a young Edward M. (Ted) Kennedy and Secretary of the Interior Stewart Udall visited the University of Massachusetts at Amherst. Kennedy is shown here with Nikaii Amarteifio, a foreign student from Accra, Ghana, who was about to enter Wesleyan and would go on to earn an M.B.A. from Harvard in 1973. Courtesy, The Walter C. and Sarah H. Jones Collection

JAMES MICHAEL CURLEY (1874-1958)

In four terms as mayor (1914-1918, 1922-1926, 1930-1934, 1946-1950), two stints in Congress (1911-1914, 1943-1946), one term as governor (1935-1937) and in every race between, James Michael Curley dominated political life in Boston, and in Massachusetts.

Curley was in jail when he ran for Board of Alderman in 1903. Being in jail helped Curley's career. He had been convicted of fraud, for taking the Civil Service exam for a poorly-educated immigrant. It was fraud, but if Curley had not done it, the man would not have gotten a job, and his family would have starved. Curley was sent to the Charles Street Jail—and to the Board of Alderman—for helping a friend.

As mayor, Curley battled with the downtown business community, railing against the Yankee enclaves of Beacon Hill and State Street and delivered services to the outlying ethnic neighborhoods. Curley built parks, schools, and sidewalks in Dorchester, South Boston, Roxbury, West Roxbury, Charlestown, and East Boston. Some of his proposals may have been partly in jest, for example, to sell the Public Garden and use the money to build parks in the ethnic neighborhoods, or to turn the State House's golden dome upside down in Andrew Square, to be a wading pool for the little children. But all were part of his lifelong, and deadly serious crusade against Boston's power brokers. By providing city services through the mayor's office, Curley also made obsolete the traditional ward bosses, whom he called "chowderheads."

Boston's business interests and ward bosses mobilized against Curley in 1918. The Republican ad-ministration elected, though, was corrupt and ineffective, and in 1922 Curley returned as a "reform" candidate. In the boom years of the 1920s Curley built bathhouses, schools, roads, a tunnel under Boston Harbor, and other public works. The Republican legislature imposed a one-term limit on Boston's mayor to keep Curley out of office, and he retired in 1926, leaving to his successor the tax bills for his projects just as the nation's economy collapsed in the Depression. Curley once again came to the rescue in 1930, as the "People's Mayor" delivering jobs and services.

Curley broke with the state's Democratic leaders, who supported Al Smith for president in 1932, by supporting Franklin D. Roosevelt. For his apostasy, and for having ridiculed them one too many times, the party leaders kept Curley off of their delegation to the Democratic convention. Their astonishment turned to outrage at the convention in Chicago, when the chairman of the Puerto Rico delegation, "Jaime Miguel Curleo," announced Puerto Rico's support for Franklin Delano Roosevelt!

Curley was elected governor in 1934, but lost to Henry Cabot Lodge for the U.S. Senate in 1936, and lost the governorship to Leverett Saltonstall in 1938. Losing to Yankee Republicans in a state-wide races was predictable, but in 1937 Curley lost the mayor's race to an Irish-Catholic Democrat from Mission Hill, Maurice Tobin. His defeat partly resulted from the kind of political trick Curley would have played on an opponent. On election day in 1937, the *Boston Post*'s front page carried a lament from William Cardinal O'Connell that "walls are raised against honest men in civic life," followed by high praise for the "honest, clean, and competent" mayoral candidate Maurice Tobin. The Cardinal had not endorsed Tobin, but the *Post* made it seem that he had. Tobin won.

Curley was elected to Congress in 1942, and when Tobin was elected governor, Curley ran for mayor of Boston. (John F. Kennedy was elected to Curley's House seat.) Curley, at the time of his election, was under indictment for mail fraud, and shortly after was convicted. In 1947 he spent five months at the federal penitentiary in Danbury, leaving City Clerk John Hynes, a quiet, competent, and obscure city bureaucrat, to conduct the mayor's duties. President Truman pardoned Curley, and, after spending a morning back at his office, the always quotable Curley told reporters, "I have accomplished more in one day than has been done in the five months of my absence." Hynes, who had prepared to slip back into honorable obscurity regarded this as a personal affront. He decided to run against Curley in 1949, though it seemed futile for the "little clerk," as Curley called Hynes, to take on the legendary "Young Jim." But Curley was no longer Young Jim, and the "outsiders" who had propelled Curley into power were now the establishment. Hynes won, and beat Curley again in 1951, and in 1955.

Curley retired to his brick mansion overlooking Jamaica Pond, tweaking his Yankee neighbors with the shamrocks carved into the shutters. Years after his death, the city decided to honor Curley with a statue. But Curley was too much for one statue, so today there are two. One is the bold "Young Jim,"

striding forward to take on the entrenched establishment. The other is an old man, seated on a park bench, like the thousands of benches he placed around the city, preparing to tell his story. When novelist Edwin O'Connor immortalized Curley and Boston politics in *The Last Hurrah*, Curley was so pleased with both the book and its protagonist that he sat down to write his own memoir. He called it, *I'd Do It Again*.

Mayor Curley is shown in a March 17th celebration in 1917—Evacuation Day— the day the hated British left Boston just before the Revolution. March 17th is also Saint Patrick's Day. Courtesy, Print Department, The Boston Public Library

The G.I. Bill of Rights guaranteed a college education to all returning veterans. This transformed the American work force, from blue collar to white collar, and also transformed higher education, making it available to millions of men and women who never would have dreamed of going to college. Here Suffolk University's Senior Class President Carroll Sheehan, and the University's President, Walter Burse, thank Congressman John F. Kennedy for the G.I. Bill. Sheehan, of Dorchester, went on to serve as the state's insurance commissioner. Courtesy, Suffolk University Archives

type of forecasting was the key to success.

THE COLD WAR

The United States emerged victorious from the war, only to discover that the world still was not safe. The Soviet Union maintained its armies in Eastern Europe, and by the end of the decade Communist regimes were in power from the Balkans to the Baltic Sea. In 1949, Communists took power in China, and the following year took control of most of Korea. Communism seemed to many a threat to the future security of the United States. Wisconsin Republican Senator Joseph McCarthy charged that the Truman administration harbored Communists and Communist sympathizers. In Massachusetts, state representative Edward J. Donlan charged that

the "long arm of Moscow has reached into the State House," and demanded an investigation of Communists in the Massachusetts government.

Massachusetts divided over McCarthy and the threat of Communism. The Catholic Church fiercely opposed Communism. While there were undoubtedly some Communist sympathizers in Massachusetts, there was also a tradition of free speech threatened both by Communism and by the anti-Communist crusade of McCarthy. When McCarthy held televised hearings to investigate Communist influence in the U.S. Army, he tangled with Joseph Welch of Boston's Hale and Dorr law firm. When McCarthy charged that one of Welch's colleagues was a Communist sympathizer, Welch responded with quiet but impassioned outrage. This nationally televised charge could ruin the young lawyer's life, and McCarthy knew it, demanding to know if the firm would fire the accused. "Have you, sir, no compassion? Have you no decency?" Welch asked. Welch charged that McCarthy was not interested in Communism, but merely in ruining lives for the sake of his own political gain.

For most Massachusetts political figures, opposing McCarthy would have been suicide. Congressman Tip O'Neill supported a law to outlaw the Communist party, and Senator John F. Kennedy abstained when the Senate voted to censure the Wisconsin Senator. Kennedy also struck up a relationship in the 1950s with the Catholic anti-Communist Ngo Diem, the future president of South Vietnam. When Kennedy sought the presidency in 1960, he warned that the world could not exist "half slave and half free," and supported the containment of Communism.

Playwright Arthur Miller visited Salem during the McCarthy hysteria, researching the 1692 Salem witch trials. His play, *The Crucible*, is an exploration of paranoia at work in a community. Though based on the events of 1692, Miller the artist deftly drew the characters as real people, with John Proctor at the end refusing to sign his name to a confession, even though to do so would save his life. His life would be meaningless without his name, and he could not confess to having been in a league with Satan if he was not. In the hysteria of the 1950s, Miller saw a parallel to the Salem outbreak of 1692. The play has since been performed throughout the world, often in societies emerging from totalitarianism. After a performance in China, a recently-released political prisoner was surprised to learn that the author was not Chinese. The interrogation scene was so reminiscent of her own brutal questioning by the Communist authorities. From these two traumatic episodes, Salem in 1692, and America in 1950, Miller created an enduring monument to human freedom and the dangers it faces.

THE CITY UPON A HILL

Ten days before he became president of the United States, John F. Kennedy addressed the Massachusetts legislature. No man, he said, about to enter high office in the United States "can ever be unmindful of the contribution this state has made to our national greatness." In crisis and in calm, Massachusetts, her democratic institutions, her principles, and her leaders had guided the nation's destiny, even before the nation was born. What Pericles had said of Athens, Kennedy said, was true of Massachusetts: "We do not imitate—for we are a model to others."

Kennedy, who had never served in the state legislature, but whose entire career had been spent on the national stage, spoke movingly of his native state, where "my grandparents were born," and where "I hope my grandchildren will be born." He had not come to say farewell to Massachusetts, but to remind the legislature, and the people of the state, of the enduring principles they all owed to the Commonwealth.

"The enduring qualities of Massachusetts—the common threads woven by the Pilgrim and the Puritan, the fisherman and the farmer, the Yankee and the immigrant," would now guide him in the "four stormy years ahead." He recalled the founders of the Bay Colony, "beset as it was then by terror without and disorder within," and their leader, John Winthrop, who set before his *Arabella* shipmates a challenge, "as they, too, faced the task of building a new government on a perilous frontier."

"We must always consider," he said, "that we shall be as a city upon a hill—the eyes of all people are upon us."

For Winthrop and for Kennedy, being a model for others was more an awesome burden than a source of provincial pride. History would judge them all, not by their competence or loyalty or stature, but by asking: were they men of courage? Were they men of judgment? Were they men of integrity? And were they men of dedication?

"Courage—judgment—integrity—dedication—these are the historic qualities of the Bay Colony and the Bay State—the qualities which this state has consistently sent to this chamber on Beacon Hill here in Boston and to Capitol Hill back in Washington."

It was both high praise, and a high challenge, to Massachusetts and to the nation.

THEY THAT GO
DOWN TO THE SEA
IN SHIPS
▲ ▲ ▲
1623 — 1923

The Massachusetts Miracle (1960-2002)

★   ★   ★   ★   ★   ★   ★   ★   ★

The famous Gloucester Fisherman looks out over Gloucester Harbor. The statue is a memorial to those who have lost their lives at sea since 1623, including the sword-fishermen in the recent book and movie, The Perfect Storm. *Photo by Justine Hill*

John Kennedy issued a challenge to the Massachusetts legislature in 1961. Every branch of government, at every level, national, state, and local, "must be as a city upon a hill—constructed and inhabited by men aware of their great trust and their great responsibilities." A week before he entered the presidency, he could not help but remember "the contribution this state has made to our national greatness," nor should the people of Massachusetts. At the end of the twentieth and beginning of the twenty-first centuries, it was clear that the people of Massachusetts, "the farmer and the fisherman, the Yankee and the immigrant" were continuing to follow Kennedy's lead.

Since 1960, Massachusetts has experienced profound economic change. But the state has built on economic difficulties to emerge stronger. The fishing industry collapsed, as over fishing eliminated the great codfish and haddock populations on George's Bank. But as this environmental catastrophe was developing, interest in the seas increased. From Province-town, Gloucester, and Boston, which had once sent out men to hunt whales, nearly a million visitors set out each year to see whales. The Gerry E. Studds—Stellwagen Bank National Marine Sanctuary, 842 square miles of water at the mouth of Massachusetts Bay, is one of the world's best places to see whales. From the brink of extinction, whales were returning in greater numbers to the waters of New England. On shore, the Center for Coastal Studies in Provincetown devoted itself to saving whales, with dramatic disentanglements and more mundane research. The New England Aquarium in Bos-

231

Professor Vannevar Bush is shown in his 1927 Massachusetts Institute of Technology laboratory where he was working on the product integraph, an early analog computer. It took four operators to run this enormous machine. Courtesy, The MIT Museum

ton, and the New Bedford Aquarium, destinations for visitors to admire marine life, are also pioneers in studying oceans and treating sick animals.

Massachusetts has benefited from the number and diversity of its citizens willing to tackle problems. The fisherman's livelihood depended on the health of the fish, while the environmentalists had an interest in protecting the marine environment. Fishermen and scientists, from the Center for Coastal Studies, the Woods Hole Oceanographic Institute, MIT and other universities, worked together to solve their common problems. Support from state and federal government, particularly from Congressman Gerry E. Studds, smoothed the way, and the work of all benefited the local economies of Provincetown, Gloucester, New Bedford, and Boston.

The confluence of various interests has benefited Massachusetts, and the

nation, in other ways. In the late 1940s, building on wartime collaboration between scientists and the military, which had led to breakthroughs in radar and jet engines, the Department of Defense supported MIT's nascent Lincoln Laboratories. Collaboration here between physical scientists and psychologists, and between researchers into analog and digital computers and acoustics such as Bolt Beranek and Newman (BBN), who also did the acoustical work for Boston Symphony Orchestra's Talbot Canopy at Tanglewood, bore rich fruit, ultimately producing the Internet. As Leo Beranek of BBN noted, "not even a modern Jules Verne could have imagined how a collaboration of physical scientists and psychologists would begin a communication revolution." Had the research been left in the hands of industrial giants in the computer or communications fields, or in the hands of the military, the crucial breakthroughs could not have been made—the leaps of faith would never have been taken.

Computer and other high-tech companies made the Route 128 ring around metropolitan Boston, "America's Technology Highway." Many of the high-tech pioneers, as is true of pioneers in general, did not survive. But high-tech industries as a whole have become a vital part of the Massachusetts economy. By 2002, Massachusetts was home to more than 250 biotechnology companies, which employed more than 28,000 people. The biotechnology industries benefited from collaborative synergy among the state's teaching hospitals and universities. Massachusetts, long a pioneer in health care, draws patients from all over the world to seek the care of some of the world's best doctors. In addition to treating the sick, the hospitals have been leaders in studying the roots of illnesses. In 1934, Sidney Farber at Boston Children's Hospital used chemotherapy to treat children's leukemia. The Dana Farber Institute has ever since pioneered the treatment of children's leukemia and cancer, with help not only from doctors and scientists, but from athletes. A visit to Dana Farber by Red Sox player Ted Williams in the 1940s helped create the Jimmy Fund, which has raised millions of dollars to study children's cancer. For Ted Williams and other players, winning the fight against children's leukemia has been one of the proudest accomplishments. Massachusetts doctors in 1953 developed a vaccine for measles, and the following year carried out a successful kidney transplant. These innovations paved the way for others, and fueled the kind of research which in the new century will change the way illnesses are combated. In 2000, scientists at MIT's Whitehead Institute were central players in the mapping of the human genome, and Massachu-

setts has continued to be the center of emerging biotechnology.

Another Massachusetts innovation, the mutual fund, transformed the nation's economy. Beginning with the fiduciary institutions of the early nineteenth century, which would manage on-shore money for the Yankee merchants off on long ocean voyages, Massachusetts became a financial center. The idea of a mutual fund, a company which exists to invest in other companies, began in Boston. These open-end investment companies and the fiduciary institutions of Boston's State Street made the city the second-largest financial center in the nation by the 1980s. In the 1990s, with reforms in the nation's banking laws, and an increasing centralization of capital, some of New England's traditional economic powers—in publishing, banking, and retailing—were bought out by investors from other places. The loss of local ownership changed the insular nature of the Massachusetts business community. But it also meant New England's integration into the world economy.

Work in Massachusetts in the twenty-first century is likely to demand high-technology skills, as is shown here in a laboratory at BAE SYSTEMS in Lexington. At BAE SYSTEMS' Infrared Imaging Systems (IRIS) people design, develop and manufacture advanced infrared components and systems used primarily by U.S. government in reconnaissance and space systems. Courtesy, BAE SYSTEMS, Lexington

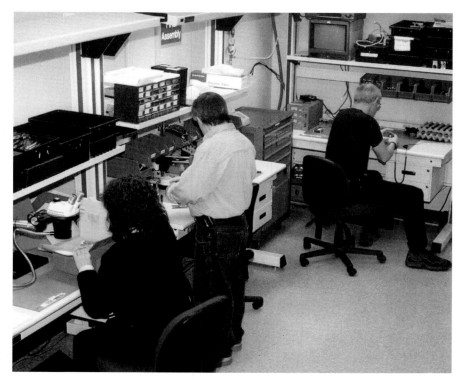

These school children were photographed for the cover of a 1975 state commission booklet on de facto segregation and its remedy. From Massachusetts State Board of Education, Balancing the Public Schools: Desegregation in Boston and Springfield, *1975*

BALANCING THE PUBLIC SCHOOLS

Desegregation in Boston and Springfield

EDUCATION REFORM

To maintain its place in the world economy, relying on technology and innovation, Massachusetts needs to maintain an educated workforce. To maintain its role as a promoter of democratic ideals, it needs educated citizens. During the 1980s and 1990s, immigration into the state increased. Many immigrants were lured by jobs in the state's high-tech or biotechnology industries, but others fled political oppression or economic devastation. To sustain an educated workforce, and to integrate immigrants into the fabric of Massachusetts, the state's educational system needed to be improved.

Public education began in Massachusetts. The oldest public school in the nation, Boston Latin, began teaching children in 1635. The state Constitution calls for education to be cherished, and requires each town to maintain public schools for the education of its children. In the 1830s, tireless reformer Horace Mann led a crusade to build and improve free public education for the children of Massachusetts.

In the 1970s, though, Massachusetts educational system was beginning to show its age. The urban schools were in a state of decay, and the explosive busing situation in Boston polarized communities who might have worked together to improve the schools for all. Proposition 2½, which limited the tax rate in Massachusetts communities, forced schools to cut their budgets, eliminating programs in music, languages, arts, and other "non-essentials." By the late 1980s, budget cuts and lackluster educational programs had taken a toll, as Massachusetts students seemed to lag behind students in other states.

The Education Reform Act of 1993 was one of the most ambitious steps in public education since Horace Mann created the state Board of Education in 1838. The state agreed to increase its aid to public schools in the 372 school districts. In return, the school districts would

the education they offered.

After mandatory testing began, school districts in which too many students failed the exam would be held accountable. The state threatened to take over failing schools to bring them up to standard. In addition, after 2001, students would need to pass their MCAS tests to graduate from high school. More important than simply identifying failure, the MCAS would identify areas of strength, and assess how well schools and school districts improved student performance.

Asians are among the latest large group of immigrants into Massachusetts. The Chantavong family of Greenfield, Laotian immigrants, came to the United States to begin a new life after the Marxist-Leninist Lao People's Revolutionary Party gained control in their native country in 1975. Photo by Samuel Pettengill. Courtesy, Special Collections and Archives, Library, University of Massachusetts at Amherst

agree to meet state standards for education. To ensure that students were being held to a higher, uniform standard, the state would create educational frameworks in critical areas—math, science, English, history, and social studies. A standardized test, the Massachusetts Comprehensive Assessment System (MCAS) test would be given to all fourth grade, eighth grade, and tenth grade students, beginning in 1998. School districts had five years to improve

Rather than a snap-shot of what students know on a certain day, the MCAS was designed to provide, over a span of years, a measurement of how much students had learned.

The Education Reform Act also allowed for the creation of charter schools. Parents, educators, for-profit and not-for-profit entities could apply to the Board of Education for a charter to run a school for five years. These charter schools would be open to all students, would receive money from school districts from which their students came, but would have complete control over their budget, and the hiring and firing of teachers. This put them outside the control of teachers unions and local educational bureaucracies, and encouraged innovation in the classroom. The Board of Education, however, could revoke a charter if the school was not performing. In 1995, the first charter schools opened. Some focused on particular themes: music, the arts, science; others offering a more traditional education. By 2002, more than 14,000 Massachusetts students were enrolled in 43 charter schools. Out of nearly 1 million students in 1,903 public schools, this

Lieutenant Governor Jane Swift became governor when Governor A. Paul Cellucci was appointed ambassador to Canada. Governor Swift was the first woman governor of Massachusetts and the first woman governor in the country to give birth while in office. She is shown here sending off troops departing to Afghanistan from Otis Air Force Base on October 4, 2001. Photo by Rose Marston, Courtesy, Office of the Governor

seems like a small number. But the charter schools have had a large impact on the school districts from which they draw students, offering an appealing alternative to parents and students seeking the best possible education.

Private and parochial schools continue to be an important alternative to public education. Massachusetts has some of the finest private high schools in the nation; schools like Groton and Andover can count among their alumni presidents of the United States. Religious schools, particularly parochial schools, provide another educational experience. Most of the 124,000 children in Massachusetts private schools are in parochial schools, nearly half of them in the Archdiocese of Boston, with its 163 parochial schools.

Attention to education on the highest levels of state government, and competition for students among public, charter, and parochial schools, has improved the education Massachusetts children receive. These educational reforms in Massachusetts provided a model for educational reform in the rest of the country. In 2002, President George W. Bush visited Boston Latin School, to acknowledge its role as a model for public education, and also to acknowledge the work of Senator Edward M. Kennedy in national educational reform. Bush, a Republican, joked that "In the coffee shop in Crawford Texas, I told them, 'Ted Kennedy's all right.'" Republicans and Democrats joined together in support of improving education for all.

MASSACHUSETTS POLITICS

Party divisions ceased to be important as the state struggled to improve its schools, but Massachusetts is one of the most politically exciting, or contentious, states in the nation. After the 1940s, the state became reliably Democratic, as voters benefited from the Democratic party's social legislation, such as the New Deal and the G.I. Bill. Democrats controlled the state legislature, and more often than not the governorship. By the 1970s, Massachusetts was so reliably Democratic that it was the only state in the union to support George McGovern in the 1972 election.

But the social turmoil of the 1970s, and demographic shifts in the state, changed this. In Boston, the controversy over school busing drove a wedge between Democratic leaders and some of their most loyal supporters. Senator Kennedy, a champion of school integration, was the target of eggs and verbal abuse when he addressed a City Hall rally in 1975. The following year South Boston Congressman Joe Moakley lost his hometown to a Republican candidate (though Moakley carried the rest of the district easily). Governor Michael S. Dukakis was defeated for renomination in 1978, and in 1980 and 1984 Ronald Reagan carried Massachusetts in the presidential election.

Voters in Massachusetts became increasingly suburban. More than a third of Boston's families left the city between 1970 and 1980. Suburban voters worried about property taxes, and many urban Democrats believed the party had abandoned them. Rebelling against the state's nickname of "Taxa-chusetts," in 1980 voters endorsed Proposition 2½ to limit property taxes. In 1982 businessman Ray Shamie, hoping to rebuild the state's Republican party, challenged Senator Kennedy's reelection. Though Kennedy won, Shamie showed that a serious challenge to the state and nation's most visible Democratic leader was possible. Shamie recruited candidates to seek local offices (long-time Republican leader John Sears lamented that many in his party saw a seat in Congress as "an entry-level position"), and in 1990 more Republicans were sent to the state legislature than had been since 1960, and Republican William Weld became the first Republican governor in 20 years.

Weld proved a popular governor, as he embraced a liberal social agenda, supporting gay rights and abortion, while opposing tax increases. But Weld lost a race for the U.S. Senate in 1996, and resigned when President Bill Clinton, a Democrat, nominated Weld as U.S. ambassador to Mexico. Conservative Republican Jesse Helms of North Carolina blocked Weld's confirmation, and

John F. Kerry was lieutenant governor from 1983-1984. He has been one of Massachusetts' two U.S. Senators since 1985 and is talked about as a presidential candidate by his Democratic party. Courtesy, John F. Kerry

the former governor moved to New York to pursue a career as a banker and novelist. Lieutenant Governor A. Paul Cellucci took office and was elected to a full term in 1998. Cellucci resigned in 2001 to become U.S. ambassador to Canada. Lieutenant Governor Jane Swift, one of the youngest people and the only woman ever to hold the office, became acting governor. But the state's Republicans, worried that Swift's popularity seemed to rise and fall erratically, in 2002 pushed her aside in favor of millionaire businessman Mitt Romney, who had challenged Kennedy in 1994, and in 2002 had helped to organize the Salt Lake City Olympics.

These Republican travails, electing governors who did not want the job, and then bumping aside ones who did, failed to make more Massachusetts voters into Republicans.

When he ran for president in 1988, Governor Dukakis said, "It's not about ideology, it's about competence." While nationally voters rejected Dukakis, and in 1990 he retired from public office, by the early 1990s voters grew nostalgic for his admin-

THE KENNEDY LEGACY

"He can do more for Massachusetts" was Edward M. Kennedy's slogan when, at the age of 30, he ran for the U.S. Senate in 1962. It was a reminder that one brother was president of the United States, another was attorney general, and that all seemed touched with political magic. His opponent, State Attorney General Edward McCormack, a talented leader, was also the scion of a political family, nephew of House Speaker John W. McCormack. McCormack mocked the neophyte Kennedy: "If your name were Edward Moore, and not Edward Moore Kennedy, your candidacy would be a joke."

Both men were right. A 30-year old Edward Moore would never be elected senator from Massachusetts. But after representing Massachusetts in the Senate for longer than any other person in her history, Edward M. Kennedy has done more for Massachusetts. For four decades, Kennedy has brought home to Massachusetts federal benefits and jobs, expanded health care and education, and been a tireless advocate for international justice and for his constituents navigating a federal bureaucracy. His candidacy may have seemed a joke in 1962, but 40 years later his legacy looms large.

The youngest of Joseph P. and Rose Fitzgerald Kennedy's nine children, Kennedy's family story is well known because it is the story of many Americans. Patrick and Brigid Kennedy met on the ship from Ireland, having been forced by famine and political oppression to flee their homes. They left with little more than their religious faith and a determination to work hard. Married in Massachusetts, Patrick found work making barrels. Their son, Patrick Joseph Kennedy, grew up to own a tavern and become a political leader in East Boston. In a society without a social welfare net, politicians could create jobs, shoveling snow, work-

ing on public building projects, sweeping courthouses, schools, and police stations. Patrick's son, Joseph P. Kennedy, earned entrance to Boston Latin School and Harvard. By the age of 30, this grandson of immigrants was a millionaire. He courted Rose Fitzgerald, the beautiful daughter of John F. "Honey Fitz" Fitzgerald, the first son of Irish immigrants to be Boston's mayor. Their marriage in 1914 was a society event, presided over by William Cardinal O'Connell, marking the rise of the Kennedys and Fitzgeralds from the brutal poverty of Boston's immigrant slums.

Closed out from the Yankee Protestant world of Boston finance, years later Joseph Kennedy would remark that he had been American ambassador to England, and that his son was a United States senator, but to many Bostonians he was still "an Irishman." The growing Kennedy family moved to New York in the 1920s. Kennedy's fortune grew as he invested shrewdly in bonds, and the fortune survived the crash in 1929. President Roosevelt recognized Kennedy's financial skills, and made him chairman of the Securities and Exchange Commission, to regulate the stock market. The entire family sailed for England when Roosevelt made Kennedy the U.S. ambassador to Britain.

When the war began, sons Joe and John could have received desk jobs, but both chose active duty, and both paid a heavy price. Joe died when his plane exploded over the English Channel; John survived the sinking of his P.T. Boat in the Solomons. The war changed the Kennedy family, and the nation. In 1946, John F. Kennedy began his political career by winning the Congressional seat held by James Michael Curley, representing the immigrant neighborhoods of his grandparents' East Boston and North End, as well as Charlestown and Cambridge. Six years later he challenged Massachusetts Senator Henry Cabot Lodge for reelection, and in a surprising upset Kennedy won the Senate seat. Eight years later, he was elected president of the United States.

Ted Kennedy managed his brother's presidential campaign in the western states, and thought of pursuing his own career in the west. But his brother's Senate seat beckoned. Years later, Kennedy spoke at Edward McCormack's funeral, recalling their bitter contest and noting his own special qualifications in 1962: "a brother who was president of the United States, a brother who was attorney general, and a father who would spare no expense to get his son elected to the Senate." Kennedy did not simply rely on his family connections. He learned how the Senate worked, and he learned how to work within it. In the 1960s he helped create the block grant program for community development, and helped create the nation's first neighborhood health care system in a Dorchester housing project. He has consistently worked to expand affordable health care for all Americans. In the 1970s he strengthened Meals on Wheels for the elderly, the Women, Infants, and Children (W.I.C.) program, and Head Start. He steered the Low Income Energy Assistance Program through Congress. A Democratic party stalwart, he has worked effectively with Republicans, such as Dan Quayle, with whom Kennedy created the Job Training Partnership Act in 1982. Under the Republican administrations of the 1980s, and the Republican Congresses in the 1990s, Kennedy has preserved and expanded the social welfare net he helped to create in the 1960s. President George W. Bush unveiled his education program in 2002, at Boston Latin School, at the side of Senator Kennedy.

The tragic deaths of John F. Kennedy in 1963, and of Robert Kennedy in 1968, forced Ted Kennedy into a national political spotlight. Delivering a eulogy to his brother Robert in 1968, at New York's St. Patrick's Cathedral, he recalled his brother's maxim, "Some men see things as they are and say, 'Why?' but he dreamed of things that never were and say, 'Why not?'" Called upon to uphold the "Kennedy Legacy," Ted Kennedy determined that it would be to seek a newer world, rather than a quest for an unreachable past.

Senator Kennedy led the international campaign against Apartheid in South Africa, and for peace in Northern Ireland. He also led a long and successful campaign to build the John F. Kennedy Library on Boston Harbor, not merely as a memorial to his brother, but as a way to call young people to public service. Each year the Library honors a distinguished individual with a "Profile in Courage" award, and its "Distinguished American" award honors a descendant of the Irish diaspora who continues to strive for the betterment of all.

Though Senator Kennedy has worked to ensure that the Kennedy legacy will be one of public service, the family has suffered continuing personal tragedy. The deaths of his brother and sister in the 1940s, the deaths of his two brothers in the 1960s, and in the 1980s and 1990s, deaths of nephews and of Jacqueline Kennedy Onassis, have cloaked the family with sorrow. But the Kennedys continue to strive to serve. Joseph P. Kennedy III, son of Robert Kennedy, distributes low-cost heating oil in Massachusetts, and served in the U.S. Congress. Kathleen Kennedy Townsend, Robert Kennedy's daughter, served as lieutenant governor of Maryland. Senator Kennedy's son, Patrick Kennedy, carrying the name of the first Kennedy in America, is a congressman from Rhode Island. After 40 years in the Senate, Ted Kennedy continues to do more for Massachusetts.

Facing page: The annual St. Patrick's Day breakfast, hosted by South Boston's senator, is one of the great traditions in Massachusetts. Politicians come to South Boston to tell jokes (mainly at their own expense), sing songs, and have fun. Here, at the 1965 breakfast, standing (left to right) State Representative Michael Flaherty, Sr.; State Senator (later Congressman) John Joseph Moakley; City Councillor Jerry O'Leary; State Representative (later Senate President and President of the University of Massachusetts) William M. Bulger; State Senator Edward Burke; and, singing, Senator Edward M. Kennedy. Seated are Robert Quinn, Speaker of the State House of Representatives; Senator Leverett Saltonstall; and Governor Francis Sargent. Courtesy, John Joseph Moakley Archives, Suffolk University

Left: The Kennedy family in 1931 at Hyannis Port did not yet include Teddy. From left to right are Bobby, Jack, Eunice, Jean, Joseph P. Sr., Rose, Pat, Kathleen, Joe Jr., and Rosemary. Courtesy, The John F. Kennedy Library

istration's unrelenting competence. His administration had launched some of the state's most imaginative projects, the Big Dig, the clean-up of Boston harbor, and improvements in the state's transportation system, which moved ahead after his retirement.

THE BIG DIG

In the 1950s, it seemed the wave of the future—to relieve automobile traffic on Boston's narrow streets an elevated highway was built through the city from Charlestown to South Station. Named for the legendary "Honey Fitz," Boston congressman, mayor, and grandfather of John F. Kennedy, the Fitzgerald Expressway, or Central Artery, was designed to carry 75,000 cars every day when it opened in 1959.

But instead of easing traffic, the Central's 27 entrance and exit ramps (in a span of less than two miles) made driving in Boston painfully frustrating. The 200,000 cars it carried every day in the 1980s idled for hours above the city, making the trip through Boston agonizing at best, dangerous at worst (with a daily accident rate four times the national average). The prognosis was that things would only get worse—by 2010, planners predicted, traffic would crawl on the Expressway, jammed for 16 hours each day.

The Expressway was old, and it was ugly. Its planners had taken little note of the 20,000 residents it displaced, or the city it carved up. More than 1,000 buildings were destroyed in order to build an ugly green barrier between the North End and downtown, and between downtown and the waterfront. The great irony was that the Expressway had been part of a bold "New Boston" planned by leaders in the 1950s. They would break the city loose from its parochial and narrow-minded past, creating a city of the future. Building the Expressway was one means toward the "New Boston." At the same time, city planners were destroying the West End neighborhood, displacing 3,500 families in the interest of "urban renewal." Originally, the Central Artery was intended only to handle local traffic. Another link would carry through traffic on a road built through the Back Bay, South End, and Roxbury. But the Central Artery's reckless disregard for the North End and Chinatown residents, and the demolition of the West End, mobilized people in other neighborhoods to save their homes. By the 1970s, mobilized residents prevented construction of the Southwest Corridor, the demolition of the West End was a text-book case of how not to renew cities, and the Central Artery stood as a rusting and dangerous monument to the shortsightedness of its builders.

Governor Dukakis, an advocate of public transportation, and Transportation Secretary Frederick Salvucci, who had grown up in East Boston when Logan Airport was trying to devour his neighborhood, knew they needed to solve this problem. But rather than expand on the mistakes of the past by building more roads, Dukakis and Salvucci proposed something more radical. They would not build on the mistakes of the past, but would dismantle them. They would build a new underground multi-lane highway beneath the Central Artery. Once the new underground road was completed, it would be able to handle more traffic than the projections for 2010, and the old, ugly eyesore above would be taken down. This would open 70 acres of parkland in downtown Boston, running from North Station to Chinatown, while solving the city's legendary traffic problems. And while construction went on below ground, the Central Artery would continue handling its daily traffic, which, it was certain, could not move any more slowly. The entire project could be completed by the late 1990s, at a cost of $2 billion.

It was one of the boldest transportation proposals ever made. Reaction at first was incredulity. "Lower the Expressway?" some asked. "Why not just raise the city?" Dukakis and Salvucci moved ahead, drawing up plans, and securing key support from Senator Kennedy, Speaker Tip O'Neill and Congressman Joe Moakley. Despite Dukakis' defeat for the presidency in 1988, and retirement from

public life in 1991, the plan moved ahead. Construction began in 1991, and the "Big Dig" became as much a part of the lives of Bostonians as baked beans and the Red Sox.

The largest public works project in the history of the world, those who have lived through the Big Dig will long remember it. The engineers and construction workers building it have used techniques and tools never tried anywhere in the world. For example, at the new underground road's lowest point, 120 feet below Dewey Square at South Station, the Expressway will cross below the subway line. Above the subway line, as another part of the whole project, a tunnel is being built for a new electric bus line. The Expressway's ceiling passes inches below the subway's tracks, and building a tunnel above the subway could force the subway tunnel down, potentially causing it to eventually crash through onto the Expressway. Engineers had to resolve this problem, and do it while the subway trains kept running between the two tunnels they were building! They devised a number of solutions, jacking up the sub-

Most of the Massachusetts Turnpike was built in the 1950s under the Eisenhower Interstate Highway program, but it did not go into Boston until the Weston to Boston section opened. This photo shows the skyline of Boston in 1965 and the spaghetti look of roads where the Turnpike met the Central Artery near South Station, February 12, 1965. Reprinted with permission of the Worcester Telegram and Gazette

Michael Dukakis was born in Brookline in 1933. He was a Democratic member of the House of Representatives, 1963-1970, then governor twice, 1975-1979, and again from 1983-1991. In this photo he was at a parade while governor. He ran for president in 1988 but was defeated by Republican George Bush. In 2002 he had moved on to teach political science and public policy at both UCLA and Northeastern University in Boston. Courtesy, Office of the Governor and by permission of Michael Dukakis

way tunnel and placing it on an enormous concrete table. Between the table's legs, which rest on bedrock, thousands of cars will pass every day, 10 stories below ground, the drivers able to concentrate on the open road rather than the feats of engineers or the skills of construction workers that has made possible their easy travel.

Unlike the initial Artery project, which attempted to rebuild the city without consulting the people who lived in it, the Big Dig has invited constant public comment. The public has forced planners to reevaluate ideas, and make the project better. To connect the new underground Artery with existing roads to the north, engineers had first proposed "Plan Z," a massive system of interchanges and cloverleafs crossing the Charles River between Boston and Charlestown. As tall as the old out-dated skyway it was replacing, "Plan Z" drew an immediate negative reaction. Forced

back to the drawing board, engineers designed an elegant cable-stayed bridge, its towers echoing the nearby Bunker Hill Monument. Named for Bunker Hill and for the late Leonard Zakim, of the Anti-Defamation League, a life-long builder of bridges between communities, the Zakim/Bunker Hill Bridge will be a fitting entry into a Boston which has not forgotten its past, or neglected its future.

The builders of the 1950s sought to free themselves from Boston's history, but the Big Dig has embraced history. The state archaeologist identified several key sites below the Expressway, and before construction began some long-buried parts of the city were revealed for the first time since the 1600s. Evidence from seventeenth-century privy holes, artifacts from colonial taverns, manufactories, and households, will allow us to better understand the Boston of Winthrop and Anne Hutchinson. Shoes, bottles, and fabrics enrich our understanding of Puritan Boston. The oldest bowling ball ever found in North America challenges that understanding. Bowling and other recreations were against the law in Puritan Boston. Who owned this 1640 bowling ball?

The Big Dig will reconnect the downtown with the waterfront, and will help reconnect Boston with its history. It was fitting that the first piece of the project to open, the tunnel connecting the Massachusetts Turnpike with Logan Airport, was named for Red Sox great Ted Williams. The "Splendid Splinter" returned to Boston for an emotional grand opening in 1995, riding a golf-cart through the new harbor tunnel which will bear his name.

When the rest of the project is completed in 2004, traffic will move smoothly underground, and downtown Boston will gain 70 acres of land where the Expressway stood. This area has been set aside as the Rose Kennedy Greenway, honoring the daughter of Honey Fitz, with 40 acres of parkland, and other parcels used for civic or cultural institutions, such as the Massachusetts Horticultural Society. Taking down the Expressway will allow the North End to connect once again with the city, and Faneuil Hall once more to connect with the waterfront.

The project has taken nearly a decade longer to finish than anticipated, and its cost has risen from $2 billion to nearly $15 billion. The escalating price tag and failure to meet deadlines threatened the project in the late 1990s, but it has since come under new management, and work has gone smoothly. When finished, the inconveniences Bostonians and visitors experienced during its building, and the traffic nightmares which made it necessary, will fade in memory. The traffic problem solved, and the ugly green roadway replaced by 70 acres of open space in the heart of the city, will give Bostonians of the next century a chance to build a "New Boston."

BOSTON HARBOR

Boston's sewer system, built between 1877 and 1884, was once regarded as the country's best. Underground pipes carried sewerage from 18 communities to Moon Island in Boston Harbor, where it was released, untreated, at high tide. The tide was supposed to carry the waste out to sea. But the tide could not keep up. By the 1930s, Boston Harbor was filthy. Shellfish were contaminated; fish disappeared. The harbor smelled so bad that to find it, it was said, just follow your nose.

This picture, taken March 22, 2002 from the 24th-floor viewing deck of the Custom House Tower near Quincy Market looking north, shows the Central Artery still above ground with great holes visible below where the new highway is being built. The Leonard P. Zakim-Bunker Hill Bridge with its A-shaped white towers is visible in the distance. When completed, the road area in the foreground will be green parkland with the highway underneath. Photo by Ruth Owen Jones

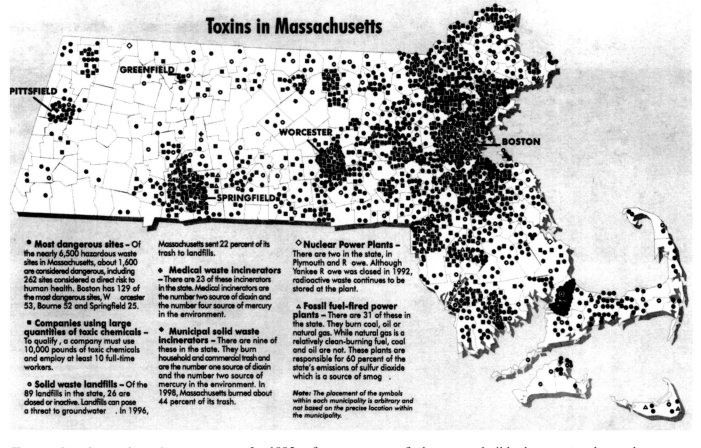

Toxins in Massachusetts

PITTSFIELD
GREENFIELD
WORCESTER
SPRINGFIELD
BOSTON

• **Most dangerous sites** – Of the nearly 6,500 hazardous waste sites in Massachusetts, about 1,600 are considered dangerous, including 262 sites considered a direct risk to human health. Boston has 129 of the most dangerous sites, W orcester 53, Bourne 52 and Springfield 25.

■ **Companies using large quantities of toxic chemicals** – To qualify, a company must use 10,000 pounds of toxic chemicals and employ at least 10 full-time workers.

○ **Solid waste landfills** – Of the 89 landfills in the state, 26 are closed or inactive. Landfills can pose a threat to groundwater . In 1996,

Massachusetts sent 22 percent of its trash to landfills.

✦ **Medical waste incinerators** – There are 23 of these incinerators in the state. Medical incinerators are the number two source of dioxin and the number four source of mercury in the environment.

◆ **Municipal solid waste incinerators** – There are nine of these in the state. They burn household and commercial trash and are the number one source of dioxin and the number two source of mercury in the environment. In 1998, Massachusetts burned about 44 percent of its trash.

◇ **Nuclear Power Plants** – There are two in the state, in Plymouth and R owe. Although Yankee R owe was closed in 1992, radioactive waste continues to be stored at the plant.

△ **Fossil fuel-fired power plants** – There are 31 of these in the state. They burn coal, oil or natural gas. While natural gas is a relatively clean-burning fuel, coal and oil are not. These plants are responsible for 60 percent of the state's emissions of sulfur dioxide which is a source of smog .

Note: The placement of the symbols within each municipality is arbitrary and not based on the precise location within the municipality.

This graphic shows where the toxins had been identified in Massachusetts as of 1999. Some are government-owned while others are private. Graphic by Kevin Barnard, Reprinted with permission from April 9, 1999 Springfield Union-News

In 1985, after a century of abuse, Judge Paul Garrity ruled that Boston's sewerage discharge violated state law. The next year, federal district court Judge David Mazzone presented the Massachusetts Water Resources Authority (MWRA) with a timetable for correcting the problems of pollution. The judge's order took a new urgency in 1988, when the harbor's pollution became an issue in the presidential election: Republican George H.W. Bush charged that Governor Dukakis, who was campaigning as an environmentalist, had failed to clean Boston Harbor. In the close election, the issue tipped the balance, and it made Boston Harbor a national disgrace.

Congressman John Joseph Moakley, who had long advocated cleaning the harbor, and had secured the harbor islands as a state park, joined with Senator Kennedy to secure federal money, under the Clean Water Act, to clean the harbor. Boston would

build the most advanced sewerage treatment plant in the world. The MWRA doubled the rates for water and sewer service, with the increase going to pay for cleaning the harbor. Federal money and Boston area consumers paid for the MWRA to build an underwater system tunnels, bringing sewerage and waste-water to a new treatment facility on Deer Island. The entire project cost $3.8 billion, involving more than 3,000 workers; the great engineering feat was completed before deadline and under budget.

The two most visible signs of progress are eight egg-shaped sludge digesters on Deer Island, and the astonishingly clear water in the Harbor. Each sludge digester holds up to 3 million gallons of sludge, which they transform into methane gas and fertilizer pellets. The sludge removed from Boston Harbor is not simply dumped somewhere else, but is transformed and recycled. Beneath the Harbor floor, tunnels bring sewerage to Deer Island where solid waste is removed and turned to fertilizer, the remaining material is disinfected, and then pumped into a nine and one-half mile tunnel under Massachusetts Bay. The remaining material is diffused gradually into the water through 55 pipes along the tunnel's last mile and a half.

The long-term effects of dispersing heavily-treated outfall into Massachusetts Bay will not be known for many years; the immediate effect on Boston Harbor is obvious. Porpoises and seals have returned to the inner harbor, and Boston's beaches have re-opened for swimming. The Boston Harbor Islands, which were once dumping grounds, have become one of the nation's newest National Parks. Visitors will board boats for the Boston Harbor Islands National Park at the John Joseph Moakley Courthouse on the South Boston waterfront, to enjoy the great outdoors in what was once the nation's largest open sewer. The transformation of Boston Harbor, from sewerage dump to environmental jewel, is one of the most remarkable feats of modern times. The metamorphosis was a result of the joint efforts of environmentalists and engineers, political leaders and community groups, and from the willingness of the 2 million MWRA ratepayers in 43 Massachusetts towns and cities to double their water bills now, in order to preserve a clean harbor for the future.

PROFESSIONAL SPORTS
Just as no one would have predicted in 1988 that one day porpoises, seals, and even people would swim in Boston Harbor—few experts predicted that the New England Patriots would be football champions in 2002. The Patriots had lost their first two games, and in their second game veteran quarterback Drew Bledsoe was

knocked down and was out for the season. But the next week, back-up quarterback Tom Brady moved the team to victory. The Patriots, Brady and Bledsoe, gave New England fans lessons in winning, but more important lessons in sportsmanship and teamwork. The players were introduced before each game not as individuals, but as a team, racing together

Champions! Adam Vinatieri is leaping for joy after his last-second kick that won the Super Bowl for the Patriots, Feb. 3, 2002. Ken Walker, who held the ball for the winning kick, is at left. Republished with permission of Globe Newspaper Company, Inc.

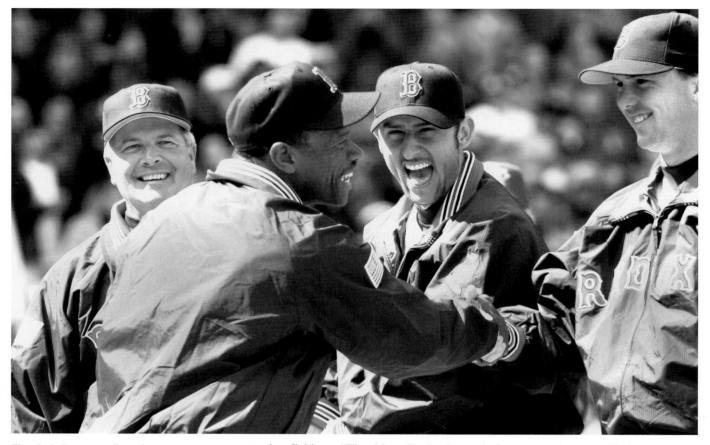

The Red Sox are all smiles as Ricky Henderson greets from left, Manager Grady Little and teammates Nomar Garciaparra and Trot Nixon on Opening Day at Fenway Park on April 1, 2002. Photo by Marla Pinsky, Reprinted with permission from the Springfield Union-News

onto the field as "The New England Patriots." When Bledsoe returned to play late in the season, coach Bill Belicheck decided to stick with the younger Brady. Disappointed, Bledsoe became Brady's mentor and showed his character in the final seconds of the Super Bowl, the score tied, telling Brady "Drop back and sling it. . . . Go win the game." Brady did, becoming the Super Bowl's youngest winning quarterback at age 24. For the team, it was a victory long in coming and for New Englanders, one long awaited.

Massachusetts had a boxing champion in 2001, when Chelsea heavyweight John "The Quiet Man" Ruiz came home with the World Boxing Association belt. Ruiz was born in Massachusetts, named for another great son of the state, John F. Kennedy (his younger brothers are Robert and Edward, his sister is Jacqueline). But he spent most of his first seven years in his parents' native Puerto Rico

before returning to Chelsea. Ruiz excels in an individual sport in which Massachusetts has long had a special place. He is Massachusetts' first heavyweight champion since bare-knucklist John L. Sullivan, who reigned in the 1880s and early 1890s, and Ruiz is the first Latino heavyweight champion. Massachusetts has produced other boxers, notably heavyweight champion Rocky Marciano, of Brockton. Another Brockton fighter, Marvin Hagler, earned the middleweight title in the 1980s. Ruiz and Sullivan, Hagler and Marciano, together form a Massachusetts mosaic. Latino and African American, Irish and Italian, each became a hometown favorite for all of Massachusetts, a state which Henry David Thoreau had once compared to a prize fighter "her fist on Cape Ann," her "bared and bended arm" of Cape Cod extending outward, and her feet "planted firmly on the Atlantic, ready to meet all comers."

Before the triumphs of the Patriots and Ruiz, no Massachusetts team had won a championship since 1986. In that memorable year the Boston Celtics, led by Larry Bird, Robert Parrish, and Kevin McHale, coached by former player K.C. Jones, set a basketball record by winning 67 of their 82 games. This was the Celtics' 16th championship—they had won 11 in 13 years (1957-1969) when Bill Russell, Sam Jones, and Bob Cousy dominated the courts. The Basketball Hall of Fame in Springfield, and the rafters of the Fleet Center, carry the banners of the Celtics glory days, and at Faneuil Hall Marketplace a bronze statue of Arnold "Red" Auerbach, long-time general manager, sits, perpetually preparing to light his victory cigar. But in the early 1990s, when Bird, McHale, Parrish, and K.C. Jones retired, and promising younger players Reggie Lewis and Len Bias died tragically, the Celtics days of glory were at least for a time put behind them.

The Boston Bruins share the Celtics' arena, and though the Bruins have not won the Stanley Cup since 1972, they have set a record by reaching the playoffs 29 years in a row (1968-1996). Team captain Ray Bourque in 2000 appeared in his 18th All-Star game, tying the record set by Wayne Gretzky. But in the closing weeks of the 2000 season, Bourque knew his own playing days were numbered, and that his Bruins would not make it to the play-offs. He asked to be traded to the play-off bound Colorado Avalanche, to give him a chance to hoist the Stanley Cup. After helping the Avalanche win the Stanley Cup, Bourque made an emotional return to Boston, bringing the Stanley Cup to share with the loyal Bruins fans. Inspired, the Bruins began rebuilding to bring back a championship of their own.

The Bruins and the Celtics played in the old Boston Garden, opened in 1928 and demolished in 1995. The old Garden had hosted boxing matches, circuses, political debates, concerts, and graduations. It would have hosted the 1965 rematch between Muhammad Ali and Sonny Liston, but Boston's District Attorney barred the fight as a "public nuisance." (Ali won

Boston Bruin Bobby Orr is shown flying across the ice in his winning goal for the Stanley Cup, May 10, 1972. Courtesy, The Brearley Collection, Faneuil Hall

A team from Georgia and one from Massachusetts clashed in the Amherst Regional High School Ultimate Frisbee Invitational in May 2002. This newest high school team sport is played on a soccer field with teams passing the disk down the field to their goal through the opposite team. If the disk falls, there is a turnover. Photo by Richard Wilkie

the rematch in Lewiston, Maine.) In the early 1990s the owners began plans to build a new arena and demolish the historic but decrepit Garden. Closing the Garden was one of Boston sports' most emotional experiences. The Bruins and Celtics each hosted farewell reunions in the fabled old venue. Bill Russell and Larry Bird stood for a final time on the parquet. Bourque, Phil Esposito, and Bobby Orr, who had flown across the net as he led the team to the Stanley Cup in 1970, skated for a final time on the ice. The new Fleet Center opened next door to the old Garden in 1995, with opening ceremonies similar to those that had closed down the Garden. Future sporting memories will be made in the new Fleet Center.

Across town, New England's most storied sporting team, the Boston Red Sox, continue to play in Fenway Park, the oldest baseball park in the major leagues (opened in 1912). In 2002 the Yawkey family trust, heirs to Tom and Jean Yawkey, who had owned the team for nearly 70 years, sold the team to new owners, who hope to bring the team its first World Series victory since 1918. The Red Sox story is not one of unrelieved futility. The real frustration for Red Sox fans comes from having good teams which make it almost all the way, but then through improbable and inexplicable events, fail to win. True Red Sox fans will still agonize over crucial missed plays or bad calls in 1946, 1948, 1978, 1986, and most years in between. After the team came within one strike of winning the World Series in 1986, fans began to speak of a "Curse of the Bambino." The theory that pitching star Babe Ruth, who led the team to its World Championships in 1916 and 1918, cursed the Red Sox for selling him to the Yankees in 1920, may comfort some. But others seek different explanations. The Red Sox occupy a special place in the hearts of New Englanders. They always seem on the verge of a championship, raising the hopes of millions, who, each spring, feel the expectant stirrings and hope that this could be the year.

The Patriots and Ruiz are the latest in a long tradition of New England sports champions. From them, the other teams can learn lessons of sportsmanship, teamwork, and discipline, and fans can see that nice guys do indeed finish first.

AMATEUR SPORTS
Massachusetts has a rich tradition of amateur athletes, both in colleges and schools, and in park leagues, recreational leagues, and just for fun. Worcester's Little League team in 2002 brought the joy and excitement of

baseball back to Massachusetts. These players—twelve years old and younger—played their way to the final round of the Little League World Series. Candlepin bowling is one of New England's most popular indoor sports, a more refined and difficult sport than the "duck pin" variety played elsewhere. Bocce courts are found in the Italian neighborhoods of Boston and other cities, and few patches of ice on Massachusetts ponds are not quickly home to skaters 0of all ages.

Every summer college baseball players from around the country come to Cape Cod, to play in one of the country's premier amateur leagues. Local families provide homes for players, who work in local stores and businesses, and form friendships which continue long after their playing days. Such stars as Mo Vaughan, Frank Thomas, and Nomar Garciaparra have spent summers the Cape League, where fans don't pay admission but pass the hat during the game.

Hockey is one of the most widely played winter sports in Massachusetts, but not all skaters are trying to land the puck in the net. Todd Eldredge of Chatham, and Nancy Kerrigan of Stoneham have represented the U.S. as Olympic figure skaters, and recreational ice-skating is popular on ponds, both natural and man-made. The Duck Pond in the Boston Public Garden, and the Frog Pond on Boston Common, are crowded with skaters every winter day.

One of the greatest Boston sporting events is the "Beanpot," a hockey tournament between Boston College, Boston University, Harvard, and Northeastern. The Boston Garden, and now the Fleet Center, hosts this lively series of games, in which the players compete for a Beanpot, but more importantly, bragging rights to being the best team among the Boston colleges. This title should not be taken lightly, as Boston College (2001), Boston University (1995), and Harvard (1989) have all won the N.C.A.A. hockey championship. Players from Massachusetts, Beanpot veterans, were part of the 1980 "Miracle on Ice," the U.S. Olympic victory over the Russians at Lake Placid. With these competitive schools in such close proximity, the arena is packed with vocal and exuberant partisans of each team. Fans of Boston University's Terriers, who had won the six previous Beanpots, in 2002 taunted the Boston College fans, chanting "Where's your Beanpot?" But when the Eagles took the lead, their fans taunted back, "Where's *your* Beanpot?"

Harvard does not award athletic scholarships of any kind, and yet has been competitive against other schools not only in hockey, winning the national title in 1989, and finishing second in 1986, but also in women's lacrosse. The Harvard women went undefeated in 1990, winning the national title, and finishing second in 1992. Few of these athletes, in hockey, lacrosse, or other college sports, go on to professional careers, but all play for the love of the game.

In the fall and in the spring, two of the world's premier sporting events draw participants and spectators to Boston. Each autumn since 1963 rowers from colleges and clubs throughout the world have come to The Head of the Charles, a rowing race along the Charles River, which separates Boston from Cambridge. Spectators line the banks of the river and the bridges spanning it, to watch the action and try to decipher the standings.

The Boston Athletic Association, founded in 1887, brought the first American track and field team to Athens for the first modern Olympics in 1896. The following Patriot's Day, April 19, 1897, 18 men ran from Ashland to Boston in the first Boston Marathon. Ten finished, led by New Yorker John McDermott, whose time was two hours, 55 minutes, and 10 seconds. Over the years the Boston Marathon grew in popularity and prestige, drawing thousands of runners from throughout the world. Women were not permitted to run until 1972, though some did enter the race "unofficially" or using only their initials.

In addition to these higher profile sporting events, communities sponsor soccer, hockey, baseball, and football programs for youth, but also programs distinct to New England's maritime culture. Towns along the coast have sailing programs to introduce the children of Massachusetts to one of the commonwealth's traditions. In Provincetown, residents are still proud of the local schooner *Rose Dorothea's* 1917 victory in the Lipton Cup race from Gloucester to Boston. A scale model of the *Rose Dorothea* has a place of pride in the town's museum, and its builder spends each summer teaching the town's children to swim and sail. Every summer in Provincetown, as in other coastal communities, dozens of small boats can be seen circling in the harbors, as children learn to catch the wind and keep their keels steady. From these beginnings in their younger years, many go on to be more experienced sailors. John F. Kennedy went into the P.T. Boat service thanks to his experience navigating Hyannis Harbor. Who knows where the wind will take the young skippers we now see navigating in Provincetown or Gloucester, Buzzards Bay or Boston Harbor?

PAST AND FUTURE

The people of Massachusetts—descendants of the Native Americans who gave the state its name, of the Yankees who built their homes in the wilderness, and the immigrants who continue to bring their own traditions to enrich the Commonwealth—continue to build their future on the strengths of the past. Home to the finest universities and hospitals in the world, Massachusetts looks ahead. But the state also cherishes its history. One of the most highly industrialized places on the planet, Massachusetts has also taken a lead in preserving its natural environment. Boston is ringed both by the Emerald Necklace, designed in the nineteenth century by Frederick Law Olmsted, and by a system of parks including the Blue Hills. A one-ton plaster model of Boston's metropolitan park system was shown at the Paris Exposition in 1900, and now these urban parks, set aside by the foresight of one generation, are complemented by the Boston Harbor Islands National Park, the newest in the U.S. park system.

Massachusetts has more history of national importance than any other state. Its history continues to be integral to the nation's, and the world's. On a peaceful September morning in 2001, two jets from Logan International Airport were hijacked by terrorists, who crashed them into New York's World Trade Center. Minutes after the second plane crashed, two fighter jets from Cape Cod's Otis Air Force Base, the East Coast's first line of defense, were above New York.

The ease with which terrorists were able to board planes at Logan forced the airport to close for a week, and its top administrators were fired. But the tragic story of September 11, and the unfolding aftermath, is more than the story of the hijackers and their victims. Massachusetts, with her universities drawing students from around the world, continues its long history as a refuge for political dissidents. Corazon Aquino lived in Newton during her husband's exile from the Philippines, and returned to her homeland in the 1980s to become president. Hamid Karzai's brothers and sisters continued to live in Cambridge while their brother began to rebuild Afghanistan after its liberation from the Taliban.

Along with leaders, Massachusetts has been a refuge for the ordinary men, women, and children caught up in the world's tragedies. In Dracut, a community of Cambodian refugees, settled in the nearby industrial cities of Lowell and Lawrence, became partners with a local farmer, John Ogonowski, who let them use his land in the traditional agricultural ways they had left behind in their ravaged country. Ogonowski was also a commercial pilot, and he was captain of one of the two jets from Logan so brutally seized that day. In his life, and in his death, he reminds us how connected the people of Massachusetts are with the rest of the world.

Cassin Young, one of the thousands of ships produced by the women and men of Massachusetts to save the world from Nazism and imperialism; monuments to the Revolutionary war, Lexington and Concord, Bunker Hill, Dorchester Heights; monuments to the industrial revolution at Lowell; the African Meeting House on Boston's Beacon Hill, and on Nantucket; the rich traditions of American art at Cape Ann and Cape Cod, and at Norman Rockwell's Stockbridge studio, and in the former mill buildings at North Adams which now house the Massachusetts Museum of Contemporary Art; all remind us of the achieve-

Plymouth, with its replica of the *Mayflower* and Plimoth Plantation; Salem, with its eighteenth century maritime history; Deerfield, with hatchet marks still testifying to conflict between European settlers and native people; the Quincy birthplaces of John and John Quincy Adams, and the birthplaces in Brookline of John F. Kennedy and in Milton of George H.W. Bush; the oldest commissioned warship still afloat in the world, the U.S.S. *Constitution*, which thundered against Tripoli and against the British, and fought her last action against a slave trader, berthed next to the World War II destroyer,

ments of the past, and point the way to the future.

The Big Dig, the harbor clean-up, the preservation of open space, the reform of education, all show the people of Massachusetts continuing to do what the generations who preceded them did. Following in the steps of Winthrop and Metacom, John Adams and Elizabeth Freeman, Frederick Douglass and Patrick Kennedy, William Smith Clark and Emily Dickinson, Isabella Stewart Gardner and John L. Sullivan, John Ogonowski and Joe Moakley—the people of Massachusetts continue to build a future, not for themselves, but for those who will come after.

Massachusetts Museum of Contemporary Art, "MASS MOCA," opened in 1999 in a 27-building mill complex joined by walkways and bridges in North Adams, the northwestern corner of the state. The galleries and performing spaces are immense, allowing performances and exhibits possible nowhere else. Courtesy, MASS MOCA

A. W. CHESTERTON COMPANY

The Chesterton family legacy originated in the United States in 1865. Thomas Chesterton, then 30 years old, along with his wife Sara and their three small children left Loughborough, Leicestershire, England and traveled to the seaport city of Liverpool. The family was headed for Australia but the ship was oversold. Thomas noticed a ship on the next pier, discovered it was bound for the United States and had space, so he announced to his family, "well, I guess we'll be Americans," and they set sail. The Chesterton family arrived at Ellis Island in New York on July 29, 1865. After a period of time, the family moved to the Boston area and settled in the town of Malden. Thomas worked as a huckster/tin peddler, his son Arthur, founder of A.W. Chesterton, began his career as a bookkeeper and a sales agent.

A. W. Chesterton lived in Brookline, Massachusetts and summered first in Winthrop and later in Scituate. A famous sailor of his day, he won many important races year-after-year. Arthur was elected Commodore of the Winthrop Yacht Club and subsequently served for four years as

About 1895 at 49 India Street, Boston, Mr. "A. W." stands in doorway, second from right.

Commodore of the Boston Yacht Club as well.

The A.W. Chesterton Company is one of the oldest and finest, family-owned businesses in America. Headquartered in Stoneham, Massachusetts, the company has been in operation for more than 118 years—incorporated in 1884—its roots dating back to 1883. Located at 49 India Street in Boston, Chesterton provided a variety of materials to local industries and the many ships that used the port of Boston. These products were displayed in an impressive 1,200-page, hardcover catalogue. Advanced Packing and Supply Company, a division of Chesterton, was created in Chicago to produce gaskets and other sealing device products for industry.

Chesterton expanded throughout the United States and continued its focus in North America until the 1960s when James (Jim) D. Chesterton became vice president of international sales. Armed with only an airplane ticket, and with no

budget for development, he headed for Europe to hire salespeople and find distributors for the company's products. Expansion into other regions of the world transformed the A.W. Chesterton Company into a global enterprise doing business in 90 countries. Jim convinced distributors to sell Chesterton products in their territories. At the same time, he pioneered a new method of bringing products and services to market. The typical distributor had an exclusive geographical area and sold products made by various manufacturers. It became essential that at least some of these salespeople receive specialized training and become dedicated to selling only Chesterton products. This would help customers improve their equipment performance by using these products. The concept of creating a "specialist" whose expertise was specifying, selling and applying Chesterton products, offered a competitive advantage and propelled the company to annual growth rates in excess of 25 percent a year for nearly 20 years.

Early Chesterton factory, Melrose, Massachusetts.

Jim, third generation Chesterton and the grandson of the founder, A.W. Chesterton, has traveled to 119 countries while holding the position of vice president of international sales for the past 20 years. He led the growth of Chesterton's international business to 27 percent per year compounded, and personally opened most of its non-USA worldwide multi-distribution accounts. In addition, Jim hired all of Chesterton's sales and technical staff—both internationally and within the United States. Consequently, his leadership led to international growth of 50 percent of total sales.

Andrew, the fourth generation Chesterton, is currently the company's CIO and responsible for the extensive training of both salespeople and customers in practices that promote cost-savings and better utilization of Chesterton products.

By the 1980s, Chesterton's global revenues had grown to an impressive $150 million. During that time, they began to manufacture new, differentiated products for sale through its distribution system. Chesterton introduced innovative products and built an outstanding reputation of providing products that are often considered superior to the competition. These products are predominately used in the maintenance, repair and operations areas of many types of equipment and industries. As customers learn the value of

Current Chairman James D. Chesterton and his wife Veronica, with President Gerald Ford.

Chesterton receives "E" Award of Excellence in Manufacturing at the White House. Pictured are Dev Chesterton and President Lyndon Johnson.

lowering overall operating costs by installing long-lived, highly-reliable products, they specify Chesterton sealing device products for use in upgrading plant equipment. The company is transforming the industry from the costly practice of plugging leaks by introducing the concept of confining fluids and gases throughout entire plants—saving significantly on the cost of leakage, while fighting pollution by keeping chemicals out of the environment and water sewerage systems. Chesterton can meet the world's strictest environmental standards and has become a leader in protecting the ecology by preventing leaks from valves, pumps, cylinders and flanges. This is accomplished through the use of more than 30,000 products it manufactures.

The Technical Products Division of Chesterton formulates maintenance chemicals used worldwide. It employs the same concept of superior and unique products while offering cost savings and durability to its customers. Acquired from Commercial Chemical Company in Lawrence, Massachusetts in the late 1960s when it had only a handful of products and one salesman, the Technical Products Division has grown to account for more

than 20 percent of Chesterton's worldwide sales.

Chesterton is distinctive, holding a number of high-tech patents and a sales and technical staff that speak all of the key languages around the world. The business grew by being discriminating in its products, by showing customers how to save on their manufacturing and maintenance costs, and by building a powerful, customer-supportive distribution and sales team. Over the years, industry has changed substantially. Today, with Chesterton's help, plants are using more sophisticated equipment, consolidating facilities, and providing improved training for their maintenance staffs. Chesterton has secured many "total" plant contracts by providing superior value through lower overall cost to the consumer. Over the past two decades service life has been extended by more than 10 times. Computers have also changed how business is conducted and who is in charge of securing particular products. When Jim Chesterton entered the company, sales were less than $1 million—consumer sales today exceed $200 million. The biggest challenge for the future is convincing Chesterton's customers that total cost, not acquisition (unit) cost—which is a small piece of the total—is in their best interest economically; that coupled with receiving plant-wide assistance from experienced Chesterton specialists.

Chesterton has always provided superior customer service. With more than 1,300 product specialists located around the world and backed by a team of professional customer service representatives and industry experts, they offer around-the-clock service focused on exceeding customer expectations. These specialists are trained to help customer's upgrade plants in industries such as paper, chemical, electric power generation, water treatment and automobile manufacturing. Over the years, Chesterton has won many prestigious awards for product excellence. It has been honored with several Vaaler

Awards from *Chemical Processing* magazine plus other magazine awards for Product of the Year. Approximately 50 percent of Chesterton's employees have been with the company for 10 years or more; 25 percent are related to each other as employees recommended the company to their qualified relatives. There are few companies that can match these statistics. Chesterton believes that its greatest asset is the dedication and "can-do" attitude of its employees. To help prove this point employee contributions are often rewarded with trips to Bermuda, Las Vegas, Disney World and other resort locations.

Throughout its 118-year history Chesterton has reinvented itself several times to maintain its prowess. As the company continues to move forward through its second century of business, new opportunities offer a bright and prosperous future. Today's markets are changing, and Chesterton has embarked on new strategies to ensure growth in the years ahead. Many of its largest customers are merging and the marketplace is becoming increasingly competitive. Proving the value of products and services while lowering plant costs are even more important today than in the past. These newly consolidated customers are focus-

Prior corporate leaders, Dev Chesterton (1902–1969) and Tom Chesterton (1906–1978).

ing their purchasing power and expect constant improvement in the value of the products they choose. Chesterton is well positioned to provide these best-value solutions through its premium quality differentiated products, services and training. Another important advantage will be an increasing array of software tools available to its customers on the Internet. These software tools will be used to help customers better understand the costs associated with operating facilities and to chart the long-term benefits of upgrading systems with Chesterton products. This will involve developing additional state-of-the-art materials and designs across all product lines; increasing the number of services provided; acquiring companies that offer complementary products and service capabilities; and forming alliances with other companies. Expansion into new markets will complement the core businesses of the company.

Chesterton will continue to focus on

Recognition for industrial contribution to the Commonwealth of Massachusetts by Governor Volpe. Left to right: Jim Chesterton, Governor Volpe, Dev Chesterton, Tom Chesterton and Dick McDermott.

progress in every areas of its business. Improving efficiencies through the use of Six Sigma and Kaizen blitz processes, reduced costs and accelerated delivery of its products are attained while continuing the around-the-clock responsiveness that has become the hallmark of the company. Chesterton manufacturing plants are ISO 9001 certified and its maintenance technical products are ISO 14000 certified.

Becoming increasingly involved in the progression of its customers businesses, Chesterton plans to help them become more competitive and prosperous in the industries they serve. Companies with exceptional technical knowledge receive a share of the gain allowing both the manufacturer and the customer to benefit from the substantial savings achieved together. Gain sharing is strategically planned for Chesterton's future. The standards of excellence established during the past 118 years will continue to propel the A.W. Chesterton Company into the 21st century.

Quincy Marketplace near Faneuil Hall, Boston, is lighted for Christmas. Photo by Justine Hill

A. W. PERRY, INC.

Since its founding in 1884, A. W. Perry, Inc. has made major contributions to the fabric and economy of the city of Boston and the South Shore region of Massachusetts. Alonzo W. Perry, originally a successful shoe manufacturer from Rockland, Massachusetts, founded the company and entered the real estate business after closing his shoe factory at 125 Summer Street, Boston. It was then that he pioneered the idea of subleasing space to other businesses. Instrumental in rebuilding the city after the Great Fire, Alonzo began leasing buildings in the city's downtown business district and subleasing the space to smaller businesses in need of office and manufacturing facilities.

Responding to the needs of the overall business community, Perry was often drawn beyond the realm of real estate. As gas lighting gave way to electricity, he

In the 1980s, A. W. Perry, Inc. assembled the block around the site of its original 1884 company office and developed 125 Summer Street, a 23-story, 463,000-square-foot first-class office building.

Alonzo W. Perry founded the company in 1884.

produced direct current that serviced a large share of Boston businesses. Early to recognize the potential in steam shipping, he acquired the Plant Line, a passenger service on the East Coast, which also carried immigrants to the United States from neighboring countries.

After World War I, Perry and his three sons, who had joined the business, focused on real estate investment. Acquiring a large number of properties in Boston and Rockland, the firm was among the largest taxpayers in both communities at that time. The company prospered as it contributed to the revival of Boston's economy after World War II. It built a tradition of service to developing businesses, originally catering to the shoe and leather manufacturing industries. Since Alonzo Perry's death in 1928, three generations of his family have managed the company, strictly adhering to his original, simple formula for success: "Establish and maintain enduring business relation-

ships by being personally involved in knowing and meeting the needs of each tenant."

Today, Perry continues to be a force in Boston and on the South Shore, focusing on the service and financial sectors in downtown and suburban locations, as well as technology and distribution industries on the South Shore. Since the early 1970s, Perry has been heavily involved in development and redevelopment of commercial and residential property. In 2001, continuing its long history of bringing industry and jobs to the Rockland area, the company completed its 200,000-square-foot One Technology Place, Rockland. This first-class office and laboratory facility is leased to Swiss pharmaceutical firm, Serono, Inc. for its North American Headquarters. This development is the first in Perry's new 200-acre section of South Shore Park, designed to meet the needs of today's technology-driven industries. Perry developed, owns and manages more than a dozen commercial properties in South Shore Park and other locations on the South Shore. It is also one of the South Shore's largest developers of residential property, planning and developing high-quality single-family subdivisions and creative communities, which respond to the needs of today's housing market.

In Boston, Perry has created properties that will have a long-term impact on the fabric of the city. In the 1980s, the company came full circle when it assembled the block around the site of its original 1884 company office and developed 125 Summer Street, a 23-story, 463,000-square-foot first-class office building. A new quality of Boston architecture is exemplified at 125 Summer Street—retaining original historic facades and incorporating many elements from its historic neighbors. In addition, the company has restored and operates several historic buildings including two that are

A. W. Perry, Inc. is perhaps most noted for its landmark building "The Berkeley at 420 Boylston," a six-story, 114,000-square-foot, 1906, Beaux Art structure which the company carefully restored in 1990. The building has been honored with several awards including the Building Owners and Managers Association-International's highest award, the International Office Building of the Year. It was the first building in Boston to be so honored.

listed on the *National Register of Historic Places*. In 1998, it completed the restoration of The Summer Exchange Building, which features one of the city's last remaining cast-iron facades, tying this property into the adjacent 101 Arch Street office complex. Perry is perhaps most noted for its landmark Berkeley at 420 Boylston Street, a six-story, 114,000-square- foot, 1906, "Beaux Art" structure, that the company carefully restored in 1990 and which was honored with several awards, including the Building Owners and Managers Association-International's highest award, the International Office Building of the Year. It

was the first building in Boston to be so honored.

A. W. Perry, Inc. continues to follow the example set by its founder, venturing into new uncharted territory. In 1996, its affiliate, Transit Realty Associates, LLC (TRA) won a contract with the Massachusetts Bay Transportation Authority (MBTA), the second largest property owner in Massachusetts, to "privatize" the MBTA's real estate department. Under this contract, TRA provides real estate asset management and consulting services for a portfolio containing over 2,000 parcels of land and 600 tenants.

Now under the management of the fourth generation of the Perry family, A. W. Perry, Inc. maintains its headquarters at Twenty Winthrop Square, the company's signature office building, renovated in the 1980s and known for its curved brick and limestone facade. In the new millennium, Perry is poised for continued portfolio growth and improvement, as it constantly strives to meet the needs of its tenants and clients, as well as the communities in which it conducts business.

In 2001, A. W. Perry, Inc. completed its 200,000-square-foot "One Technology Place, Rockland." This first-class office and laboratory facility is leased to Swiss pharmaceutical firm, Serono, Inc. for its North American Headquarters. The development is the first in Perry's new 200-acre section of South Shore Park, designed to meet the needs of today's technology-driven industries.

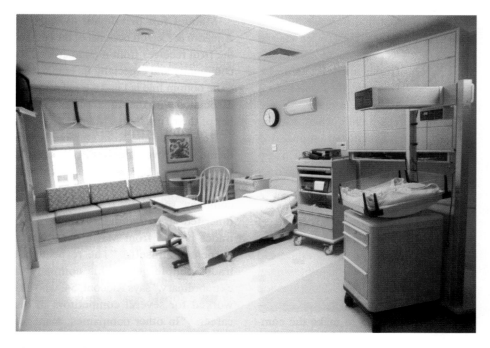

This is a view of a new labor, delivery and recovery room. This picture was taken just after CDH's new Childbirth Center opened and a few days before it was used for its first delivery.

George Hanson, a 53-year-old foreman, with the company since 1976. Hanson started as a labor steward for the unions. His job, among other things, was to make sure Aquadro & Cerruti didn't perform work that union men were supposed to do. Though Dick Aquadro saw Hanson as a thorn in his side at times, he also recognized Hanson's potential and gave him the opportunity to realize it. "Dad saw within him the ability to be a good foreman," says company President Richard D. (Rick) Aquadro.

Hanson acquired many engineering skills with Aquadro & Cerruti though he has no engineering degree. Unlike other places he had worked, Aquadro & Cerruti has been a learning experience, constantly presenting him with new intellectual challenges. "It's made my life a lot more interesting," says Hanson.

Forty-four year old Field Supervisor Dana Newell sums it up this way: "Other places hire your body and not your head—it's frustrating not to be listened to." Newell has been with the company 16 years, starting as a carpenter. At Aquadro & Cerruti, he feels like "part

of the family," and that the company has always respected his opinion.

Field Supervisor Pierre Lucas, 53, has been with Aquadro & Cerruti for 30 years. He has spent most of his professional life with the Aquadros, starting as an apprentice carpenter and "hanging on for the whole tour." Lucas stayed with Aquadro & Cerruti because of the support they give to workers who want to deliver a quality product to its customer. Where other firms might "leave you to the wolves," Aquadro & Cerruti backs up it workers. "It is easy to keep the quality of work up when you know the company is behind that," says Lucas.

Current President Rick Aquadro says it is this combination— of excellence and respect for people—that has made Aquadro & Cerruti successful. It is what he is most proud of in his family's business. "The company represents everything my family stands for: quality, fairness, and hard work," he says. "We have a tradition of strong values that has been passed down, just as the company itself was passed

down. People in the community see our name, and they know that," he adds.

Rick, 44, runs the company along with his cousins Robert J. (Bobby) Aquadro, 48 and Francis J. (Frank) Aquadro, 49. Bobby, Bob's son, is a project manager, and Frank, whose father is another of Mario's sons, is vice president. Together they are the third generation of a business that now employs an average of 50, and up to 150 people at a time—bringing in $20 to $30 million per year.

Though the office is no longer in Mario Aquadro's house, it is still in Northampton—on Texas Road—in an office built by the Aquadro's in 1960. Moving out of Northampton would be unthinkable. As the site of so many Aquadro & Cerruti buildings, the city is part of their lives and histories: it holds the schools they attended and later renovated; the churches they built and then worshiped in; and the parks they played in as children and expanded as adults.

Rick Aquadro gets particular pleasure passing the E. John Gare III parking garage in the city's downtown, a building which ameliorated the city's nagging parking problem and for which their architects won an award for design.

Three other Aquadro & Cerruti projects in Northampton were also recently honored: Northampton High School addition and renovations; Rogers Hall at Clarke School for the Deaf;

This sign welcomes people to the new Childbirth Center at Cooley Dickinson Hospital. (CDH)

The beginning stages of the Northampton parking garage. The garage was later renamed the E. John Gare III Parking Garage in memory of John Gare, a longtime local jeweler who was instumental in getting the garage built. John Gare died a few years after the garage opened.

Council as well as the advisory council for Smith Vocation Technical High School's Carpentry Program. Frank Aquadro is a board member of the Construction Industry Association of Western Massachusetts.

Rick Aquadro traces his family's philanthropic roots to his grandfather, who believed in hard work and a strong community. That made Rick and his cousins appreciate the advantages they had, which also included a strong family and a good community. "Now it's our time to give it back," he says.

As he looks to the future, Rick sees Aquadro & Cerruti growing in a controlled manner. The Aquadros take their time hiring new managers—they want people with a commitment to quality. If they grow too quickly or become too large, they might lose that commitment and they aren't willing to take that chance.

The E. John Gare III Parking Garage as seem at completion. The architects, Saski Associates, received a design award for this project.

and improvements to the People's Institute each received the city Historic Commission's Preservation Awards in May, honoring their enhancement of the city's architecture. In addition, in 1993, the Western Massachusetts chapter of the American Institute of Architects gave Aquadro & Cerruti its Built Environment Award recognizing its contribution to the construction industry for quality, responsible building.

For this reason, the present generation and the last, have made the community an important part of their lives, serving on boards and committees to better the city and contributing money to community organizations. Dick Aquadro has been chairman of the board for the Northampton Cooperative Bank for about 30 years, and served on the board of overseers for the Williston-Northampton School for a number of years in the 1960s. Bob Aquadro served on the boards of directors of several banks, including Shawmut Bank, from the late 1950s to the late 1980s. He also served on the board of trustees of the Cooley Dickinson Hospital for 15 years, was a corporator for Brightside for Families and Children of West Springfield for 12 years and is still a trustee of the Massachusetts Laborers' Health and Welfare Fund. Dick Manuel was a scoutmaster, town meeting member and volunteer fireman for many years, as well as a trustee of a local bank. He was also a management trustee of the Carpenter's Union Health and Welfare Fund, and is still a trustee of the state Laborers' Annuity Fund and a member of the local Carpenter's Apprentice Board.

Rick Aquadro serves on the boards of directors of the Northampton Young Men's Christian Association (YMCA), the People's Institute and is a member of Umass' Civil and Environmental Engineering Advisory

AU BON PAIN

In the spring of 1978, at Boston's historic Faneuil Hall Marketplace, businessman and Harvard graduate Louis Kane came across a bakery display showcasing a new line of ovens from the French manufacturer, Pavailler. Enchanted by the aroma of freshly baked bread and impressed by the quality of the product, Kane had a vision of baking wonderful, fresh French bread and making it available to commuters, tourists, shoppers, students, and residents throughout the city.

With a keen ability to discern the tastes and trends of American culture, Louis Kane quickly envisioned turning the public's increasing demand for fresh, quality food into a popular urban cafe offering "good, fast food for adults." After traveling to France to study baking methods and technology, Kane bought Au Bon Pain from Pavailler and opened bakeries in Faneuil Hall and two other Boston locations.

In his quest to nurture Boston's appetite for croissants and bread, Kane tried to run Au Bon Pain as a wholesale company much as its former French owners did. He imported French bakers to create an authentic French product but often

This Harvard Square location, one of Au Bon Pain's earliest, is an example of the many premium landmark sites which have welcomed the bakery café system.

Au Bon pain founder Louis I. Kane (1931–2002).

found himself running out of baked goods by late morning. Frustrated from losing money at first-rate retail locations, Kane was looking for ways to build the business when Ron Shaich, the owner of the Cookie Jar in Boston's Downtown Crossing, approached him. Unable to convince his customers to buy cookies before noon, Shaich asked Kane about the possibility of selling Au Bon Pain's croissants during the early morning hours. The business arrangement between Kane and Shaich

worked out well and, on February 11, 1981, the two officially created "Au Bon Pain Company, Inc."

From the beginning, Au Bon Pain has been guided by a passion for leadership, food, and hospitality. In the early '80s, the company established an innovative café manager-as-partner program that attracted the attention of restaurant business leaders and some of the country's foremost colleges and universities.

The menu items, from baked goods to sandwiches and salads, have always been special and distinctive. In 1981, Au Bon Pain led the industry in offering croissant-based sandwiches. During the late 1980s, Au Bon Pain was the first to offer sandwiches made with fresh-from-the-oven bread, premium meats, and specialty cheeses. In 1993, recognizing the growing popularity of specialty coffees, Au Bon Pain partnered with Boston-based Coffee Connection to develop its own custom-roasted blends. The company introduced its signature sourdough bagels in 1997. Over the years, the company's original product mix has grown to include menu choices that recognize the customers' desire for fresh, healthy alternatives that fit changing lifestyles and nutritional goals. Those items, in turn, have helped the company expand from offering only early morning items to featuring salads, soups, sandwiches, sweet baked goods, and specialty coffee drinks for all the hours after breakfast.

Au Bon Pain's focus on hospitality began with Louis Kane as he insisted his company do more than treat customers fairly and create a menu responsive to the customers' needs. He made sure it was easy for customers to tell company management what they liked and did not like about Au Bon Pain. And he supported the café team members' direct involvement in community activities such as Boston's annual "Walk for Hunger."

Louis Kane continued to influence the company's growth and culture until his passing in June 2000. His successor, Frank W. Guidara, assumed his leadership position with more than 25 years in the

restaurant and foodservice industry and expertise at developing restaurant businesses built on industry leadership, food, and hospitality. With his experience as president of Wolfgang Puck Food Company in Los Angeles and the prestigious Restaurant Associates in New York, Guidara is applying his proven leadership abilities to the task of managing and growing all facets of Au Bon Pain. Also critical to the leadership and success of today's new Au Bon Pain is the company's association with Restaurant Associates and The Compass Group of North America. Restaurant Associates is the owner of some of New York's finest restaurants and manager of premier food service accounts such as the Metropolitan Museum of Art, the Kennedy Center and Lincoln

Au Bon Pain President and CEO Frank Guidara and Revlon spokesperson Karen Duffy contribute to the feeding of over 45,000 volunteers and participants at the annual Revlon Run/Walk for Women's Cancer in New York City.

Center, and the U.S. Open tennis event as well as the U.S. Open in golf. In every case, detailed attention to quality, décor, and service is absolute. The multi-billion dollar Compass Group provides a level of support that has strengthened Au Bon Pain's employee programs, purchasing, and management.

The first major initiative under Guidara's leadership was to create a top-level management team by blending the best of Au Bon Pain's existing management with energetic and experienced senior restaurant leaders from outside the

company. Then he initiated the system-wide café relaunch that is transforming the cafés into lively, bustling urban marketplaces.

Featuring a contemporary French bakery café environment that is stimulating to the senses, the new café color scheme incorporates a Provencal blue taken from the woad flower that grows in Provence and a yellow which comes from the sunflowers that grow abundantly throughout France. New flooring mirrors the limestone flagstones of older French bakeries and comfortable banquettes provide for relaxed seating. With all its elements, the new Au Bon Pain décor is sensuous, stylish, and energetic.

An array of self-service options, including a bakery, coffee, sandwich, and soup stations, allow customers to select the menu item of their choice and move about quickly and easily. Au Bon Pain's continuing passion for food is expressed better than ever in its line of tasty baked goods, the addition of flavorful warm sandwiches, over 30 distinctive and nutritious soups, and more special salads than ever.

Hospitality is vital to the core Au Bon Pain values, and the new café design encourages café team members to interact more with their customers. With the new design, cafés can now more effectively serve time-sensitive customers during peak breakfast and lunch hours. By the same token, the cafés function equally well as a refuge during a busy day for those seeking a quieter break. In fact, Au

The new Au Bon Pain shown at New York City's La Guardia Airport is a stylishly seductive and abundant marketplace.

Bon Pain's exceptional and consistent hospitality is quickly becoming legendary among its core customers as well as others in the restaurant business.

The logical extension of the hospitality theme into the communities Au Bon Pain serves through direct café team member involvement continues as well. Au Bon Pain actively invests in charitable partnerships and employee volunteerism, all with an eye toward creating long-term impact for both the community and the company. Boston's Walk for Hunger and New York's Revlon Run/Walk for Women benefit from Au Bon Pain's sponsorship. The company is closely linked with America's Second Harvest across the United States with hunger walks in Chicago and Philadelphia—and with cities to be added in the near future.

Today there are over 240 Au Bon Pain bakery cafés at some of the most visible urban corners and crossroads, transportation centers, hotels, regional shopping malls, hospitals, and universities in the United States, Chile, the United Kingdom, Taiwan, Thailand, and South Korea, even though the company remains based in Boston.

With more than 3,000 employees, Au Bon Pain remains passionate about baking great bread and providing the best bakery café experience in the world. Every employee, at every level of the organization, is dedicated to delivering the same memorable experience that Louis Kane first envisioned more than 25 years ago.

BOSTON ACOUSTICS

Boston Acoustics' mission is to use its passion for sound to ensure that its customers always get the best performance and value in every product they make. Co-founded in 1979 by Andy Kotsatos, chairman, and Frank Reed, Boston Acoustics is a well-established performance and value leader in the audio industry. The company designs, manufactures, and markets high-performance speakers for use in home music and theater systems, after-market automotive systems, PC audio systems, and built-in systems.

Kotsatos and Reed met in 1968 while working for KLH Research & Development. In 1969, they joined Advent Corporation where Reed became vice president of sales and marketing and Kotsatos worked on specific design aspects of speakers. Working closely with Henry Kloss, Kotsatos "voiced" one of the great success stories of its era—the original Advent Loudspeaker. Kotsatos went on to design the highly successful Advent/2, Advent/3, and New Advent loudspeakers.

With a common belief concerning the makings of a successful audio firm, Kotsatos and Reed left Advent in 1978. Together they envisioned an enterprise committed to the design and manufacture of superior quality, competitively priced products, coupled with a retail distribution network possessing the technical expertise required to demonstrate high-performance audio product.

In 1979, Kotsatos and Reed joined forces to establish Boston Acoustics. Building upon their combined experience and complementary skills, the company has since grown to a 250-person operation, manufacturing over 200 products with worldwide distribution. During that time, Boston Acoustics has produced several products that have become classics in the audio industry, such as the legendary A40, a six-and-a-half-inch two-way bookshelf speaker. Boston Acoustics' dedicated workforce contributes significantly to the company's on-going stability and success. In fact, many of the company's original management and manufacturing personnel are still with the firm.

Sadly, in November of 1996, Frank Reed passed away. Mr. Kotsatos succeeded Reed as chairman of the board and chief executive officer. Today, Andy Kotsatos remains chairman of the board. In May 2002, Moses Gabbay was named chief executive officer, and Allan Evelyn became president. Moses first joined Boston Acoustics in 1981 as the vice president of engineering; he was elected to chief operating officer in 2000. Allan joined Boston Acoustics in November 2001 as vice president of marketing. He has also played an integral role in the growth and development of the audio industry over the past 25 years.

In 1997, the company made its first venture into the OEM (original equipment manufacturers) market with Gateway Computers. This agreement would present exciting new opportunities for Boston's expansion and lead to a profitable new business unit within the company—Multimedia Audio. Boston Acoustics' OEM relationship with Gateway continues to flourish today and is the driving force for new product development within the Multimedia Audio Group.

Boston announced its entry into the automotive OEM arena in 2002. Through a partnership with Visteon Corporation, the company will provide the Chrysler Group with premium audio systems for new vehicle lines. Much like the Gateway initiative five years earlier, the Chrysler project will provide a new channel for product development and distribution—adding a complementary business component to Boston's existing aftermarket car product division, which was launched in 1984.

Since 1984, Boston Acoustics has been a premier car audio manufacturer with innovative design and high-performance standards.

The company's design and engineering teams are engaged in the research and development of new products and materials, as well as manufacturing processes and improvement of existing products. Each of the company's products is engineered to deliver what is known as the Boston Sound™. All Boston systems, from the largest and most powerful home theater speakers to car audio components, speak in the same "voice."

Boston operates state-of-the-art automated driver manufacturing equipment, which produces units to extremely tight tolerances, greatly enhancing product sound quality and reliability. This gives the company unprecedented driver manufacturing capacity with unmatched unit-to-unit consistency.

In addition to sophisticated manufacturing techniques, such as advanced robotics and computerized quality testing, Boston Acoustics places equal significance on subjective measurements and real-world applications in the design of its products. Specifically, the ability to offer satisfying products time after time

Boston Acoustics' corporate headquarters located in Peabody, Massachusetts.

requires rigorous standards, extensive listening experience, and a full understanding of how customers actually use the products. Andy Kotsatos' words capture this discipline concisely, "It's easy to make one great speaker. The trick is to manufacture millions of them."

The company's distinctive in-house design capability has earned them numerous awards and citations. Year after year, Boston Acoustics products have earned prestigious awards from *AudioVideo International* magazine (a leading industry trade publication), the CEA's (Consumer Electronics Association's) Innovations Awards for design and engineering excellence, as well as many Best Buy, Editor's Choice, and Product of the Year recognitions from leading consumer and trade publications.

Extensive engineering resources have produced several new innovative technologies for Boston, such as its patented RadialVent® cooling, the acclaimed (and patented) aluminum VR® tweeter and the patented, acoustical tuning device, Amplitude Modification Device, (AMD™). These have produced dramatic improvements in the reproduction of sound for music and movies—Boston Acoustics never stops looking for new ways to enrich people's lives through sound.

Boston contributes to numerous charities related to music and sound, including the Boston Symphony, the

Boston Ballet, WGBH, and the Sound Recording Technology program at the University of Massachusetts, Lowell. They also make significant product donations to help schools such as the Science Discovery Museum.

In 2001, Boston Acoustics donated approximately $375,000 worth of multimedia products to the organization Gifts in Kind International, solely for the care of the ill, needy, infants and school children. It also makes donations to local food banks and shelter programs for homeless families such as Haven from Hunger in Peabody, and the Inn Between.

Finally, in memory of the lifelong pursuits of their late co-founder, Frank Reed, who believed in the American Dream and that education was key to achieving it, Boston Acoustics established the Francis L. Reed Scholarship Program. The Program awards up to $5,000 in scholarship money to eligible children of Boston Acoustics employees.

Boston Acoustics' corporate principles remain unchanged—an unwavering commitment to quality, value, and ease-of-use, working in harmony with the strength of its dealer network. After 24 years of innovative design and sound management, Boston Acoustics is solidly positioned as a well-respected market leader known for high-performance, high value products.

Boston Acoustics continues the rich tradition as a New England based loudspeaker manufacturer, providing a full line of audio products for the home.

C.H. POWELL COMPANY

In many ways the history of C. H. Powell Company is a reflection of the growth and changes in the economy of Massachusetts over the last 80 years. In providing its core services of international freight forwarding and customs clearance to exporters and importers since its founding in 1919, C.H. Powell Company has been a logistics provider in the global economy long before these terms came into common use. In March 1919, Charles H. Powell left his position as Foreign Freight Agent at Adams Express Company and set up his own business to facilitate and support international trade. In doing so, he established himself in a long line of entrepreneurs who had been responsible for the growth of Boston's shipping industry since colonial times. His original office at 88 Broad Street, with a view of Boston Harbor and close to the U.S. Customs House, accomodated Powell and five employees who saw to the details of freight forwarding in the export of merchandise and of customs house brokerage for the import of goods from other countries. One of these employees, Lillian Mackin, who had left Adams Express with Mr. Powell, played a significant role in establishing the new firm and would later become his wife.

The first customs house broker licensed in the Port of Boston, C.H. Powell Company soon assumed an international character with the opening of an office in Liverpool, England in 1925 to coordinate the shipping and storage of British wool for some of its Massachusetts accounts. The growth of the company continued in 1929 with the opening of an office at One Broadway in New York, allowing C.H. Powell to better serve its New England client base. By the 1930s New England was earning its reputation as the textile machinery capital of the world. This machinery, and subsequently its parts and related equipment, became a major export commodity for the company for the next 40 years. In the 1930s tanning materials and liquor were among the most significant imported commodities handled by the company.

A family business, back row, left to fight: Peter A. Geoffrey, Andrew F. Jr., Charles, Robert, and Steven. Front row, left to right: Peter H. Sr., Stephen, David, Andrew F., and Paul. Absent were Richard, Andrew H., and Benjamin.

During World War II, when there was little commercial demand for the services of freight forwarders and customs brokers, Mr. Powell was instrumental in setting up a cooperative in which forwarders condensed their efforts and worked as a group. He became known as the Dean of Freight Forwarders. After the War the company began to take on the character of a family business. Following his military service in World War II, Alfred Powell became the first member of the second generation to work for C.H. Powell, when he joined the company in 1946. Alfred was followed by John in 1951, Peter in 1959, and Paul in 1962, at which point all of the founder's son were active in what had truly become a family business.

During the 1950s Canadian lumber became a major import commodity for the firm. C.H. Powell handled shipments from Vancouver and Victoria, B.C., on the west coast of Canada, serving as port agents for vessels arriving in Boston via the Panama Canal. The lumber was shipped in bulk quantities and unloaded by hand at Castle Island upon arrival in Boston, then packaged and trucked to distributors. In the same decade C.H. Powell Company provided its international services to many of the major industrial firms in Massachusetts, among them Monsanto Company, Springfield; Norton Company, Worcester; and General Electric, Lynn. Upon the death of Charles Powell in 1958, Lillian Powell became president of the company and served actively and ably in this role into her eighties.

In concert with local, national and global economic development, the 1960s saw a watershed event in the growth of C.H. Powell Company. With the developing commercial viability of air freight as a service mode for international transportation C.H. Powell made a capital investment in a new enterprise providing air transportation services at Logan International Airport. Intercontinental Air Freight (Intercon) was the first company specializing in international air freight services to be located at Logan, and set the standard for the airfreight industry in Boston for many years. In addition to being the first customs broker at the airport, Inter-con was the first to operate a second shift to accommodate late arriving cargo, the first to operate an in-house computer system and the first to offer training in government regulations concerning international activities to its clients.

Powell's account base expanded to reflect the growth of the technology corridor along Route 128, including firms such as Polaroid Corporation, Honeywell Computer Systems, General Radio and The Foxboro Company. Intercon actively assisted Digital Equipment Corporation in the licensing and transport of its first overseas order. Now wholly owned by C.H. Powell Company, Inter-con has been in continuous operation in East Boston for over 40 years.

The '60s also saw the continuing exodus of manufacturing firms from Massachusetts and the rest of New England to the southeastern part of the country due to the availability of less expensive labor. Many of Powell's long-standing customers followed this pattern, especially in the textile machinery industry, with Massachusetts firms such as Crompton & Knowles, Parks-Cramer, Whitin Machine, Saco Lowell and Draper Corporation relocating their manufacturing facilities to North and South Carolina. While this trend had a negative impact on trade volume moving through the Port of Boston it also heightened the demand for trade-related services in the Southeast. In 1975 C.H. Powell Company opened offices in Baltimore, Charleston and Greer, South Carolina, expanding significantly beyond its Massachusetts base to meet this demand.

This period also saw the development of containerization as the standard mode for ocean-borne commerce. Related changes in labor rules and practices paved the way for third-party consolidation of

ocean shipments. C.H. Powell Company was one of the first firms in Boston to offer this service, an activity that it continues to provide today as the U.S. agent in the network of Damco Sea & Air, an international transportation company based in the Netherlands.

Throughout the 1960s and 1970s the import and export of consumer goods became a major factor in international trade and again Powell's roster of Massachusetts clients reflected this trend, including firms such as The Gillette Company, Ocean Spray, Franklin Sports, Spalding, Milton-Bradley and Parker Brothers. In 1973 C.H. Powell Company was a recipient of the Presidential "E" Award presented in recognition of significant contributions to the development of United States export trade.

Another significant transformation taking place during the '70s was the influx of third-generation family members into the firm. This both heightened the need for, and enhanced the ability of the company to further expand. Offices were added in Savannah (1984), Atlanta (1986), and Norfolk (1989). In the 1990s the company expanded further, opening offices in St. Louis, Los Angeles, Seattle, New Orleans, Chicago, Miami and Houston, becoming truly national in scope.

C.H. Powell Company headquarters, Westwood, Massachusetts.

While too numerous to name, (at one time or another 16 grandchildren of the founder have worked at the company) there are at present 10 third-generation and two fourth-generation family members working for the company, while Peter and Paul Powell remain active as CEO and CFO respectively.

C.H. Powell Company has a lengthy history of involvement in its industry from the local to the national level. Past and present employees have been active with the Boston Shipping Association, as well as with similar organizations at other ports, and Peter H. Powell has recently concluded two terms as the president of the industry's National Customs Brokers and Forwarders Association of America. The company has also contributed to the development of certain industry standards and its representatives are active participants in various government-industry forums.

While C.H. Powell Company looks to the future it remains proud of its past, proud of its family tradition and thankful to the many loyal and dedicated people who have contributed to its success since 1919.

DIGITAL FEDERAL CREDIT UNION

Digital Employees' Federal Credit Union was organized by Digital Equipment Corporation (DEC) in 1979. DEC, a fast-growing computer company, and at one time the state's largest employer, was looking to expand its list of employee benefits.

Unlike most financial service providers, credit unions are not-for-profit financial institutions cooperatively owned by their members. There are no stockholders. Members pool their savings, which are then loaned out to other members. Earnings after expenses are returned to the members as lower loan rates, higher savings rates, or in the way of free or low-fee services.

Their "people helping people philosophy" and democratic structure make them an attractive alternative to commercial banks and finance companies for millions of Americans. Credit unions have boards of directors made up of unpaid volunteers democratically elected by the mem-

Member Gary Miller demonstrates DCU's StreetWise Consumer Education Program Web site. He is one of thousands of members who used consumer advice on the site to negotiate better car prices.

Bill Rovington of the National Credit Union Administration (2nd from left) presents DCU's charter to John Mates, DCU's first president while Al Beatocci and Shel Davis look on.

bership. As with all credit unions, each member is allowed one vote regardless of the amount they have on deposit.

DCU, as it became known to most members, received its federal charter from the National Credit Union Administration in October 1979. On May 1, 1980 DCU opened for business in two DEC Maynard, Massachusetts facilities—Parker Street and the Mill (a former textile mill that housed DEC's headquarters). Ruth Williams of Westminster was the first mem-

ber, but by the end of the first month, DCU had 3,200 members and $2.7 million in assets.

DCU grew rapidly from its inception. By the end of 1983, DCU had over $122 million in assets. Access was important to DEC so it provided space for DCU in almost all of its facilities. By 1984 DCU had 20 branches inside DEC facilities in Massachusetts, New Hampshire, Vermont, Colorado, Arizona, and New Mexico.

In 1985 DCU moved its headquarters to 141 Parker Street in Maynard—its corporate home for the next 16 years. By this time, DCU offered its members a variety of financial services including auto loans, checking accounts, home equity loans, automated teller machines, and lines of credit. First mortgages began in 1986.

In the late 1980s, growing interest in personal computers replaced demand for DEC's mini-computers. As DEC closed many of its facilities, DCU was forced to close more than half of its on-site branches. DCU membership growth slowed dramatically.

The fall and winter of 1994-1995 proved to be a pivotal period in DCU's

DCU consolidated operations at this 83,000-square-foot facility in Marlborough, Massachusetts in October, 2001.

history. DCU introduced a large number of service improvements, new loan products, and convenient services for the membership.

The board and management, recognizing a growing credit union can provide more services and better value for members, approved a plan to expand service beyond DEC employees for the first time. By October, DCU added Quantum Corporation to its field of membership after Quantum acquired DEC data-storage operations in Shrewsbury, Massachusetts and Colorado Springs, Colorado. Over the next seven years, more than 400 companies would choose DCU for their employees.

DCU returned to a more traditional credit union philosophy after the 1994 board of director's election. A significant number of DCU fees were eliminated. In March 1995 DCU became the third credit union in the U.S. with a Web site—www.dcu.org. In April, the board named Carlo Cestra, as CEO/president. Cestra would lead DCU to dramatic growth in the coming years.

In 1995, DCU's board adopted a new mission statement—to be the primary financial institution of its members. Using

this as a rallying cry, the credit union improved many of its services and worked to give members even more options. By December, DCU was again growing.

In 1996, DCU introduced PC Branch online banking. Members quickly embraced the new service. By the middle of the following year, more than 26,000 members were active users. In 1997, DCU introduced Internet PC Branch—a web-based alternative. This service found even greater favor. By 2002, more than 54 percent (95,000) of DCU members were active users—among the highest percentage for any traditional financial institution.

DCU opened its first freestanding branch in Merrimack, New Hampshire in 1996, to better serve the families of DCU members and attract new sponsor companies. Over the next five years, DCU opened branches in Leominster, Littleton, and Marlborough, Massachusetts and in Hudson, New Hampshire.

In 1997, recognizing DCU's dramatic growth and high member satisfaction, the National Association of Federal Credit Unions named DCU Federal Credit Union of the Year. In 2001, Callahan & Associates, a credit union research and consulting firm, named DCU the fastest-growing credit union in America over the last five years.

DCU expanded its efforts to support the communities it served. In April 1996, it established the DCU Memorial Scholarship Program for graduating high school seniors. It began efforts to support Children's Hospital • Boston in 1998, raising $23,000 by year-end. By 2002, DCU had raised nearly $200,000 for children's charities. DCU also donates money to dozens of charitable causes in the communities it serves.

In 1998, Compaq Computer, Cabletron, and Intel acquired the remaining DEC business units, ending its 41 years as an independent business. DCU officially changed its name to Digital Federal Credit Union in 1999. By keeping the word digital, the credit union paid homage to its heritage for its long-time members while, for newer members, it described the high-tech financial institution DCU had become.

That same year, the board of directors defined a corporate vision for DCU—All members achieve financial well being. To attain this vision, DCU began to devote resources to unbiased financial and consumer education for its members. The StreetWise Consumer Education Program, introduced in 2001, was a direct result. It is designed to teach members money-saving ways to buy cars and homes, use financial services, protect privacy, and prevent fraud. The program won awards and praise throughout the credit union movement. In 2002, DCU also began actively promoting financial literacy among teens by teaching basic skills at area schools.

DCU consolidated its non-branch operations in 2001 at a new headquarters facility in Marlborough, Massachusetts. That facility currently houses more than 250 employees.

By 2002, DCU had grown to over $1.4 billion in assets making it the 25th largest of more than 10,000 American credit unions, and the largest in New England. It has 177,000 members and over 350 dedicated employees. DCU remains focused on improving the lives of its members.

EASTMAN GELATINE CORPORATION

Peabody, Massachusetts, a city rich in history, is the home of Eastman Gelatine Corporation. Eastman Gelatine facilities and predecessor firms have been part of that history for almost 190 years.

Settled as early as 1626, Peabody was often referred to as the "leather city" of the world. Tanneries were in operation before the American Revolution. By 1855, there were 27 leather-processing plants. The industrial section on Main Street was one of the largest known leather processing districts anywhere in the U.S. The large quantity and pure quality of the water in the city made it an ideal location for such an industry.

In 1817, a local citizen named Elijah Upton took advantage of Peabody's water resources and introduced glue manufacturing to the area. The glue plant was located on Washington Street at its present site, and was operated by the Upton family for over 80 years. The plant was almost totally demolished by a fire in late 1884, but rebuilt afterward. The American Glue Company purchased it, shortly before 1900. Glue was the only product made by the plant until 1908, when the company began manufacturing both edible and photographic gelatin. The addition of photographic gelatin was a natural one, since the only differences between glue and gelatin lie in their relative degrees of purity and physical properties. In addi-

Upton Glue Factory after the fire in November 1884.

tion, Peabody water was particularly suitable for the manufacturing of photographic gelatin due to its natural filtration through layers of sand and rock, and its mineral content.

During the 1920s George Eastman, founder of Eastman Kodak Company, was unhappy with the quality of the photographic gelatin that he was purchasing from external suppliers. When the American Glue Company liquidated in 1930, Kodak acquired the plant and the operation became a wholly owned subsidiary, known as Eastman Gelatine Corporation. This enabled George Eastman to have control over the quality of an ingredient, which was critical to the success of photographic film, his key product.

When George Eastman acquired the factory, he purchased a true turn-of-the-century property. Brick and stone buildings with soapstone and gravel roofs housed boilers, engines, pumps and steam radiators. Often the rooms used for drying gelatin were constructed with locally made bricks and flooring. A high picket fence surrounded the premises.

During the Great Depression that followed, the purchase of the glue company proved to be a great industrial boost for the city of Peabody. The company became a major local employer with as many as 350 employees on the payroll. It paid its property taxes ahead of time to help the city avoid borrowing money to meet its financial obligations in this difficult period.

The plant continued through the war years with many of its old processes and facilities in operation. In May 1954, five feet of water, caused by several days of steady rain, flooded Foster Street and the entire Peabody Square area in downtown Peabody, about one-half mile from Eastman Gelatine. At the same time, the nearby North River was at its maximum high-water level. Local fire departments and the Coast Guard were called in to evacuate local citizens. Fortunately, no lives were lost and the water receded. Company personnel participated in the clean-up and assisted businesses affected by the flood.

Eastman Gelatine has a long history of providing support to its host community. In June 1967, Eastman Gelatine leased land to the Peabody-Lynnfield YMCA for the construction of a gymnasium and office building. The company contributed land to Peabody for the construction of a new police station in 1978. In early 1980, Eastman Gelatine donated land to the North Shore Council of the Boy Scouts of America for their new offices. The George Peabody House, the birthplace of George Peabody, a wealthy businessman in wholesale dry goods and noted philanthropist in the area, was given to the city in 1986. In 1997, Eastman leased land to Peabody for the construction of a new municipal golf course.

Eastman Gelatine Corporation celebrated its 50th anniversary as part of the Eastman Kodak Company in 1980. In fact, it was Eastman Kodak's 100th

Eastman Gelatine Corporation in 1965.

anniversary during that same year.

The Eastman Gelatine facility has doubled in size over the years to its current 700,000 square-feet of production space in 40 buildings spread over 470 acres. In addition to manufacturing operations, the site contains a power plant, water treatment plant, wastewater treatment facility, research and development laboratory, quality control laboratory, engineering and maintenance departments, and administrative headquarters. More than 2-million gallons of water are pumped daily from approximately 400 water wells on Eastman's property. Also, the city of Peabody and Eastman Gelatine have a reciprocal arrangement for electrical power requirements.

The raw materials Eastman Gelatine originally used to make gelatin consisted of cattle leg bones and hide scraps of pigs, cows, and steers, which were unusable for leather. In order to loosen the hair from the hides and prepare them for the gelatin extraction process, it was necessary to put the hides in a lime solution. Hides and other trimmings are no longer used. Instead, the process begins with crushed, degreased, and dried cattle bones, a by-product of the U.S. meat packing industry.

The manufacturing process is initiated by soaking the gravel-sized bone pieces in dilute muriatic acid to remove inorganic phosphates in a soluble form. The phosphate mother liquid is treated with lime converting it to dicalcium phosphate, which is sold as a component for fertilizer and animal feed. The remaining solid, demineralized material, known as ossein, is placed in vats and exposed to a lime solution. The ossein is next washed and

Upton Glue factory in 1894.

Upton Glue factory in 1884.

treated with acid before gelatin is extracted by a series hot water soaks. The gelatin extract is filtered and passed through an evaporator to increase its concentration by removing water. The concentrated gelatin is chilled and set before being forced through nozzles to create "noodles." The "noodles" are air dried in a conveyor tunnel and form a brittle material, which is easily ground into a granular form and packaged in moisture-resistant containers.

The dry gelatin is sent by truck to Eastman Kodak Company in Rochester, New York for blending. It is then shipped to Kodak plants throughout the world for use in coating light-sensitive chemicals on

Dry rendered cattle bone as received from meat packers.

photographic film and paper to enable the reproduction of images in specific detail and color. Any dry gelatin that is not used by Kodak can be provided for pharmaceutical, edible, and other products. Liquid hydrolyzed gelatin can be supplied for edible products.

The philosophy of Eastman Gelatine Corporation is documented by its Vision statement as follows:
• We are a world class team—informed, adaptable, committed.
• We operate the world's safest plant. We are the healthiest people in industry. We protect and enhance the environment.
• We are the employer of choice.
• We supply diversified products and services with an emphasis on Photographic Gelatine. We are world leaders in our chosen technologies. We provide a competitive advantage to our customers through superior quality, outstanding delivery, and excellent financial performance.
• We are the supplier of choice.

The Vision statement sets company priorities for making decisions in consideration of people, safety, environment, quality, delivery, and cost. It provides exceptional direction for allocating resources and implementing programs. In summary, the Vision statement is the guiding light for Eastman Gelatine Corporation in any situation.

Eastman Gelatine has worked for many years to develop a family culture. There are many second and third generation family members presently employed by the company. Each employee is responsible for meeting specific goals each year relating to safety, product quality, and every other area of the business. Meeting the goals puts a great deal of responsibility in the hands of the individual. It adds up to having a highly-motivated work force. Employees are also involved in the community with the Peabody Chamber of Commerce, Citizens for Adequate Housing, the Peabody Babe Ruth League, Readers for the Peabody School System, the Peabody Education Council, the Peabody Science Fair, and the Peabody Council on Aging.

Eastman Gelatine Corporation is proud of its safety performance. It places great emphasis on providing a safe workplace for its employees. The company has been awarded the Gelatin Manufacturers Institute of America Safety Award for four different years since 1992.

It is also clear that Eastman Gelatine

Eastman Gelatine Corporation in 1998.

takes great care and pride in environmental activities. In 1989, a large and complicated project to reclaim company property where waste lime had been allowed to settle was awarded a prize from the American Consulting Engineers of New England. The land, as previously mentioned, was leased to the city and transformed into a municipal golf course. A multi-million dollar waste treatment plant addition was completed in 1998 to clean the discharge from the plant before it enters the local sewer system. In 2000, Eastman Gelatine was certified in accordance with the ISO-14001 environmental standard.

Manufacturing high quality product at Eastman Gelatine is critical to the manufacture of Kodak photographic films and papers. Kodak has presented many Quality First Supplier awards to Eastman Gelatine in recognition of their superb performance since 1990. In addition, Eastman Gelatine Corporation has been certified in accordance with the ISO-9002 quality standard since 1993.

The long-range plans are for Eastman Gelatine Corporation to complete a number of programs that will enable it to remain the employer of choice and the supplier of choice. Continuous attention will be given to employees' safety and meeting and/or exceeding environmental regulations. Quality improvement and customer satisfaction activities to provide invariant, high-quality gelatin to Eastman Kodak will be undertaken. There will be significant programs to convert waste streams, which are part of the company's disposal costs, into saleable by-products. Successful completion of these activities will ensure that Eastman Gelatine Corporation can look forward to doing business in Peabody for many years to come.

Chilled gelatin noodles about to be dried.

ELIASSEN GROUP, INC®

"When a collection of brilliant minds, hearts and talents come together ... expect a masterpiece" said an anonymous author. An appropriate quotation for the business started by Mona Eliassen in 1989.

Since graduating from Boston University, Ms. Eliassen found her talents were identifying the best information technology consultants and bringing them opportunities to enhance their skills. By doing this well, she helped many companies move critical projects to completion. She envisioned connecting companies and IT consultants and servicing those relationships for long-term success for all parties, including the staff providing that service.

As Ms. Eliassen approached her 30th birthday, she resigned from an established consulting group to take the risk of starting a firm with this vision. Within a year, with the combination of $20,000 in savings and $50,000 in borrowed money, she created Eliassen Group, Inc.® She reached out to businesses in search of high tech resources and the most qualified professionals available to get the job done.

The start was simple: a spare room in her home, a box of stationery, a new phone and a leased copier. Mona's sister, Lisa, joined her. They chose Leonardo da

Eliassen Group enjoys great feedback from their fun marketing campaign to attract companies and consultants.

Mona Eliassen, founder & CEO.

Vinci's *Mona Lisa* as their corporate symbol and later, their logo. They strived to be "the masters in the art of technology." It made sense to illustrate the importance of this with a true masterpiece.

Today, the award-winning Eliassen Group is headquartered in Wakefield, Massachusetts with offices in Cambridge, Massachusetts and Raleigh, North Carolina. The company has served more than 650 client companies, with specialized services including: contract services,

direct-hire, select services and partnership projects to deliver seamless IT solutions.

Eliassen Group commits to providing the best service possible to all its customers, both clients and consultants.

For clients, they provide just-in-time staffing to meet business objectives, by offering expert consultants. The service provided includes learning the client's needs beyond the technical requirements.

Responsiveness is critical in Eliassen's business. Eliassen responded when clients asked for a permanent staffing solution. Eliassen Group launched the Direct-Hire division to assist clients in this area. Similarly, Eliassen Select Services was created to serve large employers needing temporary staff in a cost-effective manner.

For consultants, Eliassen Group provides technical recruiters who act as career counselors. They strive to understand the needs and desired challenges of each consultant. Each recruiter specializes in a different technology and strives to operate with direct, honest feedback and high integrity. Eliassen's recruiting staff is built with committed career recruiters. Average recruiter tenure at Eliassen is more than five years.

In an industry that can experience high turnover, Ms. Eliassen has retained the quality staff that helped build the $70-million company. The loyalty is mutual. In the past two years, *Boston Magazine* included Eliassen Group in their "The Best Places to Work" survey. Workplace culture is important to the leadership at Eliassen Group.

Eliassen Group offers great benefits to its staff, including quality health and dental care. Also offered, weekly massages, health club membership reimbursement, three weeks vacation the first three years of employment, and more.

Employees enjoy an open work environment that allows them to perform their job more efficiently, including regular "town meetings" to communicate plans for the company. The culture encourages leadership and communication.

An important honor to Ms. Eliassen was her selection as *Incentive* magazine's

Eliassen Group's corporate headquarters in Wakefield, Massachusetts. Eliassen also has offices in Cambridge, MA and Raleigh, NC.

"Motivator of the Year" First Runner-Up. Ms. Eliassen shares the success of her company with her team.

An early reward by Ms. Eliassen was a trip to Paris to the Louvre to see the original *Mona Lisa*. In May 2000, Ms. Eliassen hosted her entire staff with a getaway cruise. Almost 100 people, and their guests, vacationed for three nights, visiting the Bahamas together.

Annual incentive opportunities continue to include get-away opportunities to tropical locations, like Aruba. An "Awards Banquet" is held annually to acknowledge hard work.

Eliassen Group also recognizes the importance of the support staff as members of the team.

Once a month, employees nominate eligible staff for going above-and-beyond the call of their position to assist the account executives and recruiters. Two names are drawn at random from the nominations for the "Masterpiece Award." The first place winner receives $500 and a premium parking space for the following month.

At the end of the year, one name is drawn from all the names nominated throughout the year for "Masterpiece of the Year" and a vacation valued at $2,500.

Ms. Eliassen is committed to community outreach and her employees created the Philanthropy Committee with her encouragement. Employees voluntarily deposit money from their paychecks to an account. Then the Philanthropy Committee reviews requests by staff members to support community outreach that is important to them and offers their financial support from this account. The support has more impact. An additional philanthropic effort is a paid day off for each employee to participate in a community service endeavor of their choosing, called Devote-A-Day.

Ms. Eliassen is considered a true pioneer as a woman entrepreneur. In 1998, she was included in the *Boston Business Journal's* "Top 40 Under 40" and chosen as a finalist for Ernst & Young's "Entrepreneur of the Year." She has since been inducted into the Women's Business "Hall of Fame." *Working Woman* magazine annually ranked Eliassen Group as one of the "Top 500 Women-Owned Businesses in America" since 1995. In 2001, *Boston Business Journal* listed the company first as the "Area's Largest Recruitment Firms."

Certified as a woman-owned business in Massachusetts since 1993, Mona Eliassen was ranked number eight of the "Top 100 Woman-Led Businesses in Massachusetts," based upon research compiled by The Center for Women's Leadership at Babson College and The Commonwealth Institute in 2002.

Eliassen Group has an infrastructure that allows them to deliver the best IT consultants to opportunities that enable them to grow. Clients receive talented individuals to effectively complete their goals. Eliassen staff holds the tools to provide the services in the best possible way.

Mona Eliassen has the enthusiasm and the vision to continue to build on her successes.

HERBERT H. LANDY INSURANCE AGENCY, INC.

In an industry designed for helping people, the Herbert H. Landy Insurance Agency, Inc. exemplifies the highest quality of friendly customer service and commitment. Founded by Herbert H. Landy in 1949, the Needham-based firm has provided errors and omissions insurance for professionals for more than five decades. Through affiliations with some of the leading insurance companies, Landy is the national administrator for programs that offer coverage to more than 30,000 accountants, realtors, appraisers, audiologists and other professionals across the United States.

In its second generation of management, the insurance agency has weathered some tough times, just like its founder. After graduating from high school in 1941, Herbert Landy attended Bentley College for Accounting and Finance in Waltham, Massachusetts. World War II interrupted his higher education, and he spent three years flying B-24s over Europe. After the war, he finished college and attended Northeastern University for his B.B.A. He received his master's in accounting and finance, with a minor in insurance, from Boston University in 1950.

While attending BU, Landy acquired his first insurance license and hit the

National headquarters, Herbert H. Landy Insurance Agency, Inc., 75 Second Avenue, Needham, Massachusetts.

Herbert H. Landy, chairman, Herbert H. Landy Insurance Agency, Inc.

streets selling general and auto insurance in 1949. "I worked seven days a week, canvassing businesses. I got half of the Sealy mattress account and six furniture stores." In February 1950, Helene Nelles became Landy's secretary and the second employee of the fledgling agency. She was the first in a long line of very satisfied Landy employees.

Herbert H. Landy Insurance Agency, Inc. opened its first office at 18 Tremont Street in Boston. In 1972, Landy relocated to Old City Hall, where the company remained until 1976. On the day following Thanksgiving 1976, Landy moved to Wellesley Office Park, merging its Old City Hall office and Belmont offices into one. The company's last move came on July 16, 1986, when the office was relocated to 75 Second Avenue at the Hillsite Office Building in Needham.

After its customers, the Landy agency continues to place its employees first. Landy's daughter, Betsy Magnuson, became president of the company on

January 1, 2002. Magnuson joined the company at the urging of her brother, Stephen Raskin, former CFO of Landy and now a part-time consultant to the agency.

Betsy carries on the Landy heritage of honoring commitments, to customers and employees. "People who work for Landy are like family," she says. Landy retirees return each year for the annual Christmas party and one group of retirees still meets each month for lunch. The company is dedicated to its employees, who in turn are dedicated to their customers. "We believe in the age-old adage, the customer is always right," says Magnuson, "and we teach our people to honor their commitments."

With a staff of up to 40 professionals dedicated to the profitable underwriting and distribution of insurance for professionals, Landy delivers significant advantages in risk selection, administration, agency-network management and product distribution. As a program manager, Landy works with insurance consumers, affinity groups and insurance companies, developing guides for risk selection premium structures and risk management, while providing the necessary administrative services and supporting the marketing and sales efforts of the national distribution network.

"Our long affiliation with the leading insurance companies has helped us to develop into a specialized organization, viewed as an industry leader in professional liability. This experience allows us to provide unique insight and value-added benefits not matched by other programs," according to Magnuson.

One benefit is customized software applications, designed by Landy's two in-house software programmers. "We don't buy canned software," says Magnuson. "We design it ourselves. An insurance company will tell us what they want, and we design it to meet their needs." Like her father, Magnuson keeps ahead of the technology curve and plans to "go paperless" by 2003. Landy is also looking for ways to improve its Web site and

Left to right: Gail Bellefontaine, assistant treasurer; William Garofalo, assistant vice president; Betsy Magnuson, president; Herbert II Landy, chairman; Joseph S. Flynn, vice president operation and business development; and Stephen Raskin, treasurer.

expand online opportunities for one-stop shopping.

In 2000 Landy launched its online professional liability program, which enables accountants, real estate brokers, CPA's, attorneys and audiologists to instantly receive full coverage in Landy's professional liability areas.

More than 20,000 accountants insure through Landy's award-winning accountants programs, which are endorsed by the Illinois, Oregon and Texas CPA societies. More than 7,000 Realtors in 50 states place their insurance through Landy; the National Association of Real Estate Appraisers, the National Association of Review Appraisers and Mortgage Underwriters and the International Real Estate Institute, endorse its appraiser's program.

Some of the changes that Herbert Landy and Betsy Magnuson have seen in the professional liability insurance industry include the "hard market" of the early 1980s, the Securities and Exchange Commission crisis, Y2K speculation and the current extended soft market. Advances in technology have affected the company in a positive manner. Both generations of Landy leaders are enthusiastic about technology, in particular the advance of

the Internet for applications and other transactions online. Betsy Magnuson credits Landy's consistently superior standing with its ability to implement those technological changes to improve customer service and product delivery.

Small insurance agencies are feeling the negative effects of the events of September 11. But Magnuson thinks Landy can weather the tough year without affecting the company's growth. "Lots of small agencies have folded, but we are very self-sufficient. We don't owe money

and we manage ourselves well."

Whatever the future brings for the tenacious insurance agency, Herbert Landy is convinced that success lies with more than making customers happy. The affable and generous Landy shares that success with his family and community. Plaques on his office wall give testimony to the company's generosity through programs like the Greater Boston Learning Center for Children and Northeastern University Huntington Society.

Herbert Landy was named in *Who's Who in Executive and Professionals* and received the first national award given by the National Society of Professional Accountants in 1987.

Now that he has more time for leisure, Herbert Landy is getting ready to embark on his 38th cruise with his wife Leah. He doesn't plan to retire anytime soon, and he's happy to share his formula for success. "Success is having a great family, friends, and great people to work with, and to work for." Herbert Landy's friendly formula ensures success for the next generation of Landy customers.

Left to right: Barbara Ferrell, claims and administration, 27 years with the agency; Nancy Daniels, supervisor, administrative support, 17 years with the agency; Ellen Bagley; and Betsy Magnuson, president.

JENZABAR, INC.

Jenzabar, Inc., based in Cambridge, Massachusetts, is the country's largest provider of computer software products devoted solely to running the business of higher education. The company, founded in 1998, has made a name for itself by not just offering technology solutions, but by going a further step, taking universities' systems from transaction-oriented to intelligence-oriented.

Jenzabar's central product is a concentric line of Internet technology products for universities, a virtual online community for administrators, faculty and students. Through the direction of the company's founder, Ling Chai, Jenzabar has created systems that build on the functionalities that all sectors of a university need. However, they have taken the product past basic data warehouses and data marts, allowing the system to "think" independently and help create solutions.

In a relatively short period of time Chai, also Jenzabar's president and chief operating officer, has created a company that is on the cutting-edge of its field; however, her path to reach success is, on its own, a story of true success.

In the spring of 1989, Beijing University counted Ling Chai among its graduate students in child psychology. China's Communist government had placed the 23-year-old Chai, elected president of her student government and then leader of the student dissidents, on its Most Wanted List. Her skills in organizing and exhorting students to protest marked her for execution. The movement of tanks onto the square effectively ended Chai's life as a Chinese citizen: after ten months spent in hiding, frequently in disguise, she allowed compatriots to nail her inside a shipping crate and smuggle her aboard a freighter bound for Hong Kong. Four days and five nights later, she arrived safely in that country, and traveled from there to France, and from there, with no resources and no knowledge of the English language, to the United States.

Upon arrival in this country in 1990, Chai enrolled in Princeton University's Master's Program in Public Affairs, a

Ling Chai, president and chief operating officer.

program created especially for political refugees. Recognized as an international spokeswoman for the Chinese Democracy Movement, she was twice nominated for the Nobel Peace Prize for her role in the Chinese students' pro-democracy efforts, and witnessed, in 1993, President Clinton's signing of the executive order according Most Favored Nation status to China.

After graduating from Princeton she established a career as a business consultant with Bain & Company, focusing on software computer systems companies and the emerging Internet industry. Subsequently, Chai earned her MBA from Harvard Business School. Her own student experiences in Tiananmen Square had convinced her of the necessity for free and open communication. Her industry experience, along with her student experience at Harvard, convinced her of the viability of establishing a new educational software technology company.

Jenzabar's corporate logo appears over the software development offices in Cambridge.

Jenzabar's corporate offices are located in Cambridge, on 17 Sellers Street.

Chai founded her IT start-up with $25,000 of her own savings. She secured start-up funding from several Bain & Company partners, from WebTV founder Steve Perlman, and from Paul Fireman, CEO of Reebok International, who characterized her business ideas as sound and her instincts as sharp. An additional $60 million in capital solidly established the new industry start-up.

Industry competition was fierce, with many well-funded rivals already enjoying the benefits of the burgeoning technology revolution. Jenzabar was student-focused, but soon learned its niche could be made by creating a product that centered around the administrators' needs.

In 2000, Jenzabar.com acquired four additional IT companies: CARS Information System, Computer Management and Development Services (CMDS), Quodata, and Campus America, to form Jenzabar, Inc. The newly acquired companies represented many years' experience in educational software development and management, and established branch offices in Cincinnati, Ohio; Hartford, Connecticut; Harrisonburg, Virginia;

Knoxville, Tennessee; and Ontario, California. A leading industry research group noted that Jenzabar.com's expansion into Jenzabar, Inc. created "a formidable entity dominating the small college IT marketplace."

Jenzabar.com's capabilities greatly expanded with the addition of the four new software companies, which had been previously dedicated to "back-office" operations such as admissions, registra-

Robert A. Maginn, chairman and CEO.

tion, enrollment, human resources, finance, and institutional advancement. Users could now integrate services related to prospective students (admissions), enrolled students (registration, financial aid, assisted learning, e-learning, web communication and collaboration), and alumni (fundraising campaigns and career opportunities). Practical applications included the joining of previously segmented services: students, through "one-stop" registration, could now plan a schedule of classes, register, pay their bill, access homepages for new classes, review course syllabi and assignments, and even receive e-mail greetings from teachers, all in one place.

In early 2001, Ling Chai recruited Robert A. Maginn, a senior partner and director at Bain & Company, to join the company. Since assuming the role of chairman and CEO, Maginn has positioned Jenzabar, Inc. to revolutionize the higher education software market.

Today, Jenzabar is in the process of launching I-cubed, a new program that brings together the three I's: intelligent, integrated and internet. I-cubed allows for universities to provide their students with a unique user-centric experience, seamlessly merging all the processes and relevant information that a student needs into one point of contact. The goal is to produce a program that allows not only for data-input, but a program that can actually assist with the decision-making process of the user.

The new product strategy for I-cubed includes three areas: Jenzabar's internet campus, virtual classroom and business intelligence data mart strategies. The Internet campus is where the intelligence and integration are brought together, resulting in a personalized portlet-based system.

Jenzabar is continually looking to the future. Its moniker is taken from the Mandarin word that means the best and the brightest. The company's team, led by Chai, will continue to strive to offer new and groundbreaking technological solutions worthy of the name.

KEANE, INC.

Keane, Inc. (AMEX: KEA) helps Global 2000 companies and government agencies to plan, build, manage and rationalize application software through its Business Consulting, Application Development and Integration, Application Development and Management (ADM) Outsourcing, and Applications Rationalization. The company delivers its services with world-class processes, management disciplines, and performance metrics via an integrated network of branch offices in North America and the United Kingdom, and Advanced Development Centers (ADCs) in the United States, Canada, and India. In addition to helping its customers, the company supports the communities in which it does business with an annual giving campaign, charitable contributions and involvement in a variety of community groups and activities.

Headquartered in Boston, Massachusetts, Keane, Inc. emerged from a technical revolution, which transformed the country and the Commonwealth of Massachusetts. In the 1960s, a new generation of multi-purpose computers began to flood the market, and hardware vendors grew rapidly. Data processing became one of the fastest growing professions in the state, yet few people understood the potential of this new technology.

In 1965, Chairman John F. Keane founded John F. Keane Associates, Inc. above Nichols Donut Shoppe in Hingham, Massachusetts. Keane helped businesses to bridge the gap between the power of technology and their ability to harness that technology. The company opened a series of offices in close proximity to clients, and garnered a reputation as a technically-savvy organization filled with "shirt-sleeve" consultants who rolled up their sleeves and did the tough jobs. In 1970, the company went public and changed its name to Keane Associates, Inc.

During this time, companies moved beyond financial-oriented applications and began automating functions such as purchasing, production and inven-

tory control. As a result, applications throughout many departments became functionally interdependent, and the process of developing systems to meet increasingly complex specifications became more difficult. In order to distinguish itself, through more reliable delivery—in this highly competitive environment—the company conducted post-mortems on a variety of projects, some successful, some not, to develop a clear project management approach. The resulting process, Productivity Management, became the foundation of all of Keane's application development and outsourcing methodologies.

In 1975, Keane established its Healthcare Solutions Division, then called KeaMed Hospital Systems, with its first acquisition. Keane has successfully grown its healthcare business through both internal means and acquisitions, and now offers a complete line of financial, patient care, and clinical applications for hospitals and long-term care facilities.

CEO Brian T. Keane and his father stand in front of Keane's current headquarters at 10 City Square in Boston.

At the end of the 1970s, the company changed its name to Keane, Inc.

After the company's first and only operating loss in the second quarter of 1986, Keane refocused efforts on its core IT services business, and immediately returned to profitability. It was at this time that the company began codifying its best practices and organizational experience in the management of applications within Keane's Application Management Methodology (AMM).

As the complexities of newer technology intensified, the need became clear for a standardized approach to developing business software. In order to increase the reliability and predictability of these development projects, Keane crystallized its approach through a series of Frameworks life cycle methodologies. Based on Productivity Management, these world-class methodologies can be used in a variety of technical environments. Riding a wave of success, Keane ended the 1980s as one of *Forbes'* top 200 small U.S. companies, and since then has been recognized by *Fortune* magazine, *Business Week*, *Investor's Business Daily* and *The Boston Globe* for its financial performance and management.

As Massachusetts and the nation experienced an economic downturn in the early 1990s, Keane made quantum leaps in expanding market share and geographic coverage through acquisitions. These acquisitions expanded Keane's network of branch offices across the country and added to Keane's line of healthcare products. A few years later, Keane Federal Systems was founded to meet the needs of Keane's public sector clients. With customers in over 50 government agencies, Federal Systems brings Keane's services and commercial business practices to the public sector.

By the late 1990s, Keane emerged as a premier provider for the Year 2000 "millennium bug" with its Resolve 2000 service. Keane also entered the European marketplace with Keane Ltd and launched its business consulting practice with the acquisition of Bricker & Associates, now called Keane Consulting Group. Based on Keane's growth and strong financial performance, Keane closed the 1990s by being named *The Boston Globe's* "Company of the Year" in its annual "Globe 100" listing. Also, Brian Keane was named CEO as the company began its 35th year in business.

As Keane entered the new millenium, the new CEO and management team focused the company's strategy around building a leadership position in ADM Outsourcing. This flagship offering was based upon the application management experience that Keane had developed from over 30 years of provider IT solutions for Global 2000 customers. To date, Keane has been recognized as the leading application outsourcing vendor in North America by industry analysts such as GarnterGroup and Giga Information Group. In addition, Keane has demon-

From old to new – The company's first office above Nichols Donut Shoppe and the new 95,000-square-foot headquarters set to open in January 2003.

strated great success in selling new outsourcing business, which accounted for more than 50 percent of 2001 revenue. Recurring revenue from these long-term outsourcing projects has enabled Keane to outperform, on a financial basis, most of the IT services industry.

Currently, Keane is also capitalizing on the economic downturn to gain market share and add delivery capability. In 2001, Keane acquired hundreds of new customers and enhanced its critical mass through the acquisition of Metro Information Services. In 2002, Keane strengthened its delivery model and value proposition in outsourcing via its acquisition of SignalTree Solutions, now known as Keane India.

Keane India provides customers with access to world-class offshore capabilities through a proven domestic partner at lower risk and with enhanced flexibility. In addition, Keane can now offer its customers the economic advantage of a global delivery model, enabling them to fluidly allocate work between a variety of delivery options including on-site, off-site, near-shore (Halifax, Nova Scotia), and offshore.

Most recently, Keane introduced its new Applications Rationalization service offering, which is designed to help companies identify and eliminate information systems with redundant functionality,

Keane, Inc. supports the communities in which it does business. Shown at the announcement of a $1 million gift to the Charlestown Boys & Girls Club is Marilyn Keane, CEO Brian Keane and Chairman John Keane.

non-core technologies, or that have reached the end of their useful lives as valuable assets. Applications Rationalization will enable Keane's customers to significantly reduce their costs, while increasing the flexibility and scalability of their applications. This in turn will allow companies to improve financial results or increase capital budgets to invest in new information technology.

Throughout its 37-year history, Keane has prospered by continuously enhancing its services to meet the changing needs of its customers. The company has grown from a small group of 12 consultants to over 8,000, based in over 45 branch offices in North America, Europe and India. Early next year, the corporate headquarters, which began over a dough-

Founder and Chairman John F. Keane working the phones in the early days of the company.

nut shop, will move into a new 95,000-square-foot facility at Gateway Center in Boston.

Since 1965, Keane has captured and built on its organizational experiences to help its customers prepare for the challenges of each new horizon. That is the foundation for its vision and unwavering commitment to customer satisfaction.

Keane's vision is to be recognized as one of the world's great information technology (IT) services firms by its customers, employees, and shareholders. The foundation of Keane's management philosophy is encapsulated within the following Guiding Principles.

Critical Mass—In the IT services industry, achieving critical mass is a key driver of profitability because it allows busuinesses to reduce SG&A cost as a percentage of revenue. Keane seeks critical mass at the company, business unit, account, and project levels.

Recurring Revenue & Repeat Business—Keane focuses on sustaining consistent levels of revenue growth by establishing long-term business arrangements with repeat clients.

Geographic Focus—Keane desires to maintain a high degree of geographic focus to maximize critical mass and to not dilute its efforts or investments. Keane strives to be one of the top three providers in each of the markets it serves.

Business Focus—Keane believes in the merits of focusing on only a few, synergistic business areas where it has or can achieve industry leadership.

Teamwork/Boundaryless Organization—To achieve its potential, it is essential to operate as one Keane team. All Keane employees are empowered to tap into any part of the Keane organization, regardless of geographic or business unit boundaries, to pull together the best solutions for their customers.

Operational Excellence—Keane will continue to pursue a high degree of operational excellence in how they run their business, and all employees are encouraged and expected to foster a culture of continuous improvement in everything they do.

Acquisitions—Keane recognizes that the IT services industry is poised for consolidation and anticipates using acquisitions as a cost-effective means to reduce the cycle time of gaining critical mass and enhancing cash flow.

Proactive Communications—The Company develops strong relationships with customers, employees, and shareholders through frequent, straightforward communications.

Commitment to Core Values—Keane conducts business and manages its organization in accordance with five fundamental core values. These core values are: Respect for the Individual, Commitment to Client Success, Achievement through Teamwork, Integrity, and Drive to Continuously Improve.

Invest in People & Culture—The Company is committed to building and propagating its client-focused culture through the training and development of its technical, sales, and managerial employees.

HMEA

HMEA believes in the power of dreams, not the limitations of disability. The organization provides services to over 1,000 individuals and families in 110 communities in central and eastern Massachusetts to help them achieve their highest potential. People with disabilities have the same dreams as everyone else—of satisfying work, of strong and loving relationships, of security and of respect. HMEA supports people throughout their lifetime to learn, work, and contribute to their communities as active and productive members. The service area is broad, but the mission is narrowly focused on people who face significant challenges from developmental disabilities, including autism.

Originally incorporated in 1961, the organization was first known as Wrentham Research Foundation. Located on the grounds of Wrentham State School in southeastern Massachusetts, its primary mission was to conduct research in the field of mental retardation. Studies included prevention, treatment, best practices and staff training. With the enactment of Chapter 766 in 1972, the state law requiring education for all children regardless of disability—special education services became its primary focus. The agency assisted public schools in

Brothers Michael and Matthew have benefited from Early Intervention. Services also include consultation to parents and schools, and in-home supports for children with autism and other developmental disabilities.

Eric Franke suffered a traumatic injury at age 18 which left him unable to walk or talk and with impaired cognition. Shown here at the Massachusetts State House in Boston winning an award for the courage demonstrated in overcoming these obstacles. Eric leases his own apartment and works out regularly at the YMCA. Like many people supported by HMEA, Eric gives back to his community by volunteering, most recently in the annual "Y" fundraiser. He has started a recycling business and hopes to share profits with co-workers.

developing appropriate programs and directly provided services to children on the grounds of the institution.

In 1982, the agency relocated to Franklin, Massachusetts and was renamed Horace Mann Educational Associates (HMEA) after the renowned educator who was born in Franklin. As secretary of the newly formed Massachusetts Board of Education in 1837, he tried to ensure a free public education to many more children than were being educated. He also began some of the first teacher training schools. "Be ashamed to die until you have achieved something for mankind" was an expression of Horace Mann, and the board president felt that it was especially appropriate for a nonprofit organization. The agency became a pioneer in the development of supports for adults who face significant challenges.

Today HMEA offers services for every age level. HMEA is a Specialty Early Intervention provider for children with autism from birth to age three. Services are educational and are made available in the family's home. These services continue as the child begins a pre-school program and then enters public school. HMEA staff provides clinical and educational services both in school and in the family's home, with the goal of increasing language and social interactions and decreasing inappropriate behaviors so that the child can be successful at his/her grade level. HMEA

also provides transitional services to any special needs student ages 16 to 22 who needs help with career development and community inclusion. Services are funded through local school systems.

Adults can attend a variety of day programs, based on their needs and preferences. Options range from Day Habilitation programs with nursing and therapy services to programs that secure competitive employment. People can choose from a variety of residential options as well, including group homes with 24-hour support or living in their own apartments with intermittent supports.

Other programs help families to increase their own caregiving capacity by securing services and developing advocacy skills. Family Support programs serve families whose children face complex medical issues; support elder caregivers, or families who face multiple challenges.

All services are designed to promote independence, respect, productive employment and civic involvement. HMEA's core values are choice and control— without them it is not possible to have hopes and dreams for a better future.

ROCHE BROS., SUDBURY FARMS SUPERMARKETS

On October 16, 1952 an event took place that would have a profound effect upon thousands of Massachusetts residents in the years to come.

Before the first Roche Bros. Supermarket took shape, two brothers, Pat and Bud sat with their family and asked a vital question: "What would make us different and better than any other supermarket?" The answer was based on the Roche family values, which were instilled by their parents, P.J. and Ellen. The philosophy of Roche Bros. Supermarkets is also a way of doing business, which is still followed today: Treat each customer like one of the family.

Roche Bros. Meat Market opened its doors that autumn day in Roslindale, and featured the slogan: "No Better Meats Sold Anywhere." In 1957, groceries were soon added to the 450-square-foot store, and Roche Bros. Supermarket became a major component of the Roslindale business community.

Founders Pat and Bud Roche never could have predicted that this opening would be the beginning of one of the most respected family-owned supermarket chains in the United States. They wanted their store to be different and better than any of the meat markets and grocery stores around—they accomplished this by

Roslindale Square, October 1952.

employing thousands of associates and serving hundreds of thousands of satisfied shoppers in the Greater Boston Metropolitan area.

With a focus on fresh meats, the supermarket in Roslindale quickly earned the reputation for excellent food and outstanding service. Every shopper knew that Pat and Bud Roche would always be found in their store; and could be counted on to contribute to charitable and school groups throughout the community.

Pat and Bud strictly adhered to what the family planned as a business operating profile. Customers recognized the Roche brother's dedication to their supermarket, and as a result, Roche Bros. built a strong core of repeat customers. What became evident was that these were loyal shoppers, who truly felt like they were members of the Roche Bros. family.

As a result of their success, Pat and Bud Roche took what began as one supermarket and two associates, and started adding stores as more and more shoppers traveled greater distances to "shop at Roche Bros." People would constantly ask when a Roche Bros. Supermarket was going to open in their town.

The second Roche Bros. Supermarket opened in 1959 in Needham, on the corner of Chestnut Street and Great Plain Avenue. With over 27,000 square-feet in this store alone, Roche Bros. Supermarket was determined to meet the prices of popular chains "head on," something never before conceived in a small store operation.

The 1967 grand opening of the 17,000

Roslindale store opening, October 16, 1952. Left to right: Pat Roche, parents P.J. and Ellen, and Bud Roche.

Founders Pat and Bud Roche.

square-foot West Roxbury Supermarket on Centre Street marked the company's personal involvement with the West Roxbury community. This commitment would continue to strengthen over the next 35 years and serve as a benchmark for other businesses to follow.

Pat and Bud enjoyed a personal highlight in 1970 as they broke ground for their new Westwood store. For the first time, a Roche Bros. Supermarket incorporated department concepts into one store. A bakery, florist and restaurant were new features that drew more and more shoppers every week. This distinctive design became the standard for Roche Bros. Supermarkets during the following decades.

Taking on new challenges became a part of everyday business life, as the company decided it was time to take a major step away from its local focus. The brothers looked beyond the Needham, West Roxbury, and Westwood areas, bringing the Roche Bros. way of doing business to new towns and shoppers. By 1981, Roche Bros. had expanded to five locations, opening the Natick store in 1974 and the Wellesley store in 1981.

In a bold departure from conventional type supermarkets, Bud and Pat opened their first Sudbury Farms store in 1980. This new type of supermarket pioneered unique experiences in personal service, and offered an incredible selection of fresh and prepared foods that had never been available in a supermarket setting. Sudbury Farms featured one of the largest bulk produce departments, a deli kitchen with a large variety of homemade quality entrees and side dishes, and a fresh fish department with the exclusive rights to sell Foley Fish—a brand which had only been available in the finest restaurants in the United States. For the first time, "the taste of homemade goodness" enticed an ever-increasing number of shoppers to Sudbury Farms. The response was truly positive, causing Roche Bros. to incorporate concepts like salad bars and prepared foods into all of its stores. The second

Left to right: Jay, Rick, and Ed Roche (second generation of ownership).

Sudbury Farms Supermarket opened in Randolph in 1983, followed by Needham in 1990. Sudbury Farms continues to serve as a model for the food industry for the development of its "all natural" supermarkets.

In 1988 the Millis store was built, which included all of the best features of the other stores and some new concepts as well. The Millis Roche Bros. featured the food court, an exciting, specialized department where hot and cold prepared foods were sold. The success of this store encouraged the management team to enter fresh territory. Looking at the expanding population along the Route 495 corridor, Roche Bros. opened a new 43,000-square-foot store in Bridgewater in 1992 followed by a 45,000-square-foot supermarket in Norton in 1993. Looking to the north of Boston, Roche Bros. opened a 30,000-square-foot store in Acton in 1995. With food selections and service never before offered along this stretch of Route 2, Acton is now a destination for shoppers from miles around. Boston's South Shore, one of the most competitive areas for supermarkets, posed one of Pat and Buds' greatest challenges. Opening in an area dominated by major chains, Roche Bros. built a state-of-the-art supermarket in the city of Quincy in 1996. It included a bank, dry cleaner and video store. The new Roche Bros. Quincy Marketplace became an immediate favorite, and continues to build a loyal group of shoppers.

Throughout the years, the philosophy of doing business hasn't changed. A key factor in the success of Roche Bros. Supermarkets is the ability of the owners and management team to keep talking and listening directly to the customers. This enables Roche Bros. to quickly detect changing moods, needs for new products, or shifts in purchasing trends. This strong customer contact sent a powerful message to the Roche family— the customer

West Roxbury produce department.

is looking for quality home-style prepared foods that were ready to enjoy. Burning a candle at both ends, a working couple can always use a little help, and Roche Bros. is always there with a warm meal.

As the year 2001 approached, plans for two new stores were underway. Burlington opened in December, bringing shoppers north of Boston a whole new shopping experience. A world of prepared foods, from sushi and gourmet grilled vegetables to magnificent tenderloins and crusty-bread bakery, began to draw customers from towns near and far. Burlington is now a food shopping experience sought-after by thousands of metro north residents.

Always remembering their roots, the Roche Family knew that the original West Roxbury location was no longer meeting the needs of the community. Continuing the family's dedication to strengthen the community, Roche Bros. opened the new 46,000-square-foot West Roxbury Supermarket in February 2002, a totally innovative supermarket, just blocks from their original store. Opened by Thomas M. Menino, Mayor of Boston, and noted as a dynamic step for the revitalization of West Roxbury, shoppers entering the store

were immediately impressed by the dazzling departments. Specially prepared food and chefs daily selections now gave families the possibility of selecting and individualizing meals. The choices of Angus beef, natural lamb, pork, veal, and chicken, along with Foley Fish, allow shoppers to prepare the best quality foods for their families. When shoppers enter the store, they see a field of "just picked" produce, and discover wonderful treats in the fresh pastry department. Shoppers find an irresistible world of food choices to explore.

With the beginning the new millennium, Roche Bros. made the transition to the second generation of family ownership. Pat's sons, Ed and Rick, and Bud's son Jay, assumed the leadership positions of the family owned supermarket. Today the combined company of Roche Bros. and Sudbury Farms Supermarkets is strengthened by the second generation. From one generation to the next, the family values continue: Loyalty, honesty and caring for each other. Ed, Rick and Jay proudly share the family commitment to their customers, associates and communities.

The Roche Bros. reputation for excellence is a hallmark shared by every associate.

A great energy comes from all associates, as they share the commitment that every individual who works with them and each person who shops at Roche Bros. and Sudbury Farms are to be treated as one of the family. Roche Bros. provides a major source of employment for the communities in which they operate—some corporate level associates began their career as part-time high school employees.

What marks Roche Bros. as different from other companies is the loyalty and dedication shown by their associates. As a result, in 1985, the Diamond Decade Club was created. The Annual Diamond Decade Club Dinner honors the commitment of Roche Bros. associates who have been with the company for 20 years. There is also a Service Awards Program recognizing associates who have been part of the Roche Bros. family for each five years of service.

A College Scholarship Program was created at Roche Bros. in 1990. Its goal is to encourage associates and their children to further their education and to attain their academic and professional goals. Through tuition reimbursement, qualifying associates are able to attend college level courses, which serve to enrich their professional and personal lives.

Pat and Bud Roche have set such a high standard for charity and community involvement, which remain respected and unequaled throughout the Boston area. Beginning in 1979, and continuing to this day, Roche Bros. supports the Senior Citizen's Bus in Needham. They participate in July 4th parades in their communities; donate to the local food banks and pantries; contribute to countless local charities, PTA's, religious organizations, along with school and town sports groups. Pat and Bud personally give resources and inspiration to the Catholic Schools Foundation; The Ireland Fund; Habitat for Humanity; and the Roche Family Community Center in West Roxbury. Separately, Pat strongly supports Boston College and Catholic Charities while Bud gives to the Brain Tumor

West Roxbury store opened in February, 2002.

Society; Charles River ARC; and Stonehill College.

Roche Bros. Supermarkets make it a point to give back as much as possible because the family understands the importance of building stronger, more vital communities.

At Roche Bros. and Sudbury Farms, the emphasis on personal service equals the quest to present the highest quality foods throughout each supermarket.

Families always look forward to shopping at Roche Bros., fully aware that each new department is created to make their visit enjoyable and rewarding. Exciting food courts present an ever-expanding world of choices meant to satisfy every taste. Store decors are thoughtfully planned, and food selections constantly changed to reflect the customer's desires for new, different and delicious foods.

In each supermarket, shoppers enjoy the convenience of Roche Bros. party planning service— Creative Entertaining. Equal to the finest catering services, Creative Entertaining offers complete personal and corporate catering for any occasion and any size gathering. Every catered event is given personal attention as requested by the customer. As a compliment to Creative Entertaining, Roche Bros. florist department adds the perfect touch with everything from simple floral arrangements to elaborate wedding centerpieces. Every aspect of an event is designed specifically for the individual customer.

With the opening of a new store in West Roxbury and a new location in Burlington during the past year, the company now has a total of 11 Roche Bros. and three Sudbury Farms Supermarkets, providing an answer for consumers who constantly ask "when is Roche Bros. moving to my town?"

As the company celebrates its 50th anniversary, Roche Bros. has expanded to many communities across Massa-chusetts, and proudly has a family over 3,500 members strong. Roche Bros. Supermarkets can be found in Acton, Bridgewater, Burlington, Millis, Natick, Needham, Norton, Quincy, Wellesley, West Roxbury and Westwood and three Sudbury Farms Supermarkets in Needham, Randolph and Sudbury.

For half a century, everyone at Roche Bros. has continued to hold fast to Pat and Bud's "golden rule" philosophy, which guided their first supermarket in Roslindale onto the path of success. Today Ed, Rick and Jay Roche, the management team and associates work confidently to strengthen the building blocks of the future with fresh ideas and an innovative spirit. The Roche Bros. commitment to family values and customer service remains vibrant, helping to accomplish the original goal of being "a better place to shop." Simply stated, yet rich in meaning: "Family values make the difference."

SPRINGFIELD TECHNICAL COMMUNITY COLLEGE

Much of the history of Massachusetts, from the village militia training in the 1600s to information technology and photonics, has passed through this 55-acre site on a bluff overlooking the Connecticut River. From the historic Springfield Armory to the campus of the most comprehensive community college in New England, these grounds have been an important source of innovations and economic developments.

Formalized by an Act of Congress in 1794, George Washington's approval of this site as the first national armory created a manufacturing point for weapons, from muskets to the famed Springfield Rifle, to the M1 Garand Rifle, for the next 174 years.

Improvements and innovations in manufacturing processes conceived at the Armory led to its recognition as a national mechanical engineering landmark. Thomas Blanchard did much of the early work for his famous lathe at Springfield Armory. The techniques used for manufacturing irregularly shaped parts for rifles eventually led to the development of mass production, used in producing consumer goods, and expanding the U.S. economy.

Experienced Armory employees, with the knowledge of technical innovations used here moved throughout the region, founding or influencing other companies. The Connecticut River valley, from southern Connecticut into Vermont, came to be seen as a precision corridor. Companies such as Remington, Smith & Wesson, and even Cadillac and Rolls Royce all benefited to some extent from Armory expertise.

In 1843 when Henry Wadsworth Longfellow was touring the area, he wrote *The Arsenal at Springfield* to praise education over war. A visitor in the late 1840s described the "large and handsome buildings" surrounding the spacious treed quadrangle as "appearing like the buildings of a college." The grounds were landscaped in the 1850s by commanding officer Major James W. Ripley and surrounded by an ornate fence cast from iron

The 55-acre Springfield Armory National Historic Site, including the campus of Springfield Technical Community College, with the STCC Technology Park in the background.

procured by the enterprising Ripley from cannon he had requisitioned from government storage.

Production at the Armory grew from the 30 muskets a month produced by 40 workers in 1795, to 5,000 rifles manufactured daily in 1943 by 13,800 employees. Then in 1964, the Armory was included in a cost-saving measure, and scheduled to be deactivated. At that time, the post-high school Springfield Technical Institute was established, administered by the city and funded by the city and state. It rapidly outgrew its location in an annex of Springfield's Trade High School.

Trade Principal and STI Director Dr. Edmond P. Garvey, a retired Navy commander, along with industrialist Joseph J. Deliso, Sr. and State Representative Anthony M. Scibelli, enlisting the help of Springfield Mayor Charles V. Ryan, pushed to create a community college on the Armory grounds. In September 1967, the 12th of 15 Massachusetts community colleges opened in three buildings of the Armory, with an initial class of 400 students and 20 faculty, and Dr. Garvey as founding president.

In April 1968 the Armory was officially closed, and in July the new college changed its name to Springfield Technical Community College. Associate degree

and certificate programs offered in the early years were focused on training for technical trades and later health and human service occupations. As the curricula expanded, transfer programs were added, providing the first two years of a bachelor's degree education.

By 1983 when STCC's third president, Andrew M. Scibelli, was inaugurated, the college served nearly 7,000 day and evening students with 251 full-time faculty and professional staff, in 50 programs ranging from nuclear medicine technology to computer science transfer. The college began to reach out beyond Major Ripley's fence, to establish partnerships with national and international corporations.

STCC students, as well as faculty, benefit from the millions of dollars worth of hardware, software, and expertise gained through these national partnerships and alliances. Beginning with membership in IBM Corporation's CIM in Higher Education Alliance, STCC was selected:

• By Verizon to administer the New England Next Step Program, devising corporate-specific curriculum in telecommunications and leading 11 colleges in training 1,200 Verizon employees

• By Microsoft Corporation as one of five Mentor Colleges in the nation, tasked with teaching other colleges how to teach information technologies.

• By Intel Corporation, the world's largest microchip maker, as an Intel Strategic College to assist in preparing potential employees for Intel.

• By Cisco Systems as a Regional Networking Academy, to set up and administer 10 Local Academies for Cisco certification training, through which western Massachusetts high schools received significant hardware and training.

• Again by Microsoft, as one of 13 Regional Academies in the nation

• By USAID to mentor internationally, assisting Athlone Technical College in South Africa.

In 1997, the college won the largest of its many grants from the prestigious National Science Foundation to establish the National Center for Telecommunications Technologies, a collaboration creating curriculum in telecommunications for national dissemination. NCTT is also involved in setting skills standards for American education in telecommunications.

STCC's Center for Business and Technology, established in 1985, has provided

STCC was the only institution in western Massachusetts selected by Intel Corporation as an Intel Strategic College. Students in the Electrical Engineering Technology department may qualify for scholarships and summer internships; graduates of the program are recruited by Intel.

intensive computer and other workshops for thousands of area industry professionals, often contracting with businesses to offer specialized training. CBT is the only authorized center in western Massachusetts for many industry-leading software programs and IT certifications.

Physical facilities have grown on the STCC campus, with the addition of modern brick structures for classrooms, a gym and theater, and extensive computer labs.

Throughout its 35 years, STCC has maintained strong connections with the community, originating articulation agreements with high schools as well as four-year colleges, and working with neighborhood councils. Numerous grant programs link with the community, such as the Tech Prep program which introduces regional high school students to technical careers at the college level, and the UPDATE program, providing minority teachers' aides with the first two years of a bachelor's degree which will return them to their urban classrooms as full-fledged teachers and not incidentally, role models for their students.

Thousands of STCC's health alumni, graduates of the most extensive range of health sciences programs in New England, are providing care in hospitals, doctors' and dentists' offices, and other healthcare institutions throughout

the region. Area residents can take advantage of low-cost services in STCC's student-staffed, faculty-supervised labs in dental hygiene, cosmetology, massage therapy, and a rehabilitation clinic. STCC's partnership in the Springfield School Dental Program brings urban children to the college dental assistant lab for city-reimbursed treatment.

Each year, students in liberal arts, business, and engineering science transfer programs at STCC have gone on to Smith College, Mt. Holyoke, RPI, UMass, and other fine institutions, to complete bachelor's degrees and often master's degrees. Some students already have master's degrees and have come to STCC to prepare to change careers.

STCC's depth in technology has served it well. Founded as the only technical community college in Massachusetts, STCC developed faculty expertise, extensive investment in hardware, and real-world, in-depth curriculum in engineering technologies, so that when the high-tech economy arrived, STCC was already an acknowledged expert.

Likewise, the entrepreneurial spirit encouraged by senior leadership at the college has resulted in a national reputa-

Surgical Technology students in STCC's mock operating room, one of 14 health sciences programs at the college.

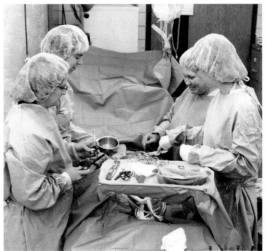

tion for entrepreneurship education and action. In 1994, Digital Equipment Co. announced that it would close the multi-building facility across the street from the STCC campus. What could have been a disastrous blow to the local community, with 1,000 jobs lost and a major location on the city's main thoroughfare potentially boarded up, became instead an entrepreneurial opportunity.

STCC's president forged an alliance of government and business leaders, reminiscent of the one that originally established the college, to purchase the facility. Originally part of the Springfield Armory grounds, the 15-acre tract was relatively unused until the last century. When the Armory closed, the site was owned by a succession of companies and used for light manufacturing and office functions.

In October 1996, ownership was transferred to the STCC Assistance Corporation, and in November the Springfield Technical Community College Technology Park opened. Due to the unusually concentrated fiber-optics resources of the immediate area, as well as the proximity to STCC s graduates and faculty, the Technology Park filled with tenant companies such as Choice One Communications, Equal Access Networks, and other primarily telecommunications businesses.

The STCC Technology Park has been

Students in STCC's Information Technologies programs may be studying subjects ranging from Microsoft certifications to Oracle, from website management to SQL, or diagnostic medical coding.

heralded as the first technology park in the United States created by a community college. In a further entrepreneurial venture, the college launched a major capital campaign to rehabilitate another building in the Technology Park, which resulted in the October 1999 opening of the Springfield Enterprise Center.

This small business incubator/accelerator, provides networked office space, office support services, and pro-bono guidance from an advisory board of local business professionals to nurture young businesses. Anchor tenants provide additional benefits and guidance to the SEC tenant companies as well as to greater Springfield. The first satellite business assistance center was established in 2002 in nearby Agawam.

Within the Springfield Enterprise Center, the STCC Entrepreneurial Institute was formed to offer entrepreneurship education. The YES! (Young Entrepreneurial Scholars) program provides National Foundation for the Teaching of Entrepreneurship curriculum to area high schools. An additional K-8 program inspires younger area students.

The Student Incubator administered by the Entrepreneurial Institute provides office space and support to college and high school student-owned businesses. The college is also embarking on a national entrepreneurship education-consulting program.

The Western Massachusetts Entrepreneurship

Three teams of area high school students designed and built replicas of medieval trebuchets (catapults) through a grant program led by STCC Engineering and Science Transfer faculty. The teams competed in catapulting water balloons at a target on the campus green.

Hall of Fame was created by STCC in 2000, to honor entrepreneurs from the past and present of the four western counties.

Also located within the Springfield Enterprise Center is the Joseph J. Deliso, Sr. Videoconferencing Center, providing area companies with a timesaving alternative to business travel. The SEC's international links, for instance to a growing Enterprise Zone in Belfast, Northern Ireland, also benefit from the video-conferencing center.

Because of the creation of over 1,000 jobs through the STCC Technology Park and the SEC, more than replacing the positions lost when the Digital plant closed, STCC was selected by the U.S. Department of Commerce/Economic Development Administration to receive the 2001 Award for Excellence in Urban Economic Development.

Life has changed in many ways on this site since the beginning of the Armory in 1794. The only weapons here now are polished exhibits in the Springfield Armory Museum, administered by the National Park Service. Manufacturing is taught here, using the latest computer-assisted processes. Technical knowledge is still disseminated throughout the region, now by STCC graduates. And the entrepreneurial spirit of Armory superintendents and innovative Armory employees has entered a new era.

MELINDA MILBERG, ESQ.

Melinda Milberg, an attorney with over 24-years experience, has a law and mediation practice in Natick, Massachusetts. She assists individuals, businesses and organizations by increasing productivity and harmony through conflict resolution, training and consultation. Active listening and creative problem solving are the key components she uses to build better teamwork and cooperation.

Born and raised in California, Ms. Milberg came to the Boston area in 1970 to attend Brandeis University as an undergraduate. She graduated magna cum laude with a B.A. in 1974, and went on to attend Boston University School of Law, receiving her J.D. in 1977. Ms. Milberg developed an interest in women's issues in college, and pursued that interest through law school and into her professional life. She was one of the founders of the Women's Bar Association of Massachusetts in 1978, an organization that has grown to a membership of over 1,200—commanding the respect of the state legislative and executive branches. Ms. Milberg also served as president of the W.B.A.in 1982, and as a board member for many years.

With a legal career that has encompassed many varied positions, Ms. Milberg served as Legal Counsel in three state agencies from 1978 through 1985. During that same time she served as a public member of the Board of Registration in Medicine, the state agency charged with the licensing and disciplining of physicians in Massachusetts. Concurrently she was also an instructor at Boston University School of Law, teaching First Year Legal Research and Writing for two years.

Ms. Milberg entered the private practice of law in Boston with Glovsky and Associates in 1985. After becoming a partner in 1995, the firm changed its name to Glovsky, Tarlow & Milberg. Her practice concentrated on employment law, estate planning and real estate. She was a contributing author to a book on Massachusetts Consumer Law, Chapter 93A, and served as faculty to the Massachu-

Melinda Milberg.

setts Continuing Legal Education Company as well as the Flaschner Judicial Institute.

During this period of time, Ms. Milberg further developed her interest in alternative dispute resolution, serving as an arbitrator with the American Arbitration Association, and as a hearing officer for state agencies. After attending a certified mediation course in October 1997, she became very interested in pursuing a career in ADR.

In June 1999, Ms. Milberg opened her own office in Natick, Massachusetts and became a mediator with various panels, as well as an arbitrator, and joined the New England Chapter of the Association for Conflict Resolution. She was appointed co-chair of the Boston Bar Association's ADR Committee in 2001—her term extends through 2003. Ms. Milberg has also expanded her training and consultation practice, providing training for employment, conflict resolution and other workplace issues to companies and organizations. Among the comments received

at seminars conducted by Ms. Milberg are: "the workshop was dynamic, well-planned and well-executed"; and the "handbook is an excellent resource." Ms. Milberg is on the list of certified trainers with the Massachusetts Commission Against Discrimination, and has also served on the panel of trainers for the University of Massachusetts' Donahue Institute.

Milberg has been married to Philip Benjamin since 1976, and they have two sons, Jason and Alex. Ms. Milberg and her husband have made a concerted effort to balance their careers, parenting and civil activities—choosing during the first several years of parenting to each work a part-time schedule. Balancing professional life, personal life and growth in all areas has been a priority, and a welcome journey. Ms. Milberg feels that she has been very fortunate to have engaged thus far in many stimulating and rewarding career and personal activities.

WHATMAN, INC.

The Whatman story began with a small, country-based English mill making fine, handcrafted paper. The business has since evolved into a dominant force in the international market for high quality scientific papers and filter products geared toward analytical chemistry, diagnostics, and life science markets. From its inception, the charter for Whatman has been to produce and market the very best products, and to sustain long-term relationships with customers based on service, technology, and mutual trust. That is the creed, which inspired James Whatman, and it remains the philosophy, which drives the company forward as the world moves into the twenty-first century.

Many stories end with a wedding. The Whatman story began with one. On August 7, 1740, in the parish church of All Saints at Maidstone, Kent, in England a marriage took place between James Whatman, a leather tanner, and Ann Harris, a widow who had inherited her first husband's newly-built paper mill. The newlyweds set about making their paper mill the finest in the land.

James Whatman assembled a highly skilled workforce of craftsmen for all stages of the paper making process. By 1753, his "Laid" papers, made on a simple mesh of wires, had an excellent reputation in Britain, and were even being exported to America. Three years later, Whatman introduced "Wove" paper, produced on a different configuration of wires in the mold, which resulted in a smoother, finer sheet. Whatman Wove paper set the standard for superior quality that was not commercially challenged for over 30 years.

James Whatman II proved to be as talented a businessman and innovator as his father. He discovered that the whiteness of paper could be improved by adding blue stone in the early stages of manufacture, further establishing the company's preeminence as a paper maker. In 1770, the Society of Antiquaries was commissioned to make a large copper engraving of an old painting

James Whatman founded the Whatman paper making company in 1740.

depicting Henry VIII meeting Francis I at the field of the Cloth of Gold. The necessary paper had to be 49.25 inches by 27 inches—bigger than any paper Whatman ever produced. James II, ever the creative problem solver, built a special machine to make the antiquarian-sized paper. The machine took 11 men to operate and the resulting sheets were so heavy that they had to be transported from Maidstone to London by boat.

By 1783, James II was running two other mills. In addition to Wove paper, he was exporting marbled paper, and paper for copper plates. He also established a reputation as a considerate and enlightened employer, occasionally paying employees a guinea, or two bo-

nus, and up to four guineas extra at Christmas.

In 1790, his protégé, William Balston took over the running of the business, however, due to James' illness the business was eventually sold. William remained at the business with his new colleagues until August 1805, when he left to start a new company at Springfield on the banks of the River Medway near Maidstone.

True to Whatman's founding traditions, William Balston was also an innovator and at the forefront of technological advances. Instead of using the nearby river as a source of power for his new company, William chose to use steam. He commissioned the renowned engineer Sir James Watt to supervise the installation of a steam engine, the first ever to be used as the main source of power for a paper mill. Inspired by his great interest in chemistry he also installed a small laboratory at the Springfield Mill. The following years saw tremendous growth for W & R Balston, as the firm was now known. Ten vats were installed at the Springfield Mill and despite a difficult economic climate, the company employed almost 250 people by 1861.

During the early years of the twentieth century, the Balston family laid the foundation for expansion into other types of paper, hiring chemists to conduct experiments to help the company maintain control of the manufacturing process. With the dawn of World War I, Balston was approached by an anxious government, which needed filter papers, particularly for steel and armament production. Previous supplies had come from Germany. Balston responded and developed the technology needed to produce the required filter paper. It was an event that would forever change the nature of the company.

As the world became increasingly fascinated with, and reliant on, advances in science and technology, making filter papers for use by laboratories, hospitals, schools as well as industry became the company's clear path to expansion. Whatman No. 1 filter paper was a key medium in the pioneering experiments undertaken in 1944 by the research scientists, Consden, Gordon, and Martin. Their work in chromatography, coupled with the parallel work that earned Martin and Synge a Nobel Prize, was a technology breakthrough

Whatman "Wove" paper set the standard for superior quality.

that enabled hospital pathologists, forensic scientists, and biochemists separate chemical compounds into individual components for analysis. By the end of World War II, the company's comprehensive range of analytical filter papers had become brand leaders under the Whatman name. New materials, such as glass and quartz micro-fibers, were being developed and incorporated into new filters that provided solutions to the ever-increasing challenges of science and industry. By 1968, Whatman filter papers were available in more laboratories the world over than any other brand.

Whatman expanded to the U.S. in 1914 when Reeve Angel International established an office in New York and was appointed the exclusive sales representative for W & R Balston in the burgeoning North American market. Having access now to U.S. government requirements during two world wars, plus the rapidly expanding industrial, scientific, and healthcare markets, contributed significantly to the company's

growth. Whatman filter products were being used in such diverse areas as coffee pots, hospital sterilizers, environmental pollution monitors, life jackets, pregnancy testing kits, and sample preparation devices for scientific research.

In the early '70s, Reeve Angel acquired the technology for manufacturing high-pressure liquid chromatography (HPLC) columns. HPLC was emerging as a powerful analytical technique capable of separating a wide range of complex chemical, biochemical, and environmental samples. HPLC instruments were developed which used high-pressure pumping systems to pump a sample through the HPLC column for separation and then through a sensitive chemical detection device, which would identify each component. Given W & R Balston's history with Whatman brand filter papers in the separation sciences, it was realized that the future of both companies would be best served by merging their interests. In 1974, W & R Balston merged with Reeve Angel International and the brand name Whatman was incorporated to form Whatman Reeve Angel, Ltd.

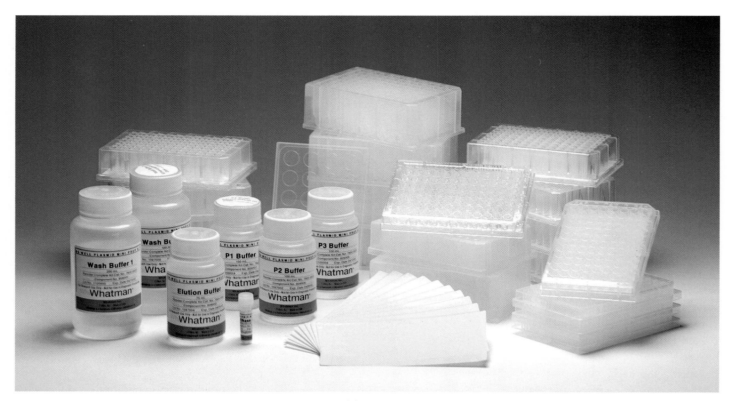

Whatman filter microplates, collection plates, and chemical buffers for purification of DNA.

Following the merger, the new company was divided into two divisions based on product technology. The Paper Division had its headquarters in Springfield Mill in the UK and the newly formed Chemical Separations Division was located in Clifton, New Jersey. The Chemical Separations Division continued to pioneer the development of HPLC Column technology along with related thin layer (TLC) and ion chromatography (IEC). Whatman was recognized as the world-leading supplier of these important analytical technologies. In addition, HPLC and ion chromatography were able to be scaled up to allow these techniques to be used on a production level for processing large volumes of material for commercial purposes. In 1983, Whatman Reeve Angel was contracted to install a Process Liquid Chromatography System at the GD Searle Company for the production of a new synthetic sweetener called Aspartame.

As Whatman paper and membranes continued to enable scientific advancements at a rapid pace, the company looked to Massachusetts for growth. In order to provide filtration and adsorption solutions for the biosciences, Whatman developed specialized membranes and media to allow the sensitive separation and analytical techniques required for biomolecular research. In 1995, the company acquired Rockland, Massachusetts based Polyfiltronics, a world-leading producer of plastic multiwell microplates. The rectangular micro-plates contain from 96 to 1584 wells in a fixed pattern and are widely used in bioresearch to allow processing of a large number of experiments in a small amount of space. It was determined that by incorporating Whatman's filter technology into the individual microplate wells, researchers could process samples even faster by eliminating time consuming pipetting steps. Today, Whatman offers a wide variety of filter microplates along with reagent chemicals for the purification of DNA and RNA in pharmaceutical laboratories researching new drugs.

In May 2001, Whatman acquired the HemaSure Company located in Marl-borough, Massachusetts. HemaSure produces a filtration system for the reduction of white blood cells (or leukocytes) in transfusion blood. Before whole blood is transfused into patients it is separated into plasma and red blood cells. Red blood cells also contain leukocytes, which may carry threatening viruses and create immunological complications in the transfusion recipient. Removing the leukocytes reduces potential complications and improves healing time for the patient. HemaSure works closely with hospitals and blood banks to ensure the quality and safety of red blood cells for transfusion.

The Marlborough and Rockland sites provided Whatman with first-hand insight into the significant pool of life sciences talent available in the Boston metro region and the potential benefits to be realized by expanding their presence in the area. Given the rapid shift of the company's focus toward life sciences, it was decided to establish Whatman's U.S. corporate research and development center in Newton, Massachusetts. The new facility is home to international product management

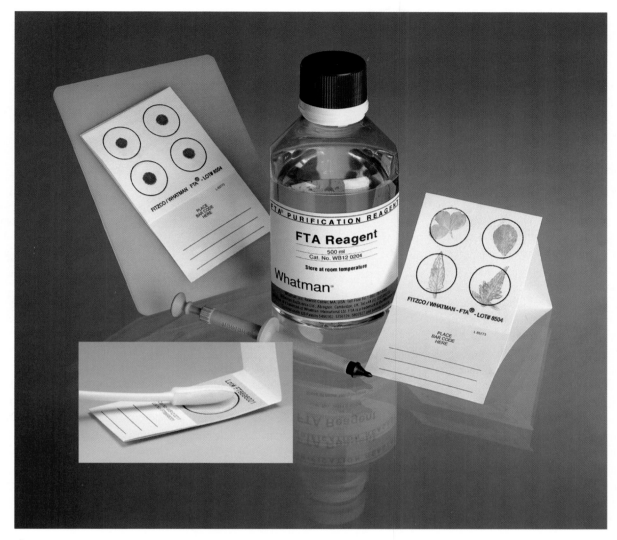

Whatman FTA® Technology revolutionizes the collection and storage of DNA samples.

and marketing as well as a major percentage of the company's R&D scientists and engineers. The Marlborough facility has been retained as the headquarters for Whatman HemaSure. It also houses U.S. corporate management and serves as a U.S. manufacturing site for blood filters. Today, Whatman employs over 100 people in its Boston metro sites.

From the new strategic location in Massachusetts, Whatman continues to develop new technologies to make tomorrow's scientific advances possible. Recently introduced patented FTA® Technology is revolutionizing the handling and storage of DNA. With this unique membrane technology, scientists

and law enforcement personnel can now collect, transport, and store DNA safely and securely at room temperature, eliminating the need for expensive ultra-low temperature freezers. Ongoing tests have confirmed that using this method, genetic material can remain at room temperature for more than 11 years.

With the new capability provided by FTA Technology, researchers and scientists in many different disciplines, in laboratories throughout the world, are discovering the benefits for archiving virtually any type of biological sample for DNA analysis: Researchers are able to store and retrieve their DNA clones with unprecedented ease. Forensic scientists are using FTA Technology to collect and store evidence and to build a criminal identification database. Ani-

mal breeders and agriculturalists can use FTA to monitor food origins and food safety. Because FTA Technology provides a simple solution for obtaining samples from remote locations, it is being used for plant studies and other field operations.

FTA Technology is just one of the exciting life science innovations that Whatman will introduce to support the important pioneering research in genomics and the emerging field of proteomics. At the Newton site, numerous projects are currently in the final stages of completion and will soon be ready for product launch.

Given his penchant for providing customers with truly innovative solutions, James Whatman would be pleased.

303

CRITTENTON HASTINGS HOUSE

A strong and vibrant organization is one that reflects its time, adapts to changing needs, and is an active leader in the community. Crittenton Hastings House, the venerable Boston institution, is an example of an organization that has stood the test of time for nearly 200 years. Spanning three centuries, Crittenton has supported generations of poor young families and today, stands as a unique mirror of Boston's and America's evolving history.

Crittenton's roots go back to 1824, when a pioneering group of women established the Boston Female Moral Reform Society to provide shelter and moral guidance to "fallen girls." Since the organization had no physical building, the Society's members brought destitute, unwed young mothers into their homes. Their friends were shocked and some ministers denounced them for being "unwomanly and for daring to face the unpleasant realities of life."

Yet, their work was essential to Boston, a city many considered corrupt. According to an 1838 prospectus, the opinion of the Hub City was dismal. Boston "is a polluted city, sending forth a corrupt influence throughout our land. The vice prevails to an alarming extent in our midst. Our grand design is to inculcate purity of heart and life: and especially to urge upon mothers their duties—to caution young ladies against the fashionable dissipation and extravagance of the present age. The society presumes on the female talent and enterprise of New England to sustain it."

An early publication by the Society called *The Friends of Virtue,* laid out its early mission:

This Society shall have for its object the prevention of licentiousness. We will extend the hand of encouragement to all such as seem penitent, and who desire to return to the path of rectitude and virtue.

The efforts of these dedicated women in the early and mid-nineteenth century were carried out within the strong religious tenor of the times. For the next 45 years, the Society grew steadily as it concentrated its efforts on rescuing young

Boston Female Moral Reform Society.

women from the streets and continuing its crusade against liquor and prostitution.

In 1869, the organization changed its name to the New England Moral Reform Society and established a maternity home and hospital in Boston's Jamaica Plain neighborhood. It was immediately filled to capacity. During this time—the post-Civil War industrialization era—a major influx of "country and immigrant women" were lured to the city by the prospects of economic success. Instead, they found themselves victims of economic and sexual exploitation. The organization's focus on providing medical care for unwed mothers and their children, reflected the beginning of the health reform movement sweeping the country, which assumed that many moral and societal problems could be cured through medical care.

This shift from a predominately religious tone to a health focus forever altered the organization, as did the arrival in 1871 of Dr. Caroline E. Hastings who became the hospital's first attending physician. Her association with the organization went on to span more than 50 years, including 24 years as the organization's president. Dr. Hastings, one of the first female physicians in the nineteenth century, was a vocal proponent of women's equality, public sanitation, and fresh air. In 1893, Dr. Julia Morton Plummer, who served as attending physician until her death in 1925, joined her.

As the New England Moral Reform Society continued its pioneering efforts, a similar organization, the Florence Crittenton Home, was emerging in Boston in the 1890s.

Charles N. Crittenton, founder.

Kate Waller Barrett.

Charles Crittenton, a wealthy pharmaceutical wholesaler, founded the nationwide network of Florence Crittenton Homes that provided shelter and moral guidance to poor, unwed mothers. After the tragic death of his four-year-old daughter Florence, he began ministering in New York's poorest neighborhoods and soon established a mission for "fallen" girls. By the mid-1890s, his vision of a network of more than 50 Florence Crittenton homes throughout the country, including Boston, became a reality. Dr. Kate Waller Barrett, a nationally recognized physician and feminist who shifted the focus of the Florence Crittenton Homes from the "rescue and redemption of prostitutes to residential and maternity care for unmarried mothers," supported him in this work.

Boston's Florence Crittenton Home shared many of the same goals as the New England Moral Reform Society. It targeted prostitution and joined forces with the Boston Police to help close down the City's "disorderly houses." In 1896, Boston's Florence Crittenton Home was established at 37 Green Street in Boston, as an all-day, all-night mission for unwed mothers. A network of Boston-area shelters soon followed, in Roxbury,

Watertown, downtown Boston, and eventually, at its present site in Brighton.

Mrs. Thomas Tyler, Boston's street matron, was one of the many women who staffed the Boston-area shelters. In 1913, a local newspaper profiled Tyler's efforts:

"Night after night she has gone about the streets and the parks, into the theatres and cafes, wherever girls are to be found, and has quietly and unobtrusively given her help where needed. The service she renders run the whole gamut of girls' needs. It varies from seeing a simple country girl safely on the right car to plucking swiftly back an equally simple girl from the final misstep. She is a friend to girls and her entire formula of service embraced in the phrase so often on her lips: She saw I was her friend. Nor is it an idle formula with Mrs. Tyler. The girls she helps are her friends—they are not cases; they are individuals who need Mrs. Tyler."

"There is no cause in New England

The open door entrance to "The House of Another Chance."

Florence Crittenton League of Compassion, Inc., 88 Tremont Street, Boston. The "Big Sister" to unfortunate New England girls.

more appealing to the general public than that of the Florence Crittenton League of Compassion," another Boston newspaper wrote of the organization that called itself "The 'Big Sister' to Unfortunate New England Girls."

For the next 56 years, the New England Moral Reform Society (which changed its name to the Talitha Cumi Maternity Home in 1924 and then, in honor of Dr. Hastings, to Hastings House in 1948) and the Florence Crittenton Home (which became the Florence Crittenton League of Compassion Inc., in 1908) operated on parallel missions. Each made an important and lasting impact in assisting unwed mothers and their children in Boston's poorest neighborhoods.

The two organizations provided housing as well as maternal and infant care, worked to build strong parenting bonds between mothers and their babies, and offered job training and educational programs that could help unwed mothers become self-sufficient.

In 1924, the Crittenton League secured six acres of land at Ten Perthshire Road in Oak Square, Brighton, once the old Peter Faneuil estate and later, the Adams estate. Harold Field Kellogg, a leading architect of the time designed the Crittenton Home and Hospital, which continues today as Crittenton's headquarters. The laying of the cornerstone took place on September 25, 1924 with Massachusetts Governor Channing H. Cox and Boston Mayor James M. Curley in attendance.

In the 1930s, the Florence Crittenton League established Boston's only complete unit for treating venereal diseases and both organizations coped with the increased demands spurred by the Great Depression. It was also in the late 1930s that the Talitha Cumi Home began reaching out to young fathers with a unique program designed to encourage strong family bonds. This focus continues today as part of Crittenton's Young Fathers Program.

Through World War II, the emphasis turned to meeting the needs of a "larger number of stranded unfortunates" and preparing them for the "after-the-war world" and "industrial independence."

Not surprisingly, the two organizations crossed paths regularly as they pursued similar goals. In 1949, the Florence Crittenton League of Compassion and

Florence Crittenton Home and Hospital, Boston Massachusetts, circa 1925.

Maternity Home and Hospital
10 PERTHSHIRE ROAD, BRIGHTON

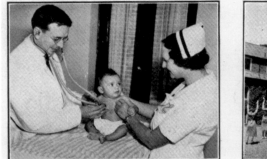

DAILY ACTIVITIES

Maternity Home and Hospital, 10 Perthshire Road, Brighton, daily activities.

Hastings House began formal plans to merge. In 1961, a Special Act of the Massachusetts Legislature authorized consolidating the two organizations into the Crittenton Hastings House of the Florence Crittenton League of Compassion, Inc., today better known as Crittenton.

During the 1950s and 1960s, Crittenton Hastings House operated at full capacity, serving more than 400 young women annually. In 1962, the first alternative high school in the Boston Public Schools was established at Crittenton so

CEO/President Elizabeth Reilinger Ph.D.

that the young pregnant women could complete their high school education.

In 1973, Crittenton Hastings House assumed yet another leadership role by opening the first fully licensed freestanding abortion clinic in Massachusetts, following the passage of the landmark Supreme Court case *Roe v. Wade*. The clinic was opened amid considerable controversy, resulting in the disbandment of many of its groups of volunteers, the Crittenton Circles, and the loss of United Way funding. At the same time, support for this service was provided by major Boston teaching hospitals, members of the medical profession, and the general public. Among them was Dr. Somer Sturgis, a leading Harvard physician, who had worked with Margaret Sanger to pioneer the development of the oral contraceptive pill. In 1999, in response to changing community needs, Crittenton discontinued its reproductive medical services.

The 1980s and 1990s saw another significant shift in Crittenton's emphasis. It became increasingly clear that societal and economic changes demanded a strong educational foundation as a prerequisite for economic independence and success. Recognizing that young at-risk families faced greater barriers to attaining and sustaining self-sufficiency, Crittenton, under the leadership of Dr. Elizabeth Reilinger, began a modern day chapter in its evolving history.

Incorporating a holistic approach and drawing on an integrated array of services, Crittenton strengthened its efforts to break

"Movin' On Up Graduates 2000."

the intergenerational cycle of poverty, pregnancy and dependency. Today the mission of Crittenton is simple: promote self-sufficiency. Ultimately, this became the core of the welfare reform movement enacted in the late 1990s by President Bill Clinton.

Today, Crittenton offers thousands of families access to programs that include housing, education, workforce development, early education and child-care, health, nutrition, parenting, and family life skills. All of these programs help young people develop the essential tools that they need to maintain stable housing, to find and to retain employment, and to support the healthy growth and development of their children.

From its earliest days in the nineteenth century, Crittenton has been on the forefront of major social and economic issues of the time. It has shifted its focus from rescuing "fallen" women and promoting social purity to fostering the health of mothers, children and families. It then turned away from viewing women simply as "victims and wronged" to respecting their capacity and desire to become independent, responsible parents, and productive members of the community.

Housing and education will continue to form the cornerstone of Crittenton's work as it moves into the future. As President/CEO Reilinger, who also chairs the Boston School Committee, has noted: "Success in the future is dependent upon success early in life and in school. It is our responsibility to make available to the young people of Boston, the opportunity for success."

Over the years, Crittenton has given hope and opportunity to thousands of poor mothers, fathers, children, and families. The generosity of Bostonians to provide the funds and support to operate its programs has made Crittenton's work possible. Crittenton, in turn, has added value to the fabric of the community. As noted by Boston Mayor Tom Menino, "Crittenton offers our young people a chance to turn their lives around. We need more Crittenton's!"

FISHER COLLEGE

Fisher College—now located on the prestigious streets of Boston's Back Bay—was originally opened in what was predominantly the working-class city of Somerville, and had its beginnings with educational entrepreneurs who believed the immigrants of that city in the early 1900s needed a way out of their un-skilled employment.

Today, the college provides courses leading to the baccalaureate degree, as-sociate degrees and certificates to tradi-tional-age college students from around the world as well as continuing education students. Yet it was a long and fascinating evolution to the present day Fisher Col-lege which keeps striving to find new ways of providing education and devel-oping the capabilities of students through continued enhancement of its educational program, delivery systems, facilities, student activities and other facets of college life.

In 1897, brothers Myron C. Fisher and Edmund H. Fisher moved from Shen-andoah, Iowa, to Somerville, Massachu-setts. They had studied education in a midwestern normal school but, unlike many others of their day, they sought new

The Fisher Business College in 1918, at 374 Broadway, Somerville, Massachusetts.

opportunities in the east. Dr. Scott A. Fisher, now interim president of the college, said of his grandfather and great-uncle: "Most Americans of the day were traveling west to seek fame and fortune but my forefathers traveled east."

The Fisher brothers started their teach-ing careers at Burdette College in Boston in 1898 but soon saw a need to open a different kind of school—one for what Dr. Fisher calls the "meat and potato folks"

who lived in places like Somerville. These were the people—many of whom were recent immigrants—who worked in factories, brick foundries, and slaugh-terhouses. Working conditions were difficult: The buildings were extremely cold or hot (depending on the season); they worked six days a week for long hours; their wages were meager. Conse-quently, the only way for them to escape harsh working conditions was to get a better job and that meant they needed access to education.

That was the need the Fisher brothers wanted to fill. And so they did when, in 1903, they opened the doors of Winter Hill Business College, which was housed in rented space in one of Somerville's Masonic buildings. The brothers went door-to-door in the neighborhood, sell-ing courses. They certainly had a good product to sell: The school was located right across the street from a streetcar station (which could be reached from Lowell and other northern towns); the curriculum was individualized and stu-dents could study whatever they needed to land the job they were seeking.

The Fisher School Business Management for Men in 1949, at 160 Beacon Street, Boston.

The first student to sign up was Alma Olsen, a Swedish immigrant. Soon after, 12 others joined her and the college was underway with its initial 13-member class. Almost immediately, the college was a huge success. Primary courses included typing—which was a new business science then—bookkeeping and penmanship. "These were all vital business skills which could provide employment opportunity to the city's vast immigrant population looking for the American dream," Dr. Fisher said. Some students walked in off the streets and started their classes right away; some stayed for a day or a week; and others stayed for years. They often paid by installment or paid on account and were granted a Certificate of Completion in some courses or just gained the skills they deemed necessary for getting a better job.

Several years after its opening, Winter Hill Business College became the northeast distributor for Royal Typewriters. Touch-typing was introduced as a subject during those years and Winter Hill was the first school in the northeast to teach it.

Over the years, the school opened—and closed—other branch institutions. The main campus moved in 1918 to a different building in Somerville; the college's name changed several times until receiving its present one. In 1939, the family reorganized the college into a

Fisher Junior College, vocal group, 1962, at 118 Beacon Street, Boston.

nonprofit institution, donating all the assets toward future development. The founders retired and their sons took over leadership of three campuses in Back Bay, Roxbury and Waltham.

In 1957, the college received authority to grant the Associate in Science degree, followed by the Associate of Arts in 1963. Fisher College was granted initial accreditation by the New England Association of Schools and Colleges in 1970. Other milestones over the century include the augmentation of the Evening Division in 1974; the introduction of an international dimension in 1992 called the Fisher International Research Seminar Trip which allows students to travel to a city in Europe for one week as part of their academic program; the re-establishment of co-education in the Day Division in 1998; and the introduction of Internet education with the first pilot course offered to continuing education students in 1998 and the formal introduction of Home-Campus in 1999—the delivery of academic courses to students in their homes through the Internet around the world.

The Fisher School for Girls, 374 Broadway, Somerville, Massachusetts.

Today, the main campus at 118 Beacon Street consists of many buildings with classrooms, a library, dormitories, student services facilities—all the facets of a modern college. Regional and specialized program accreditation has been acquired and a number of collegiate degrees are offered in business and liberal arts concentrations. Fisher College continues to enlarge its programs and offers 17 different programs in business and secretarial studies, human services and liberal arts. The school has always been an educational institution where many students with average academic backgrounds can truly learn and achieve to the best of their abilities.

Fisher College does not define its quality or excellence by how many students it excludes in the admissions process, explains Dr. Charles C. Perkins, vice president for Academic Affairs. Rather, he said, the college defines its quality by how its programs meet the needs of its students where they are academically when they enroll. "We do this by honoring their individuality; by diagnosing their individual needs, prescribing an educational plan, and placing them in courses with an appropriate level of challenge," Perkins said. "It is this institutional ability and attitude which enhances the remarkable success of our students, fulfills the professional aspirations of our faculty and staff and sustains our unique educational mission."

The school's administrative council recognizes that if Fisher College is to truly be an institution in the new century as "the small college in a world-class city," they will need to raise sufficient funds to preserve the unique and special aspects of the college, to fund more scholarships and build additional facilities to support the students. Until recently, the college did not have a formal fund-raising program but rather relied on the efforts of alumni volunteers who solicited gifts from other alumni. In 1998, however, a formal Office of Institutional Advancement was established and a development professional was hired to administer fund-raising activities. The college hopes to raise $10,005,980 for endowment funds, scholarship fund, faculty development, resident halls, architectural contingencies and academic program growth and degree augmentation.

The college administration often thinks Myron and Edmund Fisher must be smiling to think that what they began as a business school would turn out to be an educational institution approved by the Massachusetts Board of Higher Education and offering courses and programs leading to an Associate Degree in Science, a Bachelor of Science in Management and appropriate certificates of completion. The college is proud of the services it provides and the role it plays in serving underprivileged and minority students in Boston and southern Massachusetts. Minorities make up 50 percent of the college's Day Division population.

Each July, Dr. Fisher takes new employees of Fisher College on a tour—beginning in Somerville and ending in Back Bay—to provide an overview of the school's history.

In the nearly 100 years since opening

its doors, Dr. Fisher said, the college—initially a Somerville-born fledgling in higher education—has become one of Boston's leading small colleges offering degrees in a variety of Business and Liberal Arts programs.

Fisher School, accounting class in 1944, at 118 Beacon Street, Boston.

Fisher Junior College, residence hall in 1959, at Beacon Street, Boston.

To this day, business emphasis prevails in the college curricula, maintaining as well the objectives of giving a student knowledge, employability and professional security. Early students were primarily from Somerville but modern classes include representatives of all the continents in the world.

A member of a recent July tour said it was clear from her visit that although the Fisher family no longer "owns" the college, they are an integral part of its history and current welfare. "There is a sense of family among staff members, which I assume, carries over to the students," wrote Harriet Lebow after taking what Dr. Fisher calls the "Somerville Roots Tour."

Lebow said the school was created to meet the needs of its times and changed throughout the years to continue to meet those needs. Fisher College is

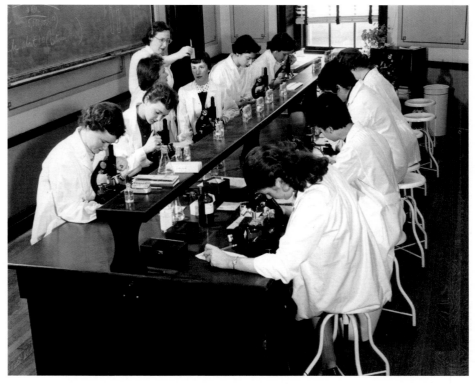

Fisher Junior College, chemistry lab, 1955.

Myers said. "Faculty and students are intellectually engaged and enjoy the challenges together."

Myers said many returning students to Fisher College attest to the significant, positive impact their education has had on them and that the energies and endeavors of adult learners in the Division of Continuing Education add significant stature to the college community. "This blend comes to life in the aura of gentility that our magnificent Beacon Street building exude," she said. "As an alumna and a teacher, I'd like to extend an invitation to members of the Boston business community to visit. Experience for yourself a dynamic learning environment involved in preparing your future employees to meet your needs right here in Boston."

The Fisher School, typing class, 1944, 118 Beacon Street, Boston.

still designed to educate lower-and middle-income students who are not being served by the area's more elite educational institutions. Whether these students were the immigrants of the school's earliest days, returning World War II veterans or the students of today, Lebow said, Fisher provided and continues to provide opportunity and a path to a better way of life.

Graduates have also praised the school and written to administrators to tell how their education at Fisher College changed their lives. Pat Senich, Class of 1959, said she has forever been grateful for her two years of training at Fisher College. "I often wish I could have stayed in Boston and gone back to school there over and over again," she said. Now in the twenty-first century, Senich can resume her educational progress via the Fisher Internet.

Karen Casey Myers, who was a member of the Class of 1968 and now is the chairman of Fisher College's Career and Professional programs, said the college community is more vibrant and energized than ever before. "Education is solid,"

HOUGHTON MIFFLIN COMPANY

An abiding sense of tradition is evident at the publishing house of Houghton Mifflin Company, as befits a firm that includes among its authors Longfellow, Emerson, Whittier, Hawthorne, Dickens, Thackeray, Tennyson, Browning, Thoreau, and Twain—a company largely responsible for making Boston the nation's literary and publishing capital for more than a century.

Houghton Mifflin had its origins at the Old Corner Bookstore at Washington and School streets in the "Golden Age" of literary Boston. Built just after the Great Fire of 1711, the bookstore was the literary center of Boston for more than a half-century. It was headquarters for the exclusive Temple Club in 1829, the Tremont in 1851, and later the Somerset, the Union and the Saturday clubs. In 1832, publishers William D. Ticknor and John Allen bought the store, but their partnership was short-lived, and Ticknor subsequently chose James T. Fields as his partner. Together they assembled one of the most distinguished groups of writers ever to share the same publishing house. They brought tact, discrimination, and generous royalties to their American and English authors while the firm took its place as a leading mid-nineteenth-century publisher. To be published by Ticknor & Fields became a mark of success among writers.

An association beginning during the Civil War with Henry O. Houghton of the Riverside Press, and later with George H. Mifflin, culminated in a merger in 1880 and the birth of the new partnership of Houghton, Mifflin and Company. By 1908 it would be a corporation.

Early on, an education department was established to publish books for a growing number of students. Today the educational publishing divisions are the backbone of the company. Houghton Mifflin is a leader in developing instructional techniques and educational materials. An extensive list of elementary, high school, and college textbooks, tests, software and other educational materials now account for the largest segment

of the business. Among the firm's best-selling educational publications are the *Houghton Mifflin Reading Program,* high school mathematics and social studies textbooks, college-level English and accounting programs and standardized tests such as the *Iowa Tests of Basic Skills.*®

Houghton Mifflin's general publishing activities have also remained important. Fine literature for children and adults is published under the Houghton Mifflin and Clarion imprints. Through the years Houghton Mifflin authors have received numerous book awards, including a number of Pulitzer prizes and American book awards, as well as Caldecott and Newbery medals for children's literature.

Publishing fine literary and educational works is Houghton Mifflin's heritage. For more than 160 years the firm's

Ticknor & Fields, forerunner of Houghton Mifflin Company, assembled one of the most distinguished collections of writers ever associated with one publisher. Here the founders, James T. Fields (left) and William Ticknor (right), are seen with one of their many authors, Nathaniel Hawthorne.

goal has been to shape information, instruction and entertainment into forms that provide unique features of value to its customers. The company develops and manages ideas and intellectual properties with the help of an extensive collection of author relationships, a staff of experienced editorial talent and a valuable storehouse of creative works.

Houghton Mifflin issues works representing a variety of viewpoints for a broad range of markets. Kate Wiggins' *Rebecca of Sunnybrook Farm;* Edward Bellamy's *Looking Backward;* Henry James' *The*

Portrait of a Lady and *The Bostonians;* Winston Churchill's six-volume, *The Second World War;* Esther Forbes' *Johnny Tremain;* and Rachel Carson's *Silent Spring* were all published by the firm as it built a list of distinguished, best-selling twentieth century authors. This list also included Woodrow Wilson, Margaret Deland and Brooks Adams, and by mid-century added Henry Cabot Lodge, Theodore Roosevelt, Amy Lowell, Archibald MacLeish, General George Patton and Field Marshal Bernard Montgomery. Its more contemporary authors include Roger Tory Peterson, who began the popular Field Guide series more than 50 years ago, David Macaulay, J.R.R. Tolkien, Howard Fast, John Kenneth Galbraith, Arthur Schlesinger, Philip Roth and Lois Lowry.

As society has moved into the information age, the firm now publishes a wide variety of materials in electronic as well as print formats. Its *American Heritage® Dictionary* is licensed to many Internet websites and e-book producers. The company's product line features video, CD, software and websites as well as books.

In the 1990s, Houghton Mifflin embarked on a significant period of expansion, beginning in 1992 with small acquisitions in the college and testing areas, which strengthened it in attractive markets. The 1994 acquisition of McDougal, Littell & Company, a highly respected publisher of educational materials for secondary schools, provided the critical mass to establish a separate secondary school division. And the 1995 addition of D.C. Heath allowed entry into the supplemental school market, significantly expanded Houghton Mifflin's College Division and added strong secondary school products, fostering the company's leadership in the high school advanced placement segment. The Great Source Education Group, established in 1996, combined the supplemental product lines of D.C. Heath, Houghton Mifflin's School Division and McDougal Littell.

The history of Houghton Mifflin Company began more than a century and a half ago at the Old Corner Bookstore at School and Washington streets in Boston.

Computer Adaptive Technologies, acquired in 1998, and Assessment Systems Incorporated, acquired in 2001, serve the rapidly growing computerized test delivery market, as CAT*ASI. The 1999 acquisition of Sunburst Communications strengthened the company in the educational technology market.

During the 1990s, Houghton Mifflin also streamlined operations and became extremely efficient, taking advantage of emerging technologies to increase productivity. Technology products became an important part of all of its lists, and new methods of delivery became routine. The Company's award-winning Education Place website receives 500,000 unique visits per month.

In 2001, Houghton Mifflin became part of Vivendi Universal, a global communications powerhouse with international scale, rich content and vast digital and distribution capacity. The company remains dedicated to providing materials that help every individual exercise the right to be educated and to offering its customers New Ways to Know.®

JEWISH MEMORIAL HOSPITAL AND REHABILITATION CENTER

In 1913, the Roxbury Ladies' Bikur Cholim Association began collecting donations to provide a haven for the chronically ill. These charitable ladies recognized that new Jewish immigrants, crowded into Boston's West End and North End neighborhoods, lacked basic medical care. Many of these newcomers found upon their arrival to this country, that few Jewish doctors practiced in the Boston area. Furthermore, communication between doctor and patient was sometimes difficult since many of these people spoke no English, and very few doctors spoke Yiddish. Moreover, many local doctors did not understand the particular social problems, religious traditions, and behavior patterns of these new immigrants. Finally, many Orthodox Jews refused to stay in hospitals where they could not eat kosher food and observe the Sabbath. Hence, the ladies of the Bikur Cholim, many of them immigrants, began a grassroots movement to build a medical institution for Jews who were suffering from long-term illness and disease and had limited places to go for treatment.

The original charter of the Roxbury Bikur Cholim Association was established in 1915. Thirteen years later, in 1928, the Association voted to establish and maintain a home for incurables. Later that same

Dedication of the Greater Boston Bikur Cholim Hospital later renamed Jewish Memorial Hospital.

year, the Association realized its goal of developing a Jewish hospital by purchasing the former Beth Israel Hospital.

A year later, in 1929, the Greater Boston Bikur Cholim Hospital, with 42 beds, was officially dedicated. A medical staff consisting of volunteer physicians was organized, and a hospital-based auxiliary was formed to support the Hospital's operations. At that time the Hospital was primarily a custodial institution, accepting patients from other hospitals who could no longer benefit from active treatment. In the early 1930s, the physiotherapy, radiology, and laboratory departments were opened. During the 1930s, 85 percent of the patients admitted to the Hospital received free care, and a majority of the financial support for the new hospital came from donations by the Jewish community.

A new three-story wing was dedicated in 1936, doubling the size of the Hospital to 87 beds. This new wing included a complete operating room, dental department,

and a kosher kitchen to ensure adherence to Jewish dietary practices. Finally, to reflect the changing focus of the institution, the name of the Hospital was changed to the Jewish Memorial Hospital in 1937.

During the early 1940s, the Jewish Memorial Hospital cared for terminally ill patients during their final days. Care remained largely custodial. Since most of the nursing homes in existence at this time were private. Poor and needy elderly had limited choices for medical care—Jewish Memorial Hospital welcomed all those in need.

Entering the new Hospital.

Awards ceremony.

The 1940s reflected a period in which the Hospital expanded its commitment to providing hospital care. A training school for nurses was established in 1940, and in 1941 a check-up clinic was opened for discharged patients. Construction of a new 36-bed annex to the Hospital was completed in 1947. New programs were added including physical therapy, hydrotherapy, and diagnostic therapies. During this period, the Hospital's focus began to move away from custodial care to active rehabilitation and treatment. Patient referrals increased, and a waiting list was established. In 1949, a professional medical social service department was

Opening of expanded programs.

established to work with patients and families on an individualized basis. A limited teaching and research program with Tufts Medical School was also started. This program helped to advance the Hospital's scientific approach to chronic illness.

For the period 1950-1960 the Hospital continued to grow and receive recognition in the medical community. For example, in 1950 a famous French post-Impressionist artist was successfully treated with cortisone for his rheumatoid arthritis and, in 1952 the first hip replacement in the Boston area took place at the Hospital. In 1954, the Hospital received its first accreditation from the Joint Commission on Accreditation of Healthcare Organizations.

Building construction continued at a rapid pace. In 1955, three floors of the main building endowed by the Kaplans were completed, increasing the size of the Hospital to 156 beds. This new construction enabled the Hospital to provide occupational therapy and expand its kitchen and dinning room areas. Moreover, an Orthodox Chapel, auditorium, research laboratory, new lobbies, elevators, and administrative offices were added. In 1962, construction of the Kaplan building was completed, and in 1964 a new nurses' residence and storage warehouse were constructed. Expansion continued and by 1968 the fourth and fifth floors of the main building and the fifth floor of the Kaplan building had been finished. Also, a new x-ray area was erected between 1966 and 1968. By the end of the 1960s, the Jewish Memorial Hospital had increased its size to 207 beds.

During the 1970s a pulmonary care unit, behavioral neuro-psychiatric unit, and rehabilitation care unit were added. In 1971, the Hospital began its affiliation with the Boston University Medical Center. This program enabled the Hospital to expand its teaching programs and develop medical

Ribbon cutting celebration.

specialties to improve patient care. That same year, a two-story addition to the annex was completed. Construction continued, and in 1972 a new ambulance entrance and linen-processing facility were built, and the pharmacy and patient rooms were renovated.

The high point of the 1980s was the dedication of the Murray Fertel Rehabilitation Wing in 1988. This new construction replaced the original 1880 building, the annex and the 1947 buildings. The new building centralized patient

Expansion of Pulmonary Care Unit.

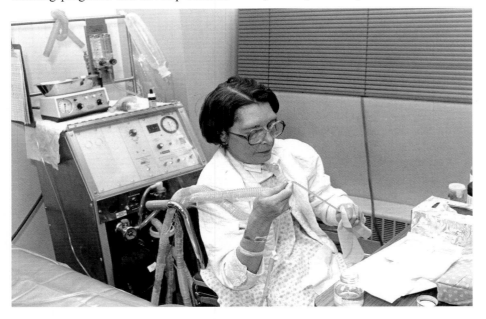

315

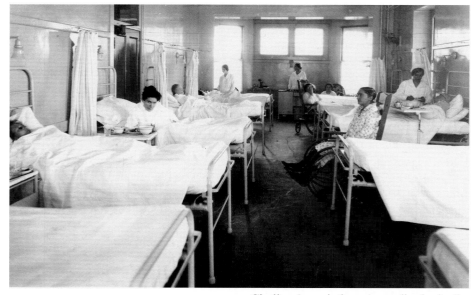

Nurses' dormitory opens in 1940.

support and rehabilitation services and offered the community a modern facility with state-of-the-art equipment.

Hospital services continued to expand in the 1980s. In 1985, a Total Parenteral Nutrition program was established for patients who were unable to take oral nourishment. In that same year, the Comprehensive Assessment and Rehabilitation Unit was opened. This unit was dedicated to treating individuals with behavioral and functional disorders and was the only one of its kind in the Greater Boston area at the time. In order to provide increased care for patients who could not breathe on their own, a Pulmonary Care Unit was established to provide services for ventilator-dependent patients in 1986.

Over its 70-year history the Jewish Memorial Hospital had grown from an institution that provided only custodial care to one that now emphasizes the active treatment and rehabilitation of patients. In order to more clearly reflect the focus of the Hospital's programs and to enhance its image as an active rehabilitation facility, the name of the Hospital was changed to the Jewish Memorial Hospital and Rehabilitation Center in 1992.

As the new century approached, the Hospital remained committed to the original goals of the Roxbury Ladies' Bikur

Cholim Association. Accordingly, in the 1990s the Hospital expanded its patient services by developing a Peritoneal Dialysis Service and Hemodialysis Service. In 1995, a Complicated Obesity Rehabilitation Environment Program was begun and later in the decade, the Hospital established new programs in cancer management and cardiac rehabilitation.

Historical Milestones for the Hospital include:

• 1913–Ladies Bikur Cholim Association, founders of the Hospital, collect

Over 1,000 volunteers have been involved with Jewish Memorial Hospital.

donations to provide a haven for the chronically ill.

• 1928–Ladies Bikur Cholim Association purchase the former Beth Israel Hospital building at 59 Townsend Street, Boston.

• 1929–Greater Boston Bikur Cholim Hospital dedicated, 42 beds.

• 1930–Physio-therapy, radiology and laboratory services opened.

• 1936–First wing completed, bed count grows to 87.

• 1937–Hospital renamed Jewish Memorial Hospital.

• 1940–Training school opened for attendant nurses.

• 1941–Check-up clinic opened for discharged patient's.

• 1945–Annex completed.

• 1947–Annex extension completed.

Introduction to facility for volunteers.

• 1952–First hip replacement in Boston performed.

• 1955–Three floors of main building completed, 156 beds —first accreditation by Joint Commission on the Accreditation of Healthcare Organizations.

• 1962–Four floors of Kaplan Building completed.

• 1964–New nurses' residence completed.

• 1966-68–Fourth and fifth floors of main building and fifth floor of Kaplan Building and new X-ray completed, capacity increases to 207 beds.

• 1971–Teaching affiliation established with Boston University Medical Center and University Hospital.

• 1980–Long-Term Care Unit dedicated, an adjunct of Boston University's Gerontology Center Long-Term Care Program.

• 1985–Comprehensive Assessment and Rehabilitation Environment (CARE) Unit opened.

• 1986–Pulmonary Care Unit expands to include services for ventilator-dependent patients.

• 1988–Dedication of Murray Fertel Rehabilitation Wing.

• 1992–Hospital renamed Jewish Memorial Hospital and Rehabilitation Center -

Hemodialysis Unit expanded.

• 1993–Complicated Obesity Rehabilitation Environment (CORE) Unit opened.

• 1994–Cardiac Rehabilitation Unit opened—Brain Injury Rehabilitation Unit opened.

• 1995–Outpatient Obesity Program opened.

• 1996–Hospital receives psychiatric license—CARE Unit expands to Psychiatric Programs.

Purchase of the former Beth Israel Hospital.

Dedication of Kaplan Building.

THE RETEC GROUP

The RETEC Group was founded in the last days of 1985, just before the year-end holidays. Their 12 employee founders (five in Massachusetts, three in Pennsylvania, four in Colorado) were all refugees from another environmental service firm, one that had been taken over by new management the previous September.

With three offices (Concord, Pittsburgh, Ft. Collins) and no backlog, the startup looked perilous. But each of the founders as well as its four external board members helped capitalize the company, and RETEC began life with enough cash to sustain operations for six months, the hoped-for break-even date for cash flow. The cash estimate proved accurate within a few thousand dollars and after six months, RETEC was on its way!

Today, that same company has reported revenues for its latest fiscal year of $115 million. In the U.S., it ranks as the 45th largest environmental firm. It has these additional distinctions: 14th largest all-environmental firm; 17th largest firm in hazardous waste work and 19th in hazardous waste contracting; 19th largest in fossil fuel work, and the 21st largest in refinery and petrochemical plant work.

RETEC now employs about 600 people in 23 offices in the U.S., coast-to-coast. The company's growth, at an annual average compounded rate of 25 percent since its second full year, has consistently been above the growth rate of the industry. Perhaps more importantly, RETEC has always been recognized as a top performer in the engineering industry, both for its profitability and for its management.

What makes the crucial difference in the factors that separate successful from failed startups? In RETEC's case, a number of factors present in the company from its beginning made the difference: values, focus, and management style.

Values have been an important part of RETEC's life, setting the company apart from many of its competitors. The company's values are posted prominently in each office and are these: (1) Clients

Inspection at a Brownfield restoration site.

are the focus of everything the company does. (2) The company's people are its strength and principal asset; they are a community; they treat each other with trust and respect. (3) Working safely is the company's top operating commitment, both at its facilities and at client locations. (4) The quality of the company's products and services is the primary influence driving its growth. (5) RETEC's people operate as one company and make decisions that benefit the entire company. (6) The company measures success by how it grows its revenues, increases its prof-

its, develops its people, and delivers business value to its clients.

These values have been crucial to decision-making at RETEC since its first day, ending arguments about what should be done, what priorities should take precedence, and how the company and its people should treat one another and their clients. More than most companies, RETEC has been and is a value-driven organization!

Site work underway at a former utility gasworks.

The environmental science and engineering market in the U.S. has always been highly disaggregated, with strong competitors on local, regional, and national scales. From its inception, RETEC decided to focus on being a national player, a gutsy assumption for a new startup with 12 people spread across three offices. What was their market? The on-site remediation of difficult-to-treat wastes, typically coal tars and oily residuals, using technologies for separation, biotreatment, and thermal treatment. Today, the company is a prime national player in that market, working with many of the nation's major utilities (coal-tar cleanup of manufactured gas plants), petroleum refiners (oily residuals from up-stream production and downstream refining), and railroads (diesel spills, tie-treating operations). The company has also branched out from its base and now provides operations and maintenance services at client sites, environmental consulting in a host of specialties, and management consulting related to best practices. Strong market focus on specific niches where it can excel is a RETEC tradition!

Always a RETEC strength, the company is known for its loose-tight style and disciplinary structure. The company is "loose" in those activities that maximize the entrepreneurial activities of its people, and uses a project management structure that deeds control and power to the individual manager on the client's site, a project manager empowered to "do the right thing." But the company is "tight" in its commitment to its values—health, safety, and quality among them —and also in its approach to financial management. Here, the company basically runs national businesses, managing the individual offices in a cost-center approach. The "one company" philosophy of RETEC shines through this structure. Many of RETEC's clients have multiple sites and use project teams drawn from across the country. The same face of RETEC shows everywhere: proud to serve clients well, a community of people who "do well by doing good!"

RETEC views the future as one requiring much work in the environmental engineering and science field, both in this country and abroad. The national and global challenges are the same: how can the people of this globe manage their natural resources both to serve current needs and to leave resources available for the future, to serve the needs of their children and their childrens' children? RETEC feels the problem of "Sustainable Development" is a major hurdle for civilization in this century, as global population and global needs soar with population growth. Business must supply solutions for the crucial set of activities that can put the U.S. and other nations of the world on a sustainable path to the future. RETEC is slowly transitioning its business to serve this new market and strong set of needs. Working with old and new clients alike, RETEC will be part of the solution to this important twenty-first century problem!

The Remediator.

A TIMELINE OF MASSACHUSETTS' HISTORY

Native peoples, Massachusett, Wompanoag, Nipmuc, and others, lived in Massachusetts for thousands of years before the arrival of Europeans.

1524 Italian explorer Giovanni da Verrazano visits New England coast.

1602 Bartholomew Gosnold visits Massachusetts Bay and Cape Cod.

1614 John Smith names region "New England" as he maps coastline.

1616–1619 Plague brought by European visitors devastates Massachusett and Wompanoag people.

1620 *Mayflower* reaches Cape Cod; English religious separatists (Pilgrims) then settle at Plymouth.

1621 Plymouth colonists make peace treaty with Massassoit, leader of Wompanoags, hold first Thanksgiving.

1623 Fishing outpost established at Naumkeag (Salem).

1624 Samuel Maverick sets up trading post in what is now East Boston.

1625 Thomas Morton establishes trading post at Merry Mount, Mount Wollaston (now Quincy).

1628 Puritans establish base at Naumkeag.

1630 Massachusetts Bay Company sends 11 ships carrying 900 Puritan settlers, led by John Winthrop, to settle at Boston.

1631 Boston designated capital of Massachusetts Bay Colony, dominated by Puritans. Plymouth Colony continues to be separate entity.

1632 Smallpox devastates native population, killing Massachusett sachem Chicatobat and many others.

1635 Massachusetts Bay banishes minister Roger Williams for heresy; he founds Rhode Island colony. Boston Public Latin School, first public school, founded.

1636 Harvard, first college in North America, founded in Cambridge.

1637 Massachusetts goes to war against Pequots, people native to southwest, in contest over lands of Connecticut.

Top: *This first Massachusetts seal was sent to the newly chartered Massachusetts Bay Company by the English governor in 1629. It was used until 1684. The Indian is saying, "Come over and help us." From* New England Magazine, *February 1901*

Bottom: *The Green Dragon Tavern was in Boston's north end near Hanover Street. Here the patriots of the Revolution are said to have met and planned their strategy. From James Stark* Antique Views of Ye Towne of Boston, *1882*

1638 Massachusetts Bay banishes Anne Hutchinson for heresy.

1640 *Bay Psalm Book* published in Cambridge, first book printed in North America.

1642 Population of Massachusetts Bay reaches 10,000.

1650 Anne Bradstreet publishes *The Tenth Muse*, first American book of poetry.

1651 First "Praying Town" for Christian Indians established at Natick.

1660 Mary Dyer, Quaker, executed on Boston Common for her religious beliefs.

1663 Roxbury minister John Eliot's translation of Old and New Testaments into Algonkian is first Bible published in North America.

1673 Boston Post Road links New York and Boston.

1675–1676 King Philip's War, led by Metacom (Philip), sachem of Wompanoags and son of Massassoit, against English colonists. Over 3,000 died.

1684 British government revokes Massachusetts Bay charter.

1686 British crown tries to incorporate all New England colonies into Dominion of New England, send Edmund Andros to be governor.

1689 Bostonians arrest Edmund

Elizabeth Freeman (Mumbet) (1742-1829) was the first slave freed because of the bill of rights in the 1780 Massachusetts Constitution. Massachusetts was the first of the states to abolish slavery. Watercolor by Susan Sedgewick, courtesy, Massachusetts Historical Society

Andros; Andros released and returned to England when Glorious Revolution topples King James II.

1691 British government grants new charter to Massachusetts; Plymouth included in new province of Massachusetts.

1692 Witchcraft hysteria in Salem; 19 accused witches were hanged.

1704 *Boston News-Letter*, first regular newspaper in America, published in Boston. Indians attack frontier town of Deerfield, killing 53 and taking over 100 colonists to Canada.

1713 Town House, now the "Old State House," built in Boston, will be seat of Massachusetts government until 1797.

1721 Smallpox epidemic in Boston, debate over inoculation.

1734 Northampton minister Jonathan Edwards begins series of religious revivals known as the "Great Awakening."

1742 Merchant Peter Faneuil builds central marketplace on Boston docks; will also hold town meetings.

1745 William Shirley leads Massachu-

setts forces against French stronghold of Louisbourg, in Nova Scotia, capturing entry point of St. Lawrence River. Britain returns Louisbourg to France at end of war.

1765 To pay for Seven Years War, British Parliament passes Stamp Tax. Violent protests in Boston and other ports. Sons of Liberty organized.

1768 After repealing Stamp Tax, Parliament passes Townsend Duties. Boycotts in Massachusetts. Two British regiments arrive in Boston to enforce law.

1770 Boston Massacre; British troops fire on mob of Boston civilians, killing five.

1771 Thomas Hutchinson, great-grandson of Anne Hutchinson, appointed governor; will be last civilian royal governor.

1773 Boston Tea Party, in protest of British tax and trade laws, Bostonians destroy two cargoes of tea. Phillis Wheatley's *Poems on Various Subjects* published in London.

1774 Parliament closes port of Boston, suspends Massachusetts government. Assembly continues to meet as Massachusetts Provincial Congress, adopts Suffolk Resolves calling for resistance

to British authority. General Thomas Gage arrives to govern rebellious province. Massachusetts calls other colonies to send delegates to a Continental Congress.

1775 Fighting between local militia and British regulars at Lexington and Concord (April 19). Battle of Bunker Hill, June 17. Continental Congress, on motion from John Adams, sends George Washington to command army which has surrounded Boston.

1776 Using cannon captured by Henry Knox at Fort Ticonderoga, Washington forces British to evacuate Boston, March. Continental Congress, Bostonian John Hancock, President, declares Independence July 2; Declaration first read in Boston on July 18.

1780 Massachusetts adopts state Constitution, written by John Adams. John Hancock elected first governor of Massachusetts.

St. Augustine's cemetery is the oldest (1818) Catholic cemetery in the northeastern United States. It was begun by the French-American Friar Jean-Louis Cheverus, the first Bishop of Boston, but the cemetery and chapel (1819) are now primarily used by Irish-Americans in South Boston where it is located. Photo by Ruth Owen Jones

1781 Massachusetts courts rule that slavery is inconsistent with liberty promised in new state Constitution.

1786 Tax protests in Hampshire, Berkshire, Worcester counties culminate in Daniel Shays's attempt to seize Springfield armory; ship *Grand Turk* sails from Salem, opening Massachusetts trade with China.

1787 General Benjamin Lincoln leads state forces in suppressing Shays's rebellion; John Hancock elected governor, pardons rebels.

1788 Massachusetts ratifies new Constitution, but proposes Bill of Rights.

1789 John Adams of Braintree (now Quincy) elected vice president under new government; President George Washington visits Massachusetts.

1790 First federal census shows Massachusetts population 476,000 (second largest of 13 states). Massachusetts is only state with no slaves.

1791 Massachusetts Historical Society founded. Nantucket whalers sail to Pacific for first time.

1794 Building begins on Middlesex Canal to connect Merrimack and Mystic rivers.

1797 U.S.S. *Constitution* launched. John Adams becomes president.

1799-1801 Theodore Sedgewick, Federalist, speaker of U.S. House of Representatives.

1800 John Adams defeated for re-election. Massachusetts population 675,000 (second largest of 15 states).

1801 Crane Paper Mills established at Dalton. Crane continues to make paper for U.S. currency.

1803-1805 Captain Edward Preble of Maine commands U.S.S. *Constitution* in war against Tripoli; William Eaton

of Brimfield leads marines and Tripolitan forces in northern Libya.

1806 African Meeting House built in Boston.

1807-1811 Joseph Varnum, Massachusetts Republican, elected speaker of U.S. House of Representatives.

1808 Embargo closes American ports.

1809 Handel & Haydn Society, first professional orchestra in U.S., founded in Boston. Massachusetts population 701,000 (fourth largest of 17 states).

1812 Printer Isaiah Thomas founds American Antiquarian Society in Worcester. U.S.S. *Constitution* defeats British frigate *Guerriere*.

1813 Boston Manufacturing Company in Waltham produces cotton textiles. British frigate *Shannon* defeats U.S.S. *Chesapeake* off Boston Light; Captain James Lawrence's dying words, "Don't give up the ship!"

1820 As part of Missouri Compromise, Maine separated from Massachusetts. Massachusetts population 523,287 (seventh largest of 23 states).

1824 John Quincy Adams of Quincy elected president.

1825 Glassworks established at Sandwich.

1826 Horse-drawn railroad built in Quincy to haul granite to build

Top: *John Brown (1800-1859) avidly opposed slavery. Here he is shown organizing African Americans in Springfield where he lived in the early 1850s. He moved to Kansas where he and his sons led the anti-slavery massacre at Pottawattomi. He then tried to lead an uprising of slaves at Harper's Ferry in 1859 for which he was hanged. From Mason A. Green,* Springfield: 1636-1886, *1888*

Bottom: *This is a bronze bas relief in memory of the 54th Regiment Massachusetts Volunteers, the first black regiment to go into the Civil War. Recruited across Massachusetts, New England and New York, trained near Boston, they were led by young Robert Gould Shaw, a white volunteer (shown on horseback). Shaw died with many of his men in the assault on Fort Wagner, South Carolina, where they fought bravely. The movie* Glory *is about this Regiment. The memorial by Augustus Saint Gaudens is across the street from the State House on Beacon Hill, Boston. Photo by Paul C. Jones*

Bunker Hill Monument and other buildings in Boston; community of Lowell chartered, will become manufacturing center.

1828 Blackstone Canal connects Worcester with Narragansett Bay. In Holyoke, South Hadley Falls dam provides industrial waterpower.

1829 David Walker publishes his *Appeal to the Colored Citizens of the United States.* Ames Company begins making shovels and swords in Chicopee.

1830 Massachusetts population 610,408 (eighth largest of 24 states).

1831 William Lloyd Garrison begins publishing *The Liberator* in Boston.

1833 Osgood Bradley of Worcester designs first railroad passenger coach.

1834 Protestant mob burns Ursuline Convent in Charlestown.

1837 Mary Lyon opens Mount Holyoke Seminary in South Hadley; will become first women's college in America.

1839 *Lowell Offering*, literary magazine by and for Lowell mill-workers, begins publication. Charles Goodrich invents process for creating vulcanized rubber.

1840 Massachusetts courts rule that workers have right to organize into unions and to strike peaceably. Massachusetts population 737,699 (eighth largest of 26 states).

1841 Frederick Douglass, fugitive slave living in New Bedford, makes his first public anti-slavery speech at Nantucket. Transcendentalists found Brook Farm, cooperative in West Roxbury.

1843 College of the Holy Cross founded in Worcester.

1846 Elias Howe of Spencer patents home sewing machine.

1847-1849 Robert C. Winthrop, Whig, Speaker of U.S. House of Representatives.

1850 Massachusetts population 994,512 (sixth largest of 30 states).

1851 Donald McKay launches *Flying Cloud*, fastest clipper ship ever built. Herman Melville writes *Moby Dick*.

1852 Boston Public Library, nation's first free public library opens.

1853 Horace Smith and Daniel

In 1902, the first Aero Club in the United States was founded in Boston as a ballooning club (before the invention of the airplane). The club was interested in the new airplanes being developed, and they helped financially with experiments. Balloonists often ascended far inland to avoid getting blown out over the ocean. Here the gas balloon Centaur *is going up in Pittsfield in 1907. From* Navigating the Air, *1907*

Wesson begin manufacturing guns in Springfield.

1854 Anthony Burns, a fugitive slave, returned from Boston to slavery.

1856-1857 Nathaniel P. Banks, American Party, Speaker of U.S. House.

1859 Ebenezer Butterick of Sterling invents standardized paper patterns for clothing.

1860 Springfield lithographer Milton Bradley publishes *The Checkered Game of Life.* Massachusetts population 1,231,066 (sixth largest of 33 states).

1862 Oneida Football Club, first football club in U.S., begins playing its games on Boston Common.

1863 Massachusetts 54th Regiment, composed of African Americans, suffers heavy losses in siege of Fort Wagner, South Carolina. Massachusetts Agricultural College, later the University of Massachusetts, founded at

Amherst, first class graduates 1871.

1865 Maria Mitchell of Nantucket becomes Vassar's first professor of astronomy; Massachusetts Institute of Technology opens in Boston; both Massachusetts Agricultural and M.I.T. founded under Morrill Land Grant act.

1866 Mary Baker Eddy founds Christian Science movement in Lynn.

1867 New England Conservatory founded.

1869 State creates nation's first Bureau of Labor Statistics to collect data on working conditions.

1870 Massachusetts population 1,457,351 (sixth largest of 37 states).

1872 Boston fire destroys much of city, property losses exceed $70 million.

1874 Legislature limits workday of women and children in factories to 10 hours.

1875 Smith College founded; as Mt. Holyoke remained a "seminary for women" into the 1880s, Smith also claims to be the first college for women in the United States.

1876 Alexander Graham Bell sends message over telephone.

1880 Massachusetts population 1,783,045 (seventh largest of 38 states).

1881 Boston Symphony Orchestra founded.

1882 John L. Sullivan of Boston becomes heavyweight boxing champion.

1883 George S. Parker of Salem publishes first game, "Banking," first Parker Brothers game.

1890 Massachusetts population 2,238,947 (sixth largest of 42 states).

1891 Dr. James Naismith invents basketball in Springfield.

1897 Boston opens first subway line in United States. First running of Boston Marathon, from Hopkinton to Boston, on Patriot's Day.

1900 Massachusetts population

This 1907 view of High and Dwight streets in Holyoke shows the new automobiles, trolleys and still horse-drawn vehicles all competing for the road. From a 1907 postcard, courtesy, Owen Jones Pictures

Fenway Park, Boston, Mass.

Above: The Red Sox were born as the "Somersets" in 1901. They won the first World Series ever played in 1903, and began playing at Fenway Park in 1912. They are shown here in 1916 during the Golden Age of Fenway Park (1912-1918). Babe Ruth was the Red Sox pitcher from 1914 to 1919. From a postcard sent in 1916, courtesy, Owen Jones Pictures

2,805,346 (seventh largest of 46 states).

1901 Guglielmo Marconi puts Transatlantic Wireless Station into operation at Wellfleet.

1903 Boston Pilgrims (later Red Sox) beat Pittsburgh in first World Series.

1909 Edward Filene opens Automatic Bargain Basement in Boston.

1910 Massachusetts population 3,366,416 (sixth largest of 46 states).

1912 Fenway Park opens. Bread and Roses strike by Lawrence textile workers.

1914 Cape Cod Canal opens. David Walsh is first Irish-Catholic elected governor. Boston Braves win World Series.

1918 German submarine shells Cape Cod coastline; led by left-handed pitcher Babe Ruth, Boston Red Sox win World Series for sixth time; flu epidemic kills tens of thousands.

1919 Boston police strike; Governor Calvin Coolidge rejects arbitration by Samuel Gompers. Senator Henry Cabot Lodge helps block U.S. entrance into

League of Nations.

1919-1925 Frederick H. Gillett, Republican, Speaker of U.S. House of Representatives.

1920 Charles Ponzi bilks thousands in New England out of millions of dollars; Calvin Coolidge elected vice president. Harvard wins Rose Bowl. Massachusetts population 3,852,356 (sixth largest of 48 states).

1921 WBZ, New England's first radio station, begins broadcasting in Springfield (will move to Boston in 1924).

1923 On death of President Harding, Coolidge becomes president.

1926 Robert Goddard, Clark University professor, successfully demonstrates liquid-fuel rocket.

1927 Nicola Sacco and Bartolomeo

Vanzetti executed for 1920 murder; later are exonerated.

1929 Boston Bruins win Stanley Cup. Conductor Arthur Fiedler leads Boston Pops in their first "Esplanade Concert."

1930 Massachusetts population 4,249,614 (eighth largest of 48 states).

1938 Hurricane kills 650 people in New England.

1939 Flooding begins in Swift River Valley to create Quabbin Reservoir; Bruins win Stanley Cup.

1940 Massachusetts population 4,316,721 (eighth largest of 48 states).

1941 Bruins win Stanley Cup. Ted Williams bats .406, last player to hit over .400.

1942 General Electric tests first jet engine at Lynn plant. Cocoanut Grove fire in Boston nightclub kills more than 400.

1947-1949 Joseph Martin, Republican, Speaker of U.S. House of Representatives.

1947 Edwin Land announces one-step photographic process, forerunner of

327

Polaroid Instant Photography.

1948 Democrats have majority in Massachusetts House of Representatives for first time in history; Thomas P. O'Neill, Jr., elected speaker. Warren Spahn leads Boston Braves into World Series, where they lose to Cleveland Indians. WBZ-TV goes on air, first television station in New England.

1950 Brink's robbery in North End nets thieves $2.7 million. Massachusetts population 4,690,514 (ninth-largest of 48 states).

1952 In upset, John F. Kennedy defeats incumbent Senator Henry Cabot Lodge for U.S. Senate. Thomas P. "Tip" O'Neill elected to Kennedy's House seat.

1953-1955 Joseph Martin Speaker of U.S. House of Representatives.

1953 Boston Braves move to Milwaukee.

1954 Malcolm X, formerly Malcolm Little of Roxbury, opens Muhammad's Mosque 11 in Dorchester.

1957 Boston Celtics win first cham-

NOVEMBER 1, 1933
Eastern Standard Time

BOSTON-MAINE AIRWAYS CENTRAL VERMONT AIRWAYS

BOSTON
AND
PORTLAND, ME.
WATERVILLE, ME.
BANGOR, ME.
CONCORD, N. H.
WHITE RIVER JCT., VT.
MONTPELIER-BARRE, VT.

pionship; will dominate basketball world for next decade, winning 11 championships in next 13 years.

1960 John Fitzgerald Kennedy elected president, defeating ticket of Richard M. Nixon and Henry Cabot Lodge. In his last at-bat in the major leagues, Ted Williams hits home at Fenway Park. Massachusetts population 5,148,578 (ninth largest of 50 states).

1961 Cape Cod National Seashore established, preserves over 5,000 acres

---

Left: In 1933 the new Boston and Maine Airways, a child of the B & M Railroad, had regular routes from Boston to Portland, Maine and other New England cities. The yellow airplanes were Stinson SM-600s, nicknamed the Yellow Birds. From a 1933 schedule folder, courtesy, Owen Jones Pictures

Below: In 1939, after removing four towns, the state began flooding the Swift River Valley in the center of the state to create the 18-mile-long Quabbin Reservoir as Boston's water supply. Flying over the lost town of Dana one can see the Old Pottapaug Pond, now part of the reservoir beyond. Courtesy, Owen Jones Pictures

of outer Cape for future generations.

1962-1971 John McCormack, Democrat, Speaker of U.S. House of Representatives.

1962 Edward M. Kennedy defeats Edward McCormack for U.S. Senate.

1965 Boston district attorney Garrett Byrne refuses to allow Muhammad Ali – Sonny Liston rematch at Boston Garden; fight held in Lewiston, Maine.

1966 Edward Brooke, African American Republican, elected to U.S. Senate. Celtics star Bill Russell becomes first African American coach in N.B.A.

1967 In "Impossible Dream" season, Carl Yaztrzemski wins baseball's "Triple Crown," leading in homeruns, batting average, and runs batted in, and Red Sox win pennant. Lose World Series to St. Louis, 4 to 3.

1969 Computer engineers from Bolt, Beranak, and Newman (BBN) create two computers which can communicate with each other, foundation of the Internet.

1970 Massachusetts population 5,689,170 (10th largest of 50 states).

1972 With Bobby Orr flying across net, Bruins win Stanley Cup; First "Figawi Race" from Hyannis to Nantucket; Massachusetts only state George McGovern carries in presidential election.

1974 Charlestown Navy Yard closes.

1974-1976 Busing crisis in Boston schools.

1975 Boston Red Sox win pennant; Carlton Fisk's dramatic home run in game six ties Series, though Cincinnati wins game seven.

1977-1987 Thomas P. O'Neill, Jr., Speaker of U.S. House of Representatives.

1980 Massachusetts population 5,737,093 (11th largest of 50 states).

1985 Federal Judge David Mazzone orders clean-up of Boston Harbor.

1986 Boston Celtics win basketball championship for 16th time. Red Sox lose World Series to New York Mets in seven games.

1988 Governor Michael S. Dukakis is Democratic nominee for president, loses to George H.W. Bush.

1990 Eleven masterpieces of art, including works by Vermeer, Rembrandt, Degas, and Shang dynasty bronze, stolen from Isabella Stewart Gardner Museum in Boston. Massachusetts population 6,016,425 (13th largest of 50 states).

1991 Construction begins on the "Big Dig."

1993 Education reform act mandates new state educational standards, testing of students, allows opening of charter schools.

1995 Ted Williams Tunnel opens, connecting Logan Airport with South Boston, easing traffic in other harbor tunnels.

2000 M.W.R.A. completes $3.8 billion construction of sewerage treatment

College students protested the war in Vietnam at the gates of Fort Devens in Ayer on November 11, 1965. Reprinted with permission of the Worcester Telegram and Gazette

facilities, Deer Island plant and outfall pipe. Massachusetts population 6,349,097 (13th largest state).

2001 John Ruiz of Chelsea becomes first Latino heavyweight boxing champion. Acting Governor Jane Swift, first woman governor of Massachusetts, is first governor in nation to give birth to twins. Congressman Joe Moakley dies. Terrorists hijack two jets from Logan Airport, crash into World Trade Center, killing thousands and bringing United States into international war against terrorism.

2002 New England Patriots win Superbowl.

PICTURE RESEARCHER'S ACKNOWLEDGMENTS

The pictures in this book represent the cooperative efforts of dozens of people from museums, local historical societies, libraries, colleges, federal, state, and municipal agencies, private publishers, business archives, and various generous individuals who opened their normally private collections for history. Several artists offered new work to illustrate this volume, and photographic copy work from very old books and prints, as well as photography of objects, was done skillfully by several others. Finally, over 350 pictures were gathered from over 70 different sources. While the sources are credited elsewhere, I would like to take this opportunity to thank all of the people who contributed to the work of this book as well as an earlier version. It was certainly a team effort to produce the beautiful result. I especially want to thank the following people who went well beyond the obligation of their positions to be helpful with pictures, background information, and support for the project over the many many months of research.

Special thanks go to artists Jim Gipe, Evan Jones, Justine Hill, the late Marie Litterer, John Martin, Sam Pettengill, Paul Sherry, and Wilbert Smith for offering new work to be published for the first time in this book. At the University of Massachusetts Photo Services, Paul Carew, Jean Crossman, Brenda Lily, Fred Moore, and Kathryn Stadler did excellent work while Donna Meisse and then Joan Gloster dependably coordinated it all. Hill Boss, Barbara Jones, Walter and Sarah Jones, and Eugene Worman kindly lent antique books, prints, postcards, and other Massachusetts objects from their private collections.

At the University of Massachusetts DuBois Library Betty Brace gave special help, and there in Special Collections and Archives Ute Bargman, John Kendall, Michael Milewski, Steve Robinson, and Linda Seidman were always enthusiastic and willing to help with the research. Thanks go to Daniel Lombardo, Marty Noblick, and Tevis Kimball at Special Collections and Archives in the Jones Library, Inc. in Amherst. Special thanks to Wendy Watson at Mount Holyoke College Art Museum, and to Elaine Trehub and Peter Carini in the Mount Holyoke College Archives. Kerry Buckley at Historic Northampton and Elise Bernier Feeley and Blaise Bisallon at Forbes Library Northampton are appreciated as well as Michael Goodison at the Smith College Art Museum in Northampton. Barry Moser of Hatfield also generously let us use his woodcut of Emily Dickinson. At the Berkshire Athenaeum in Pittsfield, Ruth Datenhardt and Kathy Reilly were especially supportive with material from the western counties. Bernice O'Brien, Donna Stimpson and Robert Mallace helped at the Dept. of Environmental Management in Pittsfield. Jo DiVieglia at the National Grid and Kelley Smith at Yankee Atomic checked into the photograph of the nuclear power plant that Bill McGee had supplied us. In North Adams at the exciting new Massachusetts Museum of Contemporary Art, MoCA, Katherine Myers jumped to our aid with many choices. From Springfield's Connecticut Valley Historical Museum Gail Nessell and Barbara Plant gave generously of their time and expertise, and Jim Gleason was especially hard working at the *Springfield Union News* Library. Douglas Stark, despite being in the middle of new building construction, helped us at the Basketball Hall of Fame, Springfield. In Worcester at the *Telegram and Gazette*, Editor Harry Whitin deserves a handshake, while Elizabeth Hooke at the American Red Cross and Mary Jane Blasdale at the New Bedford Whaling Museum cheerfully came through and Mary Corrigan deserves a raise at BAE Systems in Lexington for all the invaluable coordinating she did.

In Boston at the John F. Kennedy Library it was Alan Goodrich who was quick to help. In the Massachusetts Art Commission at the State House, Susan Greendyke Lechevre was wonderfully accomodating, and over at the Massahcusetts Archives at Columbia Point, Richard Kaplan, Elizabeth Marzuoli and Stephen Kenney were essential. Rose Marston speedily helped us at the Governor's Press Office, and former Governor Michael Dukakis personally sent us an update. Margherita Desy was splendid at the *U.S.S. Constitution* Museum and the venerable Massachusetts Historical Society, Ross Urquhart and later Nicholas Graham knew which illustrations would be useful. Christine Brody helped at the Isabella Stewart Gardner Museum, and Aaron Schmidt has always been willing come to our aid at the Boston Public Library Prints Department. At the Museum of Fine Arts, Boston, Jane Hankins and then Lizabeth Dion and Christopher Atkins efficiently did their jobs providing photographs of art works and permissions. At the Christian Science Church, Ruth Whittaker helped, and at NStar (formerly Boston Edison) Priscilla Korrell and later James Connelly provided us with their oldest photos.

Thanks go to the authors Judith Freeman Clark and Robert Allison and Editor Carolyn Martin at American Historical Press for all of their suggestions and encouragement. And finally, love and appreciation to my husband Paul C. Jones for support of every sort.

Gratitude is extended to all who helped, but of course, the responsibility for the historical accuracy of the book lies only with the authors and picture researcher. In a book of this scope, people and events are treated all too briefly, and depth of coverage is simply not possible. Certain subjects and people are featured, others left out, but it is hoped that readers will be inspired to dig further into Massachusetts history because of something found here.

— Ruth Owen Jones

BIBLIOGRAPHY

Ahlstrom, Sydney E. *A Religious History of the American People.* New Haven: Yale University Press, 1972.

Allen, Oliver E. "The State of Medical Care, 1984." *American Heritage* 35:6 (Oct.-Nov. 1984) 33-40.

Bearse, Ray, ed. *Massachusetts, A Guide to the Pilgrim State.* 2nd ed. Boston: Houghton Mifflin Co., 1971.

Boorstin, Daniel J. *The Americans. the Colonial Experience.* New York: Random House, 1958.

_____ *The Americans. The National Experience.* New York: Random House, 1965.

_____ *The Americans. the Democratic Experience.* New York: Random House, 1973.

Booth, Robert. *Boston's Freedom Trail* Globe Pequot Press, 1981.

Brown, Richard D. *Massachusetts A Bicentennial History.* New York: Norton, 1978.

Commonwealth of Massachusetts, Annual Reports of the Metropolitan District Commission, for the years 1937, 1938, *1939.* Public Document #48.

Commonwealth of Massachusetts, Report of the Post-War Rehabilitation Commission. Boston: Wright and Potter Printing Co., 1945.

Davis, John H. *The Kennedys Dynasty to Disaster.* New York: McGraw-Hill, 1984.

Demos, John. *A Little Commonwealth.* New York: Oxford University Press, 1970.

DiCarlo, Ella Merkel. *Holyoke - Chicopee. A Perspective.* Holyoke, Mass.: Transcript-Telegram, 1982.

Fuller, Linda K. *Trips and Trivia. A Guide to Western Massachusetts.* Springfield, Mass.: Springfield Magazine, Inc., 1978.

Garraty, John A. *The American Nation, A History of the United States to 1877.* 2nd ed. New York: Harper & Row Publishers, 1971.

Greene, J.R. *The Day Four Quabbin Towns Died* Athol, Mass.: The Transcript Press, 1985.

_____ *The Creation of Quabbin Reservoir.* Athol, Mass.: The Transcript Press, 1981.

Handlin, Oscar, and Arthur Schlesinger,

et al. *Harvard Guide to American History.* New York: Atheneum, 1967.

Handlin, Oscar. *The Americans. A New History of the People of the United States* Boston: Little, Brown and Co., 1963.

_____*The Uprooted* 2nd ed. Boston: Little, Brown, 1973.

Higginson, Thomas Wentworth. *Massachusetts in the Army and Navy during the War* of *1861-1865.* Boston: Wright & Potter Printing Co., 1895-96.

Historical Data Relating to Counties, Cities, and Towns in Massachusetts. Boston, 1966.

Hodgson, Godfrey. *America in Our Time. From World War II to Nixon, What Happened and Why.* New York: Random House, 1976.

Hofstadter, Richard. *America at 1750.* New York: Random House, 1971.

Holbrook, Stewart H. *The Old Post Road* New York: McGraw-Hill, 1962.

Hugins, Walter. *The Reform Impulse, 1825-1850.* New York: Harper and Row, 1972.

Jones, Landon Y. *Great Expectations. America and the Baby Boom Generation.* New York: Random House, 1980.

Kaufman, Martin. "Step Right Up, Ladies and Gentlemen . . . " *American History Illustrated* 16:5 (August 1981) 38-45.

Kelley, Robert. *The Shaping of the American Past.* 2nd ed. New Jersey: Prentice-Hall, 1978.

Lakis, Stephen J., ed. *The Political Almanac, 1987-88.* 2 vols. 4th ed. Centerville, Mass.: Almanac Research Services, 1987.

Massachusetts Needs in Urban and Industrial Renewal, August 1960. House #3373.

Massachusetts Population Growth and Redistribution, 1950-1960. Publication #397. (Cooperative Extension Service and Experiment Station).

The Massachusetts Primer. Massachusetts Taxpayers Foundation, Inc., 1986. *Massachusetts Proposals for Better Industrial Relations. The Report to the Governor's Labor-Management Committee.* House 1875.

Morgan, Edmund S. *The Puritan Family.* Revised ed. New York: Harper and Row, 1966.

A Quality of Life. An Assessment of *Massachusetts.* Prepared by Arthur D. Little, Inc., for the Commonwealth of Massachusetts. 1972.

Reid, William James. *The Building of the Cape Cod Canal* New York: Oxford University Press, 1977.

Robbins, Peggy. "The Country Cheered Wildly When Jenny Lind Came to America." *American History Illustrated* 16:3 (June 1981) 29-35.

Tree, Christina. *Massachusetts, An Explorer's Guide.* Vermont: Countryman Press, 1979.

Trout, Charles H. *Boston, The Great Depression and the New Deal* New York: Oxford University Press, 1977.

Vexler, Robert I. *Massachusetts A Chronology & Documentary History.* Dobb's Ferry, N.Y.: Oceana Publ., 1978.

Weinstein, Allen, and R. Jackson Wilson. *Freedom and Crisis, An American History. Vol. 2, Since 1860.* 2nd ed. New York: Random House, 1978.

Wheller, Leslie. "Lucy Stone: Wife of Henry Blackwell." *American History Illustrated* 16:8 (Dec. 1981) 39-45.

Whitehall, Walter Muir, and Norman Kotker. *Massachusetts, A Pictorial History.* New York: Charles Scribner's Sons, 1976.

Young, Allen. *North of Quabbin.* Miller's River Publishing Co., 1983.

INDEX